Cheat Sheet

Banff National Park & the Canadian Rockies For Dummies, 1st Edition

Backpacking Checklist

Clothing

- ❑ Long underwear
- ❑ Wool sweater, down vest, or fleece jacket
- ❑ Rain-proof pants and jacket
- ❑ Hat and gloves
- ❑ Shorts, pants, and shirt
- ❑ Extra socks
- ❑ Boots with good support
- ❑ Sandals or runners for fording streams and wearing at camp

Shelter

- ❑ Tent with waterproof fly
- ❑ Backpack, sleeping bag, sleeping pad
- ❑ Stove, fuel, pot, dishes, utensils
- ❑ Enough food for an extra day
- ❑ Water filter or purification tablets

Other Necessities

- ❑ Wilderness Pass
- ❑ Topographic map and ⌐mpass
- ❑ Waterproof match⌐   flashlight, and extra battery
- ❑ First aid kit, r⌐
- ❑ Signaling   ⌐, mirror)
- ❑ Emer⌐
- ❑ S⌐   sunscreen, lip balm
- ❑ ⌐   gs, toilet paper
- ❑ ⌐ nife, and water bottle

KT-162-423

Banff National Park & the Canadian Rockies For Dummies, 1st Edition

Cheat Sheet

Top Spots to Watch for Wildlife in Banff National Park

Bow Valley Parkway (Highway 1A), between Banff Townsite and Lake Louise: coyotes, mule and white-tailed deer, black bears, grizzly bears, bighorn sheep, elk

Icefields Parkway (Highway 93 North), north of Lake Louise: moose (north of Saskatchewan Crossing), bighorn sheep, mountain goats, black bears, grizzly bears

Lake Minnenwanka Loop, near Banff Townsite: bighorn sheep, grizzly bears, elk

Vermilion Lakes Drive, Banff Townsite: elk, coyotes

Ten Tips for Watching Wildlife Wisely

1. Keep your distance from animals. Use binoculars or your camera's telephoto lens to get a better view.

2. The best times of the day for photography are dawn and dusk, when animals are most active.

3. Keep in mind that it's against the law to feed or disturb wildlife in the park.

4. Never approach the park elk. They like lots of space. And they get rather nasty when people get too close.

5. Be alert for wildlife near the highways, especially at sunrise and sunset. Remember that animals are unpredictable. If you do spot a deer, sheep, or other animal near the road, slow down and be prepared to stop. There's a good chance that others are nearby.

6. Avoid causing traffic jams or "animal jams" along the road. If you stop to look at wildlife, pull over only when it's safe to do so and stay in your car. Don't stop along the Trans-Canada Highway except in an emergency.

7. Check in with park visitor centers for the latest news on wildlife sightings and warnings.

8. Keep your dog on a leash.

9. Read the Parks Canada brochure, Bears and People, available at park visitor centers.

10. Pack plenty of film and spare batteries.

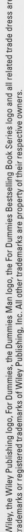

WILEY

For Dummies: Bestselling Book Series for Beginners

The fun and easy way™ to travel!

CANADA

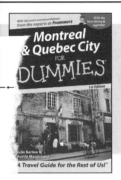

Also available:

America's National Parks For Dummies

Arizona For Dummies

Boston For Dummies

California For Dummies

Chicago For Dummies

Florida For Dummies

Los Angeles & Disneyland For Dummies

New Mexico For Dummies

New Orleans For Dummies

New York City For Dummies

San Francisco For Dummies

Seattle For Dummies

Washington, D.C. For Dummies

RV Vacations For Dummies

Walt Disney World & Orlando For Dummies

EUROPE

Also available:

England For Dummies

Europe For Dummies

Ireland For Dummies

London For Dummies

Paris For Dummies

Scotland For Dummies

Spain For Dummies

OTHER DESTINATIONS

Also available:

Bahamas For Dummies

Honeymoon Vacations For Dummies

Mexico's Beach Resorts For Dummies

Vancouver & Victoria For Dummies

Available wherever books are sold.
Go to www.dummies.com or call 1-877-762-2974 to order direct.

WILEY

Banff National Park & the Canadian Rockies

FOR

DUMMIES®

1ST EDITION

by Darlene West

WILEY

John Wiley & Sons Canada, Ltd

Stevenson College Library
Bankhead Avenue
EDINBURGH EH11 4DE

Banff National Park & the Canadian Rockies For Dummies®
Published by
John Wiley & Sons Canada, Ltd
6045 Freemont Blvd.
Mississauga, Ontario
L5R 4J3
www.wiley.ca

National Library of Canada Cataloguing in Publication

West, Darlene

   Banff National Park and the Canadian Rockies for dummies / Darlene West.

Includes index.

ISBN 0-470-83414-5

1. Banff National Park (Alta.)—Guidebooks. 2. Rocky Mountains, Canadian (B.C. and Alta.)—Guidebooks. I. Title.

FC219.W43 2004   917.123'32   C2003-906727-0

Printed in Canada

1 2 3 4 5 TRI 07 06 05 04 03

Distributed in Canada by John Wiley & Sons Canada, Ltd.

For general information on John Wiley & Sons Canada, Ltd., including all books published by Wiley Publishing, Inc., please call our warehouse, Tel 1-800-567-4797. For reseller information, including discounts and premium sales, please call our sales department, Tel 416-646-7992. For press review copies, author interviews, or other publicity information, please contact our marketing department, Tel: 416-646-4584, Fax 416-236-4448.

For authorization to photocopy items for corporate, personal, or educational use, please contact Cancopy, The Canadian Copyright Licensing Agency, One Yonge Street, Suite 1900, Toronto, ON, M5E 1E5 Tel 416-868-1620 Fax 416-868-1621; www.cancopy.com.

About the Author

Darlene West laces up her hiking boots and heads for the Rockies as often as she can. She called Calgary home for more than two decades before recently moving to Oliver, British Columbia, where she divides her time between traveling, writing, and learning how to grow grapes. Her articles have appeared in many publications, including *Canadian Geographic*, *Canadian Living*, *The Globe and Mail*, and *Runner's World*. She is also the author of *Frommer's Calgary*.

Dedication

For Ken, who ensured that we will always return to K-Country.

Author's Acknowledgments

Many thanks to the people I met on my travels through national and provincial parks in the Canadian Rockies and in the nearby communities of Canmore, Golden, Invermere, and Radium Hot Springs — the innkeepers, hoteliers, bed and breakfast owners, resort operators, and local residents who helped me get to know their neighborhoods, and the parks people and visitor bureau staff who answered my questions and offered advice. A million thanks, as well, to the friends in Calgary whose company I have been lucky enough to enjoy on countless trails and adventures in Kananaskis Country and Banff National Park. I'm grateful to all of you for helping create this book. Above all, thanks to John, for putting up with me while I wrote it.

Publisher's Acknowledgments

We're proud of this book; please send us your comments at canadapt@wiley.com. Some of the people who helped bring this book to market include the following:

Acquisitions and Editorial

Associate Editor: Michelle Marchetti

Developmental Editor: Karen Alliston

Copy Editor: Allyson Latta

Cover Photo: J.A. Kraulis/Masterfile

Back Cover Photo: PhotoDisc, Inc.

Production

Publishing Services Director: Karen Bryan

Publishing Services Manager: Ian Koo

Project Manager: Elizabeth McCurdy

Project Coordinator: Robert Hickey

Layout and Graphics: Pat Loi

Proofreader: Pam Erlichman

Indexer: Belle Wong

John Wiley & Sons Canada, Ltd.

Bill Zerter, Chief Operating Officer

Robert Harris, General Manager, Professional and Trade Division

Publishing and Editorial for Consumer Dummies

Diane Graves Steele, Vice President and Publisher, Consumer Dummies

Joyce Pepple, Acquisitions Director, Consumer Dummies

Kristin A. Cocks, Product Development Director, Consumer Dummies

Michael Spring, Vice President and Publisher, Travel

Suzanne Jannetta, Editorial Director, Travel

Publishing for Technology Dummies

Andy Cummings, Acquisitions Director

Composition Services

Gerry Fahey, Executive Director of Production Serviceds

Debbie Stailey, Director of Composition Services

Contents at a Glance

Maps at a Glance

Table of Contents

Introduction

S o, you're off to Alberta to visit Banff National Park. Banff. Already, you can *see* yourself. Skiing through bowls of waist-high powder or hiking across a flower-filled meadow. Hear the word *Banff*, and *click*, you envision majestic peaks. Banff shouts stellar mountain scenery and outdoor adventure. You can visualize the Canadian Rockies in your dreams. Which makes trip planning kind of exciting.

Now, just hold that image of snow-capped peaks and emerald lakes in your mind's eye for a minute, and ponder this: The actual Banff is every bit as stunning as the one in your imagination. Maybe more so. Indeed, many scenes in Banff National Park and the Canadian Rockies will sweep you off your feet (figuratively speaking), broaden your horizons and probably illuminate your mind. (Don't worry. You needn't adopt a lotus position; I'm only suggesting that in your travels through the Rockies, you may find yourself shifting to a higher level of awareness . . . far, far, from the office.)

I'm sure it's obvious by now that I think you've made a superb vacation choice. Buying this book was a smart move, too. It was designed to make trip planning effortless and fun.

About This Book

This book isn't intended to be devoured in one sitting — or even read from cover to cover. It's more like a reference tool (although I hope you'll find it a bit more compelling than the average encyclopedia). It's organized so that you can quickly zero in on the resources you need. It contains the key information you require to plan your visit to the Canadian Rockies and to make the very best use of your available time once you get there.

I don't bury you in an avalanche of extraneous details (although I do point you in the direction of numerous sources of further information on many topics). I simply help you choose the park or region that's best for you and lend a hand with vacation planning.

Perusing this book is rather like sitting down with an old friend who has just returned from a lengthy excursion through the Canadian Rockies. You'll pick up valuable tips on what to do, what to see, and where to sleep and eat. (But you won't have to suffer through any boring home videos.)

Conventions Used in This Book

To help you find your way around quickly, all the sections on individual cities and towns contain the same type of information on what to see and do, where to stay and eat — and in a parallel format. The same goes for chapters on national and provincial parks.

My recommendations on hotels and restaurants include price information to help you plan your budget. I use a system of dollar signs to represent the cost of a night in a hotel or a main course in a restaurant. Here's how to interpret the dollar signs:

Cost	Hotel	Restaurant
$	C$100 and under	C$10 and under
$$	C$100–C$150	C$11–C$20
$$$	C$150–C$250	C$21–C$26
$$$$	C$250 and more	C$27 and more

Under each review, you'll find the hotel or restaurant address, followed by the telephone number in bold type, and specific price information. Hotel rates, based on double occupancy, are the high season *rack rates* (before any discounts). Usually, you can get a break on the rack rate, and many hotels offer further cuts in off-peak travel seasons. For tips on saving money on your accommodation, refer to Chapter 4, *Planning Your Budget* and Chapter 8, *Booking Your Accommodation*.

I use the following abbreviations to indicate the main credit cards that are accepted by the hotels, restaurants, and attractions that I review:

- **AE** (American Express)
- **DC** (Diners Club)
- **DISC** (Discover Card)
- **MC** (Master Card)
- **V** (Visa)

In the major centers — where you have lots of accommodation options — I divide my hotel recommendations into two categories: my personal favorites and the runners-up. Don't hesitate to check in to any of these establishments: They're *all* good places to stay.

Foolish Assumptions

In writing this book, I made some assumptions about you and your needs as a traveler. Here's what I assumed:

- ✔ You may be an inexperienced traveler, looking for help planning a visit to Banff National Park. You want advice on when to go and what to do.

- ✔ You may be an experienced traveler who hasn't had much time to explore the Canadian Rockies and wants expert advice when you finally do get a chance to visit.

- ✔ You're not looking for a book that tries to tell you everything there is to know about the Canadian Rockies and that lists every hotel, restaurant, and attraction. You just want accurate information on the best places and the top experiences.

How This Book Is Organized

This book is user-friendly. It's divided into six sections, each addressing a certain aspect of your visit to the Canadian Rockies. Within each section, you find a handful of chapters that delve into more specific details about trip planning and visiting specific mountain parks and communities. That way, you can skip past topics that don't interest you and head straight for the information you need.

Part I: Getting Started

This first part gets you acquainted with Banff National Park and the Canadian Rockies. I point you in the direction of the most spectacular scenery and offer tips on where to spot wildlife. I even propose an itinerary that you can follow, day-by-day, if you wish — or simply use as a blueprint for designing your own travel game plan. Either way, you'll have a solid sense of what you can reasonably expect to see and do in the time you have available. Part I also includes some budget-planning advice and a few travel tips for those with special requirements or interests, including families, seniors, people with disabilities, and gays and lesbians.

Part II: Ironing Out the Details

Here, I get into the nitty-gritty of trip planning, with tips on flying (or driving or busing) to Banff National Park and suggestions on getting around once you arrive. Turn to this section if you're looking for advice on whether to plan your trip alone, with help from online resources, get some assistance from a travel agent, or turn things over to a tour operator. Part II also helps you figure out where to stay in the national and provincial parks in the Canadian Rockies and neighboring communities. I sum up your lodging options, and offer dollar-saving tips. And I answer some questions you may be pondering (or that perhaps have not even occurred to you), such as what to do if your wallet is stolen and whether you need travel insurance.

Parts III, IV, and V: The Destinations

These sections are the real meat of the book: They feature the places you'll visit, with suggestions on how to get there, where to find information, what to see and do, where to stay, and where to find the best meals. In each section, I cover national and provincial parks in a particular region, along with nearby "gateway communities" you may wish to stay in or explore.

Part III deals with Banff and Jasper National Parks, including destinations such as Lake Louise, Moraine Lake, and the Icefields Parkway. There's a chapter on Banff Townsite, with hotel and dining tips. I also include a separate chapter on the city of Calgary, partly because I happen to know the city intimately, but more importantly, because you'll likely end up flying into the Calgary International Airport, and you can probably use some guidance on what to see in Calgary before you head for the mountains.

Part IV covers three destinations in southern Alberta: Canmore, a rugged little mountain town just outside Banff National Park; Kananaskis Country, a collection of provincial parks and protected areas on the eastern slopes of the Rocky Mountains, and Waterton Lakes National Park, a wild and slightly off-the-beaten-track area near the Alberta/ Montana border.

In Part V, I take you across the Continental Divide into British Columbia. If you've already visited Banff and Jasper in Alberta, definitely the most well known of the Canadian Rockies parks, you may want to budget some time on this trip to motor through Yoho and Kootenay national parks in B.C. Part V fills you in on where to find the top scenery and suggests some awesome hikes. This section also includes a chapter on the town of Golden, where you may want to park yourself for a few days of skiing or white-water rafting. For travelers looking to *really* escape the crowds, I also cover three provincial parks in British Columbia: Hamber and Mount Assiniboine, which you can only get to on foot (unless you fly in) and Mount Robson, west of Jasper, which protects the highest peak in the Canadian Rockies.

Part VI: The Part of Tens

This section is rather lighthearted, which is not to say the material included is unimportant. Quite the opposite. This is the part of the book that tells you how to get high (legally) in the Canadian Rockies, for example, and where you can find indestructible trail snacks.

Quick Concierge

The appendix at the back of this book functions much like a good hotel concierge: It provides handy local information and key telephone numbers.

You'll also find some worksheets (the yellow pages) that you can use to plan your trip. They're useful for tallying up budget items, comparing airlines, noting hotels and restaurants you want to visit in specific destinations, and mapping out itineraries.

Icons Used in This Book

Throughout this book, you'll notice five different icons in the margins. These little pictures alert you to important travel planning information. Here's what they mean:

This icon points out advice that will help you make the most of your trip. It highlights suggestions on how to plan your time and budget.

This icon is a little "warning" symbol. It lets you know about areas and situations you need to be aware of or plan ahead for, such as steep trails, one-way streets, and highway routes with few service stations.

This icon highlights restaurants, hotels, and attractions that are especially hospitable to children.

When you spot this icon, it means you're going to read about a hotel, restaurant, or attraction that I consider a particularly good deal.

This icon highlights places that are well worth seeking, even if it means going a little out of your way.

Where to Go from Here

To Banff National Park, of course, or to Yoho, or to Waterton Lakes or to Jasper. Heck, why not visit all of them? When you start flipping through this book, you'll hear the call of the mountains. You may choose to unwind for a week in an out-of-the-way cabin or strike out on a wide-ranging tour. In any case, even if you're a thorough planner and a stickler for detail, you needn't concern yourself with investigating every hotel, motel, restaurant and bar in the park, town, or city you intend to visit. I've done the hard work. (Which explains why I need a month off.) You can concentrate on the hiking, the skiing, and the scenery.

Part I
Getting Started

The 5th Wave   By Rich Tennant

"Yes sir, our backcountry orientation programs are held at the Footblister Visitor Center, the Lostwallet Ranger Station or the Cantreadacompass Information Pavilion."

In this part...

If this is your first trip to the Canadian Rockies, where do you start? This part helps you devise a plan. I give you a rundown of the destinations covered in this book and offer tips on when to visit — the best months to ski, to hike, to see wildlife, or to catch festivals and events. I even include itineraries, so you can get a handle on how much of the Rockies you may be able to experience during your travels. Budget information is here, too, so you can figure out how much you can afford to see — along with ideas for stretching your dollars further. This part also provides tips for traveling with kids, suggestions on finding deals for seniors, hints for travelers with disabilities, and resources for gay and lesbian travelers.

Chapter 1

Discovering the Best of the Canadian Rockies

In This Chapter

▶ Enjoying the scenery

▶ Discovering the wildlife

▶ Exploring the great outdoors

Saying you've decided to visit the Canadian Rockies is a bit like saying you're planning to see Canada.

You can experience the Rockies by fleeing to the wilderness with a backpack and a cook stove or, if you prefer, checking into a posh resort and heading straight for the spa. Myriad combinations are doable, as well: the Canadian Rockies region includes more than 23,000 sq. km (nearly 9,000 sq. miles) of national and provincial parkland along with bordering towns and cities. The whole area does share one common theme, though: spectacular mountain scenery. (Yes, it does look like the postcards.)

In this chapter, I reveal some of the natural attractions that drew travelers here in the first place, point you in the direction of majestic mountain scenes, and offer tips on where to spot wildlife.

Stepping Back in Time

Canada's first national park — indeed the country's entire system of national parks — originated with the country's first health spa, in the town of Banff, more than a century ago. To get the lowdown on the history of **Banff National Park,** start with a visit to the **Cave and Basin National Historic Site** in Banff Townsite (Chapter 13).

The story, which you can find out more about at the historic site, begins in the late 1800s, with the Canadian government busy building the Canadian Pacific Railway (CPR) to link the country from the Atlantic coast to the Pacific. When the railroad reached the Rocky Mountains, three CPR workers discovered hot springs flowing from the side of a mountain. Likely looking ahead to retirement, these men attempted to stake a claim to the hot springs. Arguments broke out, and in 1885 the prime minister of the day, Sir John A. Macdonald, stepped in and declared the mineral waters and the surrounding 26 sq. km (10 sq. miles) a national treasure, to be owned by all Canadians.

This area, initially called Rocky Mountain National Park, was later renamed Banff National Park, and has since been expanded to encompass 6,641 sq. km (2,564 sq. miles).

Railway workers were by no means the earliest arrivals in the Canadian Rockies. Archaeologists believe that Aboriginal people lived in the area 11,000 years ago. More recently, in the 1700s, the Cree, Kootenay, and Plains Blackfoot tribes hunted and fished in the mountain passes. European fur traders and explorers arrived in the next century. Many mountains and other natural features were named by John Palliser and other members of the British North American Exploring Expedition, who ventured through the Rockies in the mid-1800s. Alberta's **Kananaskis Country** (Chapter 16) and the Kananaskis River were named by Palliser in honor of an Aboriginal.

It was the CPR, though, that planted Banff on the tourist train circuit long before the development of highways through the mountains. Indeed, a CPR director chose the name "Banff" in honor of his homeland of Banffshire in Scotland. This was well before the development of highways through the Rockies, so in order to get there you had to ride the train.

Railway officials recognized right away the potential of the spectacular Rocky Mountains as a travel destination. CPR manager William Van Horne famously remarked, "If we can't export the scenery, we'll import the tourists." Having spent a fortune developing the national railway, the CPR had considerable incentive to lure wealthy visitors to the Canadian Rockies.

Van Horne and his colleagues set about building a chain of luxury hotels, beginning with the magnificent Banff Springs Hotel, overlooking the Bow Valley, which opened in 1888. The **Fairmont Banff Springs Hotel** (Chapter 13) is a national historic site and the landmark most associated with Banff today. Development of a resort on the shores of Lake Louise, the **Fairmont Chateau Lake Louise** (Chapter 13), got under way soon after.

The Canadian Pacific Railway pushed west, crossing the Rockies between Alberta and British Columbia over the Kicking Horse Pass, laying the steepest stretch of track in North America. For safety's sake, this leg of the railway, called "Big Hill," was ultimately rerouted through creatively engineered **spiral-shaped tunnels,** which are used to this day. In British Columbia's **Yoho National Park** (Chapter 19), created in 1886, you can stop at a viewpoint on the Trans-Canada Highway to watch trains wind through the tunnels.

The Canadian government established **Jasper National Park** (Chapter 14) on the northern border of Banff in 1907, the same year a northern railway line was proposed for the Yellowhead Pass. **Kootenay National Park** (Chapter 20), between Banff and Radium Hot Springs in British Columbia, was created in 1920.

Today, national parks focus on protecting nature and wildlife. Before 1930, however, industries such as mining and logging were allowed. That explains why you can explore the remains of a former coal-mining center, at **Bankhead,** when you visit the town of Banff (Chapter 13).

Waterton Lakes National Park (Chapter 17) in southern Alberta along the Canada–United States border, was established in 1895, largely due to the efforts of a southern Alberta rancher who wanted to see the historically and environmentally unique area preserved. Early tourists arrived from the United States, traveling to Montana by train and north to Waterton Lakes by bus. The **Prince of Wales Hotel,** now a national historic site, opened in 1927. A few years later, Waterton was united with Montana's Glacier National Park to form the Waterton–Glacier International Peace Park, a symbol of goodwill and cooperation between Canada and the United States.

When you tour around Waterton and southern Alberta, you're bound to come across the name **Kootenai Brown.** John George Brown, who was born in Ireland, was the earliest settler in the Waterton area and the park's first superintendent. (He was called "Kootenai" because of his association with the Kootenay tribe of southeastern B.C.) You can visit Brown's cabin at the **Kootenai Brown Pioneer Village** in Pincher Creek, just outside Waterton Lakes National Park.

Among other celebrated figures in the Canadian Rockies are numerous mountain guides, outfitters, and climbers. Some, such as **Bill Peyto** and **Tom Wilson,** worked for the CPR during construction of the railway and chose to stay in the Banff area. A cabin that Peyto built in the 1890s is now part of the **Whyte Museum of the Canadian Rockies** (Chapter 13) in the town of Banff. A mountain in the Bow Valley bears the name of another legendary outfitter, **Jimmy Simpson,** who arrived in Canada from England in 1896. **Walter Wilcox,** an American student from Yale University, who explored and climbed in the region in the 1890s, named a number of mountains and lakes in the Lake Louise area. Wilcox and his group were the first to reach the summit of **Mount Temple.**

Although the Canadian Rockies were promoted as a tourist attraction from day one, travel to the region in the early years was really only feasible for the affluent. Major tourist traffic started only after highways enabled visitors to reach the Rockies by car. You can still take a luxury rail trip through the Rockies, however. **Rocky Mountaineer Railtours** (☎ **800-665-7245;** Internet: rockymountaineer.com) runs various tours between Calgary and Vancouver along the historical train route.

Checking Out the Scenery

The Canadian Rockies contain some of the most impressive scenery in the world. Because of their exceptional geological features and unspoiled beauty, the four national parks of Banff, Jasper, Kootenay, and Yoho, together with the British Columbia provincial parks of Hamber, Mount Robson, and Mount Assiniboine, are recognized as a United Nations **World Heritage Site.** The Waterton–Glacier International Peace Park, with its rich and diverse wildlife and outstanding scenery, has earned the same designation. That puts the Canadian Rockies in the same category as the Pyramids, the Acropolis, the Galapagos Islands, and other natural and manmade wonders.

Setting the scene

The mountains you see when you travel through the Rockies are quite young, relatively speaking. They were formed millions of years ago, when sediments that had piled up on the beds of ancient seas caused the earth's surface to shift, lifting and folding enormous blocks of sediment. On mountainsides in **Yoho National Park**, paleontologists have found fossils of animals that inhabited the seas 500 million years ago. Over time, erosion, wind, water, and ice shaped and sculpted the mountains, producing their angular peaks.

The Rocky Mountains stretch more than 4,800km (3,000 miles) from Alaska, through Canada and the western United States. They're part of the Cordillera system, the largest mountain chain in North America. Because they form the Continental Divide, which separates rivers that flow west from those that run east, the Rockies are sometimes referred to as the "backbone of North America."

In Canada, the Rockies span 1,200km (740 miles), separating Alberta from British Columbia and extending from the U.S. border north into Yukon Territory. The tallest peak is **Mount Robson** (3,954 meters/12,972 feet). Many others exceed 3,000 meters (9,842 feet).

The Canadian Rockies are grouped into four ranges, based on the age and geological makeup of the mountains. The **Western Ranges** are found in parts of Kootenay and Yoho national parks and in the B.C. provincial parks. The **Main Ranges**, which include the peaks of the Continental Divide, such as **Mount Victoria** (visible from Lake Louise), are among the oldest rocks. The **Front Ranges**, which you find in both Banff and Jasper, include Mount Rundle in Banff and Roche Miette in Jasper. The most easterly ranges are the **Foothills**.

If you start your trip in Calgary, as many people do, the Rocky Mountain Foothills loom in the distance as you motor west through the **Bow River Valley** along the Trans-Canada Highway, also known as Highway 1. A detour south at Highway 40 will take you through the Kananaskis River Valley and over the Highwood Pass, the highest drivable pass in the country.

Back on Highway 1, en route to Banff, you pass the town of Canmore and spot three frequently photographed and easy-to-recognize mountains (on your left): the **Three Sisters.** These peaks, individually called Big Sister, Middle Sister, and Little Sister, were originally named the Three Nuns, since they were thought, when capped with snow, to resemble praying nuns.

In Banff National Park, a drive along the **Bow Valley Parkway** gets you off the fast lane (the Trans-Canada Highway) so that you can slow down and reflect on your surroundings.

Driving slower on the Bow Valley Parkway, also called Highway 1A, isn't optional, by the way. The speed limit here is 60 kph (37 mph).

Along the parkway, which begins just west of Banff Townsite and runs to the village of Lake Louise, you're treated to awesome views of some popular peaks, including **Castle Mountain,** which you'll have no trouble identifying thanks to its fortress or castle-like appearance. James Hector of the Palliser Expedition named this castle-like stunner in 1858. Nearly a century later the peak was renamed Mount Eisenhower in honor of the United States president, but eventually the original name was restored. The tall pinnacle that juts up on the southeast end is called Eisenhower Tower.

From the Bow Valley Parkway, if you head south into British Columbia, you follow the Kootenay Parkway down through the steep walls of **Sinclair Canyon** to **Radium Hot Springs,** where you can break for a dip in the hot pools.

For scenery of a cooler nature, drive north of Banff on the highway to **Jasper National Park.** The route name alone — **Icefields Parkway** — prompts you to pack a coat. This 230-km (143-mile) highway, which parallels the Continental Divide and offers views of glaciers, is a signature Canadian Rockies excursion. If you have the time (and energy), it's also a spectacular cycling route in the warmer months.

Quick trips to summits

If you lack the time or the urge to scramble up a mountain, you can still take in the scenery from several mountaintops (without renting a helicopter) by riding a gondola. Tickets for sight-seeing gondolas in the Canadian Rockies usually cost C$17 to C$25 (US$12 to US$18). Some gondola operators offer sight-seeing trips only in summer. The Banff Gondola, which delivers you to the top of **Sulphur Mountain** for a panoramic view of Banff Townsite, runs year-round. In Lake Louise, you can take a gondola to the top of **Mount Whitehorn** while admiring the world-famous lake with Mount Victoria rising beyond it. The Jasper Tramway, which is the highest in Canada, whisks you to the top of **Whistlers Mountain**. You can spot Mount Robson, the highest peak in the Rockies, as well as various neighboring peaks, rivers, and lakes. In Golden, British Columbia, a gondola at the **Kicking Horse Mountain** ski resort offers splendid views of the **Columbia River Valley.**

Watching for the Wildlife

The Canadian Rockies are famous for wildlife-viewing opportunities. Banff National Park alone is home to more than 50 species of animals, ranging in size from ground squirrels to grizzly bears. The chance to see wildlife — from your car or on the hiking trail — is one of the most thrilling aspects of travel in the mountain parks.

Bear in mind — no pun intended — that it's unwise (and illegal) to entice, feed, or disturb animals in the parks.

Among the larger critters, you may see the following:

- ✔ **Bears:** Although both black and grizzly bears live in the Rockies, black bears (which, despite their name, may be black, brown, or blond) are easier to spot from the highway, since they prefer the lower valleys, whereas grizzlies generally keep to the high country. Grizzlies are larger — some weigh as much as 500 kilograms (1,100 pounds) — whereas the largest black bears are less than half that big. Bears are easiest to spot in the spring and fall. Keep your eyes peeled when you travel the Icefields Parkway between Banff and Jasper national parks (Chapter 14). Cameron Lake in Waterton Lakes National Park (Chapter 17) is a good spot to look for grizzly bears in particular (bring your binoculars). You may also see grizzlies on the slopes under the Lake Louise Gondola (Chapter12).

On highways in Banff and other parks in the Rockies, you see cars clustered along the side of the road where somebody has spotted a bear. When you pass these **"bear jams,"** be sure to slow down in case an animal — or a tourist — darts across the highway unexpectedly. If you decide to pull over, make sure it's safe to do so and stay in your car. Park officials encourage drivers not to stop when they see bears. Besides being aware of the potential for accidents, they're concerned about bears that get so accustomed to human contact that they're no longer afraid of people and begin to pose a danger. Often, these animals end up having to be destroyed.

- ✔ **Deer:** Both mule deer and white-tailed deer are found in the parks. The mule deer, which sports huge ears and has a black tip on its white tail, is more common. The best place to see mule deer is Waterton Lakes National Park (Chapter 17), particularly in the townsite. In Banff, watch for deer along the Bow Valley Parkway, especially around Johnston Canyon (Chapter 12).

- ✔ **Elk:** Chances are good that you'll see elk in your travels, even if you don't venture far from the towns of Banff or Jasper (Chapters 12 and 14). These huge animals (bull elk can weigh up to 450 kilograms/1,000 pounds) look pretty tame, especially when you see them nibbling on flowers and shrubs in people's front yards. But they're actually the most dangerous animals in Banff, so keep your distance (at least 30 meters/100 feet, or three bus lengths). Be especially cautious in calving season (mid-May through June) and in the fall mating season. And never come between a cow elk and her calf or between any group of elk.

- ✔ **Bighorn sheep:** The Rockies support large populations of bighorn sheep. Good places to look for them include the road to the Sunshine Village ski area, Mount Norquay Road, or on the Minnewanka Loop in Banff National Park (Chapter 12); near the Visitor Information Centre or at Red Rock Canyon in Waterton Lakes National Park (Chapter 17); and around Sinclair Canyon in Kootenay National Park (Chapter 20). The adult males are easily recognized by their big, curved brown horns. Ewes have short, spiky horns.

- ✔ **Mountain goats:** Differentiated from sheep by their longer, shaggier coats and pointed black horns, mountain goats are numerous in the Rockies although harder to catch sight of given their preference for high, rugged terrain. You may see them on the Icefields Parkway in Jasper — there's a good viewing spot about 38km (24 miles) south of Jasper Townsite (Chapter 14); on the Plain of Six Glaciers hike in Lake Louise (Chapter 12); or on the road to Takakkaw Falls in Yoho National Park (Chapter 19).

Visitor information centers in each park offer information on recent wildlife sightings. It's a good idea to check in with them, especially if you plan to go hiking.

Getting Active

Most people consider hiking the activity of choice in the Canadian Rockies (for help planning a hiking itinerary, see Chapter 3; for recommended hikes, refer to the chapters on specific parks), but the mountain parks and gateway communities offer nearly unlimited opportunities for other outdoor adventures.

Golf courses in the Rockies are hard to top for majestic surroundings. Tee off in the shadow of Mount Kidd in gorgeous Kananaskis Country (Chapter 16) or gaze at Mount Rundle and Sulphur Mountain when you hit the links in Banff (Chapter 12). In the Radium Hot Springs region on the western slopes of the Rockies, you can take in views of both the Rockies and Purcells — and enjoy a golfing season that often runs from March to October.

Mountain biking is permitted on specific hiking trails (check with park visitor centers). The Nordic Centre in Canmore (Chapter 15), built for the 1988 Winter Olympics, features 72km (45 miles) of trails. For more daring downhill adventure, check out Mount 7 in Golden, British Columbia (Chapter 18).

The Rockies are also ideal for **road biking,** whether you want to tool around near the townsites or tackle a longer cycling excursion such as the Bow Valley Parkway (Chapter 12), the Icefields Parkway (Chapter 14), or the Kootenay Parkway (Chapter 20).

Can't decide which ski hill to check out? If you base yourself in Banff or Lake Louise, you can conveniently sample the **downhill skiing** or **snowboarding** at three area resorts: **Lake Louise, Mount Norquay,** and **Sunshine Village** (Chapter 12). If you're staying in Calgary, it's easy to spend a day on the slopes at **Nikiska** or **Fortress Mountain** in Kananaskis Country (Chapter 16) and slip back to the city for dinner. West of the Continental Divide is the latest addition to the ski scene in the Canadian West — **Kicking Horse,** in Golden, British Columbia. Look for challenging terrain and memorable dining.

For cross-country skiing, visit the **Canmore Nordic Centre**. From there you can whip along trails developed for Olympic athletes. Venture into a snow-covered wilderness in nearby Kananaskis Country. Or, try one of the national parks. Banff alone offers 80km (50 miles) of groomed trails.

Chapter 2

Deciding When and Where to Go

In This Chapter

▶ Selecting your park (or parks)

▶ Choosing the best season

▶ Catching the top events

*N*ow that you've settled on a trip to the Canadian Rockies, you'll want to pin down a more precise itinerary and determine when to visit. This chapter helps with those decisions. I give you a rundown of the top destinations, discuss the pros and cons of traveling at different times of the year, and provide a calendar of events. This book, by the way, definitely doesn't cover everything you could see and do in the Canadian Rockies. I'm assuming you're planning a holiday — not a year-long sabbatical. I select the top destinations and the best attractions, so you don't waste a minute of your vacation time going anywhere unworthy of your attention.

The Parks and Gateway Communities

The sections on each national park region in this book include information on nearby towns or cities that you may want to stay in or visit during your travels. I start with Calgary, Alberta, which — if you're flying to the Canadian Rockies — is probably where you should launch your trip. After that, I cover the popular parks of Banff and Jasper, along with a few lesser-known destinations in the Alberta Rockies, then move west to parks and communities in British Columbia.

Calgary

Calgary offers all the amenities you'd expect in a city of 1 million people, including first-rate restaurants and oodles of shops. On the cultural and entertainment front, most of the main attractions are in and around downtown, and convenient to investigate on foot. If you're the outdoorsy type (and I'm assuming you are, since you bought this book), you can meander along riverbanks, through parks, and around downtown on an extensive network of trails. The Rockies are so close you can see them. For information on Calgary's attractions, including the Calgary Stampede, see Chapter 11.

Banff National Park

Banff boasts more restaurants, more hiking trails, and more ski hills than any other park in the Canadian Rockies. And you won't get lonely exploring it all — Banff also attracts the most tourists. Given that it's only about a 90-minute drive from Calgary, it's feasible to visit the park's top sights on a day trip, but if you can stay longer, you have plenty of hotels to choose from. For details on where to stay and what to do in Banff, see Chapters 12 and 13.

Jasper National Park

Jasper isn't exactly remote — the Yellowhead Highway runs right through the park and the Icefields Parkway conveys busloads of travelers up from Banff. But this park is definitely less visited and less glitzy than its neighbor to the south. If your ideal Rockies vacation involves a secluded log cabin and exhilarating backcountry treks, you should be content in Jasper. You can also slip over to Mount Robson, the highest peak in the Rockies, which is just 95km (59 miles) away. For more information on visiting Jasper, see Chapter 14.

Canmore

Canmore, Alberta, is so close to Banff that it's practically at the park gates. So why would you stay here, when you could just as easily be in Banff? Fewer tourists, for one thing. Canmore also offers great golfing, Olympic-standard cross-country skiing, and some fine hiking. This mountain town is a bit of a mecca for outdoor types, so just being here makes you feel fit and rugged, even if you only hang out in the coffee shops in your hiking shorts. For suggestions on where to stay in Canmore, see Chapter 15.

Kananaskis Country

For years, guidebooks have been describing Kananaskis Country as Alberta's secret. Which makes you wonder if by now the secret's out. All the same, you can definitely expect lots more space and solitude in this huge wilderness region on the eastern slopes of the Rockies than what you find in the neighboring national parks. And wilderness *is* the main attraction. This Alberta provincial parkland and protected area contains a few hotels (and lots of campgrounds). But don't look for your favorite burger chain.

Waterton Lakes National Park

Many visitors to the Rockies miss this gem, because it requires a detour to the southern corner of Alberta. But once you've been to Waterton, it's tempting to keep coming back. This park has a wild feel — as Banff no doubt did decades ago — with deer strolling through the townsite. If you have the time, you can tag on an excursion into Glacier National Park in Montana, just across the border. Waterton is essentially a summer destination. It isn't officially *closed* in winter, but there's not much open, either.

Golden

Staying in Golden, British Columbia, is rather like basing yourself in Canmore, Alberta: You're outside the national park gates, but still pretty close to the action. If you like outdoor adventure, you'll be in good company in this unassuming mountain town, which also makes a handy base for visiting Yoho and Kootenay national parks. For tips on exploring the Rockies, Golden-style, see Chapter 18.

Yoho National Park

Now we're really getting away from it all. Yoho is a small park with enormous appeal for hikers. Trails are far less traveled here than those in nearby Banff. The top spot to trek — and one of the best in the Rockies — is Lake O'Hara. For advice on how to get there, see Chapter 19.

Kootenay National Park

You won't get lost in this park: There's only one road. The protected region spans a few kilometers on either side. Kootenay contains numerous natural attractions, including hot springs. If you drive through the park's southern gate, you end up in a village of about 700 people, many of whom (judging by the local restaurant offerings) like eating Wiener schnitzel. To find out what else is on the menu, see Chapter 20.

British Columbia Provincial Parks

If you're fond of escaping to destinations that your friends have never heard of, consider a fly-in fishing trip to Fortress Lake in Hamber Provincial Park, near Jasper. Or maybe a cross-country ski excursion to Mount Assiniboine, which is squeezed between Banff and Kootenay national parks. You could also earn bragging rights by backpacking to Berg Lake on the north side of Mount Robson, the highest peak in the Rockies. For the scoop on access to these wilder-than-wild places, see Chapter 21.

The Secrets of the Seasons

Traveling in the mountains means being prepared for everything. Conditions can vary widely from one area to another, depending on elevation, winds from glaciers, position of surrounding valleys, and numerous other climatic influences. Mountain weather is famous for changing dramatically, not only from one place to the next but from one minute to the next. It can snow any time of year. (Even in Calgary, you occasionally wake up to a blanket of white stuff in August.) Weather in the Rockies may be sunny, rainy, and snowy all in the same afternoon.

So when do you visit and what do you pack? In general, you can count on summers being warm and sunny (although short), with average highs in July, the balmiest month, reaching 22° Celsius (72° Fahrenheit) in the town of Banff. The coldest weather hits in January, with average lows of –15° Celsius (5° Fahrenheit) and the possibility of a bone-chilling –30° (–22° Fahrenheit). On the plus side, Alberta boasts more hours of sunshine than any other province, and even frigid winter days are normally clear and bright. Another bonus: A chinook wind can usher in spring-like conditions in the heart of winter.

Spring is generally pleasant — daytime temperatures may reach
14° Celsius (57° Fahrenheit) in May and 18° Celsius (64° Fahrenheit) in
June. But June is also the month when you're most apt to get caught
in a shower (or a wet snowfall), and evenings are quite cool. If you're
hiking, trails at higher elevations are apt to be covered in snow until
the end of June. Fall can be glorious, with crisp air, bright skies, and
golden autumn colors.

Any time of year, keep in mind that the higher you go, the colder it
gets. Expect the mercury to dip by 1 degree for every 200m (656 feet)
of elevation you gain.

Ultraviolet radiation is stronger at higher elevations, so be sure to wear
sunscreen, even if it's cloudy.

Table 2-1		Town of Banff Average Temperature (C/F degrees) and Rainfall (mm/in.)										
	Jan	*Feb*	*Mar*	*Apr*	*May*	*June*	*July*	*Aug*	*Sept*	*Oct*	*Nov*	*Dec*
High	−5/22	0/32	4/39	9/48	14/58	19/65	22/72	21/71	16/61	10/50	1/34	−5/22
Low	−15/5	−11/12	−8/17	−3/26	2/36	5/41	7/44	7/44	3/37	−1/30	−8/17	−14/7
Precip	2.4/.09	1.7/.06	1.6/.06	10.5/.4	42.4/1.7	58.4/2.3	51.1/2	51.2/2	37.7/1.5	15.4/.6	6/.2	2.8/.1

Warm winter winds

California has its Santa Ana, southern Alberta has the chinook: a warm dry wind
that sweeps across the foothills. If you happen to arrive in Calgary in mid-January,
geared up in a ski jacket and toque, only to discover joggers in T-shirts and
shorts — it's a chinook day. Enjoy!

A chinook wind, or snow eater as it was called by the native people of Alberta, is
caused by the influence of the Rocky Mountains on air masses flowing in from the
Pacific Ocean. Temperatures can soar by as much as 20° Celsius (36° Fahrenheit)
in a matter of hours.

People prone to migraines say that the warm winds trigger headaches. Others
blame them for depression. Medical scientists have even investigated whether
chinooks cause strokes (and concluded that they don't). But for southern
Albertans, the arch of wispy, white cloud in the western sky that heralds the arrival
of a chinook is a signal to shed coats and boots and fire up the barbecue.

Spring

If you head for the Canadian Rockies in the spring, you definitely get through the park gates ahead of the crowds. A few other reasons to visit early in the year:

- ✔ It's a great time to photograph wildlife. Animals often feed in the lower valleys in April and May, when the ground is still covered with snow at higher elevations.

- ✔ You can get a better deal on a room. Many hotel owners cut their rates from about April to mid-May, since the ski crowd has left but the hiking season hasn't really begun.

- ✔ You probably won't have to wait in line for anything.

On the other hand:

- ✔ June is the month when you're most apt to end up wearing your raingear.

- ✔ While the major highways through the parks remain open year-round, side roads to some sites are seasonal. Depending on conditions, they may not open until June.

- ✔ Some trails at lower elevations are doable, but it's early for serious hiking. Many areas are wet and muddy, while higher slopes are still covered in snow.

Summer

July and August are definitely the nicest months of the year to experience the Canadian Rockies. Here's why:

- ✔ The weather is on your side. The postcards and posters you see of hikers in shorts and T-shirts were more than likely photographed in July. Summer in the Rockies is short, but it's fabulous: Alpine wildflowers are blooming and days are long and warm.

- ✔ You can dine alfresco at a Calgary cafe or on a hiking trail in Banff or K-Country.

- ✔ The major attractions in all the parks are up and running.

Then again, consider these reasons why you should *not* visit the Rockies in summer:

- ✔ Everyone else does. Hiking trails are busiest, highway traffic is at its worst, and the most popular sites and attractions are so crowded you may get cranky.

✔ The Rockies are prone to thunderstorms in late July and early August.

✔ Don't look for bargain rates at hotels: It *is* peak season, remember, and I'm not talking about the perfect time to view mountain peaks.

Fall

September, October, and early November are attractive in more ways than one:

✔ The kids are back in school; the summer crowds have departed.

✔ In early fall, weather is often just as agreeable as that in summer and you may catch fall spectacles such as a salmon run on the Fraser River near Mount Robson or a valley of golden larches or aspen in Banff.

✔ Many hotels and resorts drop their rates in late fall, before the ski hills open.

Keep in mind, however, that while it isn't winter yet, it isn't exactly summer either:

✔ Although you can still expect some bright, sunny days, it's getting downright cold after sundown. And if the forecast calls for precipitation, it probably doesn't mean rain.

✔ Even though rates may be lower, you won't have as many hotels and resorts to choose from in some parts of the Rockies. Some places shut down for the winter around mid-October.

Winter

If you're planning a winter vacation, you're in luck:

✔ The Rockies are stunning, draped in snow.

✔ If you ski, snowboard, or snowshoe, you have plenty of powdery terrain to explore: Banff National Park alone offers three ski resorts, not to mention 80km (50 miles) of cross-country trails.

✔ You can catch special events that are great for kids, such as Christmas parades and ice-carving competitions.

But winter travel does have some drawbacks:

✔ Snow and ice make for unpredictable and sometimes treacherous driving conditions. You need to allow more time to travel, and be prepared for delays. Some side roads are shut down altogether in winter.

✔ Resorts and attractions in some parts of the Rockies, including many log cabins near Jasper Townsite and most hotels in Waterton, are closed.

✔ With the ski season in full swing, hotel rates in Banff head back to the high peaks.

Hitting the Big Events

In addition to the events I list here, numerous other festivals and events take place throughout the year in Calgary, Banff, and other communities in and around the Canadian Rockies. For the latest information on what's happening during your visit, check in with Internet: www.tourismcalgary.com, www.banfflakelouise.com, www.go2rockies.com, or www.tourismcanmore.com.

January

Banff/Lake Louise Winter Festival: Through the month of January, you may catch winter festival contests and social activities in both communities. The winter festival has been a Banff tradition since 1917. For more information, call the Banff/Lake Louise Tourism Bureau at ☎ 403-762-8421 or visit Internet: www.banfflakelouise.com.

Ice Magic International Ice Sculpture Competition: In mid-January, ice carvers from around the world arrive at Lake Louise to transform blocks of ice into fantastic sculptures. To check competition dates, call the Banff/Lake Louise Tourism Bureau at ☎ 403-762-8421 or visit Internet: www.banfflakelouise.com.

February

Calgary Winter Festival: Calgarians celebrate winter with 10 days of events in Olympic Plaza and other city venues. The annual festival takes place in early February. For program details, call ☎ 403-543-5480 or visit Internet: www.calgarywinterfest.com.

March

Canmore Ice Climbing Festival: Both novice and expert ice climbers will find something of interest at this event, held in early March: equipment demos, clinics, slide shows, and competitions. Call ☎ **403-609-0480** or check out Internet: www.canmoreiceclimbingfestival.com.

April

Earth Day Celebrations: Check with the community you're visiting to see what activities are on in celebration of this worldwide environmental event. In Calgary, the Alberta Wilderness Association's Climb for Wilderness takes place in mid-April. More than 1,000 participants head for the top of the Calgary Tower — on foot. Visit Internet: www.alberta wilderness.ca. Also look for events in Banff. (Note: On Earth Day, April 22, Banff Avenue is closed to vehicles for part of the day.)

May

Canadian Food and Wine Festival: Hosted by the Fairmont Chateau Lake Louise, this annual event is a chance to sample culinary specialties from across Canada and take in seminars, tastings, and talks by visiting chefs. For more information, call the Banff/Lake Louise Tourism Bureau at ☎ **403-762-8421** or visit Internet: www.banfflakelouise.com.

Golden Wildlife Festival of Birds and Bears: If you visit the mountain town of Golden, B.C., in the second week of May, you catch this celebration of the spring migration, which features guided walks, workshops, canoe trips, and children's events. Call ☎ **800-622-4653** or 250-344-5901 or check out the line-up at http://birdsandbears. redshift.bc.ca.

Wings Over the Rockies: This week-long birding festival in the Columbia Valley includes nature walks, tours, field trips, presentations, live music, and a festival for kids. Call ☎ **888-933-3311** or 250-342-3210, extension 100, or visit Internet: www.adventurevalley.com/wings.

June

Calgary International Jazz Festival: Jazz, blues, and world beat take the stage in various downtown Calgary venues in late June. For festival information, call ☎ **403-249-1119** or check out Internet: www.jazz festivalcalgary.ca.

Mount 7 Psychosis Mountain Bike Race: Golden, B.C., hosts this single-track downhill event in late June. It's billed as the world's longest downhill mountain bike race. If you're feeling fearless, you can sign up at www.pinkbike.com.

July

Banff Summer Arts Festival: At the Banff Centre, catch performances from across the arts spectrum: opera, theater, dance, music, and others. Events are held in July and August. Call the Banff Centre Box Office, ☎ 800-413-8368, or check out Internet: www.banffcentre.ca.

Calgary Folk Festival: This four-day festival in downtown Calgary's Prince's Island Park celebrates musical innovation from across Alberta and around the globe. It's held in late July. Call ☎ 403-233-0904 or check Internet: www.calgaryfolkfest.com.

Calgary Stampede: For 10 days in July, the entire city of Calgary gets into the western spirit. Wranglers and Stetsons are de rigueur. The Stampede starts in early July, with a parade (on the first Friday) to kick off the festivities. Get tickets by calling ☎ 800-661-1260 or 403-261-0101. For information, visit Internet: www.calgarystampede.com.

August

Canmore Folk Festival: International folk, blues, and country music performers hit the stage in the mountain town of Canmore for Alberta's longest running folk festival. It's a great family event, and it takes place rain or shine on the first long weekend in August. Call ☎ 403-678-2524 or check out Internet: www.canmorefolkfestival.com.

Trans Rockies Mountain Bike Race: They call it the toughest mountain bike race in the world. With 600km (373 miles) to cover and 12,000m (39,369 feet) of elevation gain, who's going to argue? The seven-day wilderness trail race runs from Fernie, B.C., to Canmore, Alberta. It's held in early August. Call ☎ 877-622-7343 (in Canada) or ☎ 480-922-4732 (in the U.S.) or visit Internet: www.transrockies.com.

September

Melissa's Road Race: Thousands of runners head to Banff National Park in late September for this popular annual road race in the town of Banff, which includes a 22-km (13.7-mile) and a 10-km (6.2-mile) event. Register online at Internet: www.melissasroadrace.ca.

Spruce Meadows Masters Tournament: This internationally renowned show-jumping center in Calgary is considered one of the top equestrian facilities in the world. Spruce Meadows hosts four major show-jumping championships. The Masters, held in early September, is the richest in the world with more than C$1.5 million in prize money. Call ☎ 403-974-4200 or visit Internet: www.sprucemeadows.com.

October

Festival of the Eagles: If you visit Canmore in mid-October, when the golden eagles head south, you may catch a weekend of special events. Besides watching eagles, you can learn more about them on guided walks, presentations, and various migration-oriented celebrations. Call the town of Canmore special events line, ☎ **403-678-1878,** or go to www.gov.canmore.ab.ca. (Click on "Town Departments," and go to "Special Events".

November

Banff Festival of Mountain Films: This annual festival, held in early November at the Banff Centre, features the world's best mountain films and speakers. Tickets are available from the Banff Centre box office, ☎ **800-413-8368**. To see what's showing, visit www.banffcentre.ca.

Banff Mountain Book Festival: Book buffs gather at the Banff Centre to take in readings, presentations, signings, a book fair, and other literary events — all with a mountain theme. It's held in early November. Call ☎ **800-413-8368** or visit Internet: www.banffcentre.ca.

Banff Santa Claus Parade: The town of Banff gets the Christmas season under way in late November with a parade that travels across Elk Street and along Banff Avenue. Following the parade, festivities in Central Park include photo ops with Saint Nick. For more information, check in with the Banff/Lake Louise Tourism Bureau at ☎ **403-762-8421** or visit Internet: www.bannflakelouise.com.

December

World Cup Downhill Ski Races: Here's your chance to watch the top skiers on the planet in action. The World Cup races are held at Lake Louise in Banff National Park in early December. You find schedule information for both the men's and women's races at www.worldcup winterstart.com.

Chapter 3

Four Great Itineraries

In This Chapter

▶ Motoring through the Alberta Rockies

▶ Heading across the Great Divide

▶ Entertaining the kids

▶ Breaking in your new hiking boots

A great way to see the Canadian Rockies is to book a cabin or a campsite in the park of your choice and hike, bike, or sightsee from there. If you haven't made up your mind about where to head for, or if you're the type of traveler that likes to see as much country as you possibly can, the itineraries in this chapter will give you an idea of what's reasonably doable in a week (or two).

I include an agenda that will appeal specifically to kids, and another tour geared to maximizing your time on the trails. For all of these itineraries, I assume that you're flying into Calgary, that you're renting a car, and that you're staying in hotels or cabins (rather than campsites). I also assume that you're traveling in summer, when all the attractions and side roads in the parks are open.

Seeing the Canadian Rockies in One Week

Okay, that's a bit misleading. You can't really see everything in the Canadian Rockies in seven days, unless you want to set a world record for time behind the wheel. But you can see the top sites in a particular region. Here's a seven-day game plan for touring through the Alberta parks of Banff, Jasper, Kananaskis Country, and Waterton Lakes.

Spend **Day 1** checking out the city of **Calgary.** I recommend itineraries (and suggest good restaurants) in Chapter 11.

On **Day 2,** head out on the highway (that's the Trans-Canada Highway, or Highway 1) and drive west to **Banff National Park.** In Banff Townsite, take a ride up **Sulphur Mountain** on the gondola (as long as the weather's decent so that you can appreciate the view). Visit the **Cave and Basin National Historic Site** and take a drive up to the **Banff Springs Hotel.** Later in the day, motor over to **Lake Louise** along the **Bow Valley Parkway** and take a stroll around the lake. Spend the night in Lake Louise. For suggestions on where to stay, see Chapter 12.

On **Day 3,** grab a coffee and a muffin at **Laggan's** in the Samson Mall, and then head up to **Jasper** along the **Icefields Parkway.** Give yourself time to stretch your legs and admire the views. Pay a visit to the **Columbia Icefield Centre.**

Spend **Day 4** seeing the sights around **Jasper Townsite.** Rent a bike on Patricia Street. Or drive up the Maligne Valley to **Maligne Lake,** where you can take a boat tour, go for a hike, or rent a canoe.

On **Day 5,** follow Highway 93A south of Jasper to the **Mount Edith Cavell** Road. If you get an early start, you beat the crowds admiring **Angel Glacier,** and also have time for a short hike or stroll before you head for **Canmore,** where you spend the night.

On **Day 6**, drive east on the Trans-Canada Highway to Highway 40 and travel south through **Kananaskis Country** to **Longview.** From Longview, follow highways 22 and 6 to **Waterton Lakes National Park.** Take a boat cruise on **Upper Waterton Lake** (tours run as late as 7 p.m. in July and August). Enjoy a before-dinner drink in the lounge at the historic **Prince of Wales Hotel.** Have dinner at the **Lamp Post Dining Room** in Kilmorey Lodge (if you have a reservation) or the **Little Italian Café.**

On **Day 7**, allow at least three hours to return to Calgary on Highway 2, through High River.

Seeing the Canadian Rockies in Two Weeks

This trip takes you through the mountain parks in both Alberta and British Columbia. To begin your excursion, follow the first five days of the one-week itinerary, above, to see Banff and Jasper, but instead of heading for Canmore, take an extra day in Banff National Park. **Hike the Plain of Six Glaciers Trail,** or pay a visit to **Moraine Lake.** Walk up **Tunnel Mountain.** Go for a hike or take a picnic lunch to **Minnewanka Lake.**

On **Day 7** drive west to **Field,** British Columbia, in **Yoho National Park,** making a stop at **Takakkaw Falls.** Have lunch in Field at the Truffle Pigs Café or the Kicking Horse Lodge, and then drive a few kilometers down the highway to see **Emerald Lake.** Later in the day, head for Golden.

Spend **Day 8** in **Golden.** Go rafting on the **Kicking Horse River** or take a float trip on the **Columbia River Wetlands.** If you feel like splurging on dinner, check out the Eagle's Eye restaurant at the **Kicking Horse Mountain Resort.**

Drive south on Highway 95, on **Day 9,** to the village of **Radium Hot Springs.** Take it slow today. Have a dip in the hot springs pools (just inside the **Kootenay National Park** gates), explore some of the walking trails around Radium Hot Springs or in the national park (see Chapter 20), or wander through Invermere. Spend the night in Radium Hot Springs.

On **Day 10,** travel north along the **Kootenay Parkway** and head east to **Canmore.** Take a stroll along the Bow River before dinner, or go for a hike (or rent a mountain bike) at the **Canmore Nordic Centre.**

Spend **Day 11** exploring **Kananaskis Country.** Hike to **Lillian Lake,** or if you have lots of energy, try **Mount Indefatigable.**

Follow the end of the seven-day itinerary, above, to travel south to Longview, visit **Waterton Lakes National Park,** and return to Calgary. You have an extra day in Waterton Lakes, so hike the **Crypt Lake Trail** or pack a picnic and head for **Cameron Lake** or the **Red Rock Parkway.**

Enjoying the Canadian Rockies with Kids

This itinerary assumes you want to see as much as possible, without spending too much time behind the wheel in one stretch. It takes you through Kananaskis Country, then into Banff and Jasper national parks. Since the cost of traveling with the family tallies up fast, I include free alternative activities for some of the sites and attractions that charge admission.

On **Day 1,** let the kids go wild at the Calgary Zoo, with a lunch break at the Kitamba Café, or take them to western Canada's biggest amusement park, **Calaway Park,** where they can ride the double corkscrew roller coaster or, on a hot day, get drenched on "Shute the Chutes." Kids also enjoy a visit to **Prince's Island Park** and the **Eau Claire Market** area, downtown, where in summer you're apt to see buskers, clowns, and jugglers. Check out the colorful cows at the **Udderly Art Legacy Pasture** (free admission) on the second floor of the Centennial Parkade at 9th Avenue and 5th Street SW.

Spend **Day 2** visiting **Kananaskis Country.** Go horseback riding at **Boundary Ranch** and stop at **Rick Guinn's Steakhouse** for corn on the cob or a burger at lunch. Alternatively, pack a picnic and explore the kid-friendly (easy) hiking trails in **Bow Valley Provincial Park.** At **Sundance Lodges,** you can sleep in a tepee. Or, spend the night in nearby Canmore: if you stay at **Canadian Rockies Chalets,** you get your own kitchen.

Have a leisurely morning, and then drive into **Banff National Park.** On **Day 3** and **Day 4,** see the sights in and around Banff Townsite. Ride the gondola up **Sulphur Mountain** or take a boat cruise on **Lake Minnewanka.** Stroll **Banff Avenue** and stop for ice cream or fudge. Ride the shuttle bus to **Sunshine Meadows** (it's the Sunshine Village ski area during winter) where you find 12km (7.5 miles) of easy, high-alpine trails.

On **Day 5,** drive to **Jasper National Park** with a stop at the Columbia Icefield Centre, where you can take a **Snocoach** tour on the Athabasca Glacier. Head for Jasper Townsite and stay in a cabin at **Bear Hill Lodge.**

On **Day 6,** spend the morning in Jasper. Tour the townsite. If you missed the Banff Gondola, ride the **Jasper Tramway** to the top of the Whistlers. Later in the day, drive down to Banff. Then, it's an easy trip to Calgary on **Day 7.** If you have time to spare, see **Canada Olympic Park** or visit the **Calgary Science Centre.**

Hitting the Trails in the Canadian Rockies

This trip assumes that you're in the Canadian Rockies to hike. Period. You bypass some top attractions in and around cities and towns to steal more time in the wilderness. Once you've decided which area you plan to visit, invest in a hiking guide. In Calgary, **Mountain Equipment Co-op** carries a good selection. You also find packs, boots, and other hiking gear here and in neighboring outdoor shops.

On **Day 1,** drive to Banff National Park. While Banff, on the whole, is busier than other parts of the Rockies, you can't beat the selection of hikes. If the trail you have your heart set on happens to be a grizzly bear's current favorite hangout, or if it's simply in poor condition, you can select something equally spectacular without traveling far. Check in with the **Banff Information Centre** in Banff Townsite for trail reports and weather warnings. You have time for a half-day hike. What about Sulphur Mountain? It's the highest peak near the townsite, and you can always ride the gondola back down.

While you spend **Day 2** and **Day 3** hiking in the Banff and Lake Louise area, stay at **Baker Creek Chalets** on the Bow Valley Parkway (or more economically, at the **International Hostel** in Lake Louise). Chapter 12 includes some great day hikes. Staff at the visitor centers in Banff and Lake Louise are always happy to point you in the direction of top trails and let you know where the wildflowers are blooming.

On **Day 4,** slip over to **Yoho National Park** and stay at **Cathedral Mountain Lodge** (or if you prefer, at the **Whiskey Jack Hostel**) while you hike in the **Takakkaw Falls** region on **Day 5** and near **Emerald Lake** on **Day 6.** The park visitor center is in Field. Don't forget that if you want to visit the **Burgess Shale** fossil site, you need to hike with a guide. See Chapter 19.

Get an early start on **Day 7** to fit in a short trek in the **Canmore** area on your way back to Calgary.

An alternative to the above excursion is to divide your hiking days between **Kananaskis Country** and **Waterton Lakes National Park.** (Or, if you're fortunate enough to have the time, add this tour to the Banff–Yoho itinerary.) Spend the first half of your trip in K-Country (Canmore has the best selection of nearby hotels). Hike in the **Lillian Lake–Galatea Lakes** region in Kananaskis Valley or head farther south to Peter Lougheed Provincial Park and check out the trails that kick off around the Kananaskis Lakes. From Kananaskis Country, follow Highway 22 and Highway 6 south to Waterton Lakes. Hike to **Bertha Lake** or **Crypt Lake.** On your final day, give yourself at least three hours for the drive back to Calgary.

Chapter 4

Planning Your Budget

. . . .

In This Chapter

▶ Budgeting your travel costs

▶ Avoiding costly surprises

▶ Cutting costs

. . . .

*T*he last thing you want, after a trip through the Canadian Rockies, is to return home to a mountain of bills. In this chapter, I show you how to determine a price tag for your vacation and suggest ways to avoid unexpected costs.

Adding Up the Elements

Although it's hard to predict precisely how much you'll spend on travel, coming up with a reasonable estimate is fairly straightforward. Just run through the trip (in your head, with a pencil in your hand), starting with the cost of getting to the park of your choice, and estimating your expenses for lodging and meals. Next, figure in the park entry fees and admission to hot springs, museums, and other attractions you want to take in along with costs of sports and activities such as skiing. Don't overlook small items, such as souvenirs, which can swiftly add up.

The following sections help you pull together the numbers to prepare your budget. (Whether you stick to it or not is up to you.) You can also use the budget worksheets at the back of this book. After you arrive at a total, add in about 15% for unexpected costs.

Transportation

Transportation represents a significant chunk of your travel budget, but you can nail the costs down before you leave home. Start with your plane ticket (see Chapter 6 for tips on getting a low airfare). Then, tally up your expenses to rent a car, including taxes and gas costs. (Make sure that the car you rent includes unlimited kilometers (mileage).

For more on transportation, refer to Chapter 7, where you find tips for keeping car rental costs down. I also explain your options for traveling through the Canadian Rockies by bus or on the train.

Lodging

Accommodation, like transportation, is fairly easy to budget for. Your costs will depend on where you stay and when you go. Hotel costs are highest, for the most part, in the Calgary–Canmore–Banff region and lowest in the smaller towns around the B.C. parks, such as Golden and Radium Hot Springs. In every area, rooms are at their priciest in the peak summer travel months of June through September.

Remember, too, that you do have alternatives to hotels. In many parts of the Rockies, you find B&Bs, small inns, and hostels. And a spot for your tent or trailer in a campground costs only around C$20 to C$25 (US$14 to US$18) per night.

Eating out

Restaurant meals can devour a big slice of your travel budget, but as with lodging, you can save money if you're flexible. Gourmet eateries in Calgary and Banff charge C$20 (US$14) and more for entrees, so a dinner for two can easily set you back C$80 (US$56) even before you see the wine list. High-end spots in resorts throughout the national parks are in the same league. But you can also find cafes, cafeterias, pizzerias, and other casual spots where you eat for significantly less.

Except in Banff and Jasper, you won't see fast-food chains in the national and provincial parks. But you will discover local equivalents. And even the smallest towns feature local coffee shops and bakeries where you can get an inexpensive breakfast or lunch.

Throughout this book, I use dollar signs to indicate the price range of each restaurant that I recommend. The dollar signs are based on the cost of a main course, and represent the following price ranges (in Canadian dollars):

$	under $10
$$	$11 to $20
$$$	$21 to $26
$$$$	$27 and more

The easiest way to trim your dining bill is to fix some meals yourself. Stock up on food at the grocery store, deli, or bakery (either in the park or the nearest gateway community) and have lunch on the road or on the hiking trail, where you can enjoy scenery to rival the view from any restaurant. Look for hotels that include cooking facilities, or at least a microwave and a fridge. Motels and cabins in some areas provide picnic tables and barbecue facilities for guests.

Table 4-1   What Things Cost in Banff National Park

Item	C$/US$
Ticket for the Lake Louise sightseeing gondola (1 adult)	19.94/14
Bicycle rental (daily)	30/21 to 42/29
Green fees at the Banff Springs Golf Course (July)	150/105
Snowshoe rental (daily)	9/6.30
Lift ticket at Lake Louise ski hill (1 adult)	57/40
Room at Post Hotel (expensive)	300/214 to 400/280
Room at Buffalo Mountain Lodge (moderate)	215/151 to 245/171
Room at Bumper's Inn (inexpensive)	125/88
Souvlaki at Barpa Bill's	5/3.50
Dinner entree at Post Hotel (expensive)	30/21 to 40/28
Dinner entree at Coyotes (moderate)	14/9 to 24/17
Admission to Whyte Museum of the Canadian Rockies (adult)	6/4.20

Table 4-2	What Things Cost in Calgary
Item	*C$/US$*
Day pass for the public transit system	5.60/3.92
Taxi from the airport to downtown	25/18
Room at the Palliser Hotel (expensive)	179/125 to 329/230
Room at the Best Western Calgary Centre (moderate)	99/69 to 139/97
Pita with falafel at Aida's	5/3.50
Dinner entree at Catch (expensive)	20/14 to 42/30
Dinner entree at Buzzard's Cowboy Cuisine (moderate)	12/8 to 15/11
Tickets to the Calgary Stampede rodeo	22/15 to 46/32
Admission to the Calgary Tower (adult)	10/7

Park fees

To visit the national parks of Banff, Jasper, Kootenay, Yoho, and Waterton Lakes, you require a park pass. You can pay by the day (C$14/US$9 covers everyone in your car at most parks; it's C$10/US$7 per day at Waterton Lakes) or invest in an annual pass (C$89/US$63), which is good for all the national parks in the Canadian Rockies, along with other national parks across Canada (27 in all), for one year from the date on which you purchase it.

The provincial parks of Kananaskis Country in Alberta and Mount Assiniboine, Hamber, and Mount Robson in British Columbia don't charge park admission fees.

Hiking is free, in both national and provincial parks, unless you stay overnight in the backcountry, in which case you require a permit. Count on C$8 (US$6) a night in the national parks, or C$56 (US$40) for an annual pass. To reserve a campsite before your backcountry trip, you pay a C$12 (US$8) reservation fee. For information on backcountry camping in provincial parks, refer to the chapters on individual parks.

Budgeting for attractions

Assuming you like the outdoors (if not, you may have the wrong guidebook), you can enjoy a fabulous Rocky Mountain holiday without buying tickets for anything. You can step out of your car, nearly anywhere, and stroll, hike, ski, or snowshoe through some of the most amazing mountain scenery in the world. It's awesome just to *be* in the Rockies. Which isn't to say that you won't be tempted to check out museums, spas, or sightseeing tours. In Parts III and IV of this book, where I cover specific destinations, you find prices for top attractions in each area. A few sample costs: a (family) tour of Canada Olympic Park in Calgary is C$35 (US$24); entry to Radium Hot Springs pools is C$6.50 (US$4.55) per person (adults); a ride on the Jasper Tramway is C$20 (US$14) per person (adults).

Activities

A day on the slopes in the Canadian Rockies will set you back about C$50 to C$60 (US$35 to US$42) — just for your lift ticket. But that assumes you're purchasing a one-day pass on the ski hill. Multi-day tickets work out cheaper, and you can do even better by buying a package that includes accommodation and lift tickets. Many hotels and motels in Banff offer ski packages. (Check Internet: www.banff lakelouise.com.) Other companies package together lift tickets, accommodation, meals, park passes, and transportation. Package prices are cheapest early and late in the season and higher around Christmas and during the prime ski season, from about mid-February to mid-April.

Golfers can find similar packages for hotels and green fees, with the best bargains offered in May and October. Some resorts also offer discounts if you golf mid-week.

Shopping

If you're a compulsive buyer, this category is probably where your travel budget normally spirals out of control. The good news (from a budget perspective) is that after you get through Calgary and past the town of Banff, you probably won't need much shopping money in the Canadian Rockies, because there simply aren't many places to shop. You do find small towns in or near the national and provincial parks where you can stock up on essentials, buy souvenirs, and find outdoor gear and books.

Nightlife

A few nights out on the town in Calgary (at the theater, at a concert, in a nightclub) can make a dent in your budget, but when you escape to the mountains nightlife generally means a glass of wine in the hotel lounge or a beer in the local pub. If you're in a campsite, you can often catch park interpretive programs in the evening, which, along with sunsets and views of the night sky, are free.

Keeping a Lid on Hidden Expenses

The price you're quoted for a motel room, a rental car, or a sandwich in a deli — in other words, just about anything you purchase — isn't the price you actually pay. Be sure to budget for the following costs so that they don't catch you by surprise.

Calculating the sales tax

Throughout Canada, you pay a 7% federal Goods and Services Tax (GST) on most products and services you buy. If you're a visitor to Canada, you can claim a rebate of the GST on many items. The tax rebate is available mostly for purchases you take out of the country; you can't recoup the GST you pay on meals, for instance, or on liquor, tobacco, transportation costs, or gasoline. Rebate application forms are available at many tourist information centers and duty-free shops. For more information, visit Internet: www.ccra.gc.ca/visitors.

Provincial taxes vary from one province to the next. In Alberta (Banff, Jasper, and Waterton Lakes national parks and Kananaskis Country) there's no provincial sales tax, but hotels charge a 5% (nonrefundable) accommodation tax.

In British Columbia (Kootenay and Yoho national parks and the provincial parks of Hamber, Mount Assiniboine, and Mount Robson), you pay a (nonrefundable) retail sales tax of 7.5% on most purchases, including rental cars. There's no provincial tax on food and restaurant meals. Books and magazines are also exempt. The provincial tax on hotels in B.C. is 8%.

Getting tips on tipping

Another cost you may overlook is tipping. Tips or service charges aren't usually included in your restaurant bill, unless you're dining with a big group, in which case some establishments add the gratuity to the tab (be sure to check your bill). The usual practice for good service in a restaurant is to tip your server 15% to 20%. Tip hairstylists and taxi drivers around 10%. Porters and bellhops usually get C$1 to C$2 per bag, and if you spend a few nights in a luxury hotel or resort, it's customary to tip the chambermaids a couple of dollars per night.

Cutting Costs

By now you've probably figured out that it's cheaper to head for the wilderness than to hang around in a city or resort town, but here's some additional advice on keeping expenses in check.

- ✔ **Go off-season.** If you travel at nonpeak times (in April and May, for example, ahead of the prime hiking season, or in late October, before the ski crowd arrives), you'll find hotel prices much lower than in peak months. Some rates are cut by nearly half.

- ✔ **Travel midweek.** If you can travel on a Tuesday, Wednesday, or Thursday, you may find cheaper flights to your destination. When you ask about airfares, see if you can get a cheaper rate by flying on a different day.

- ✔ **Reserve a room with a refrigerator and coffeemaker.** You don't have to slave over a hot stove to cut a few costs; many rooms have mini-fridges, coffeemakers, and even microwaves. Buying supplies for breakfast will save you money — and probably calories.

- ✔ **Always ask for discount rates.** Membership in AAA, frequent-flier plans, trade unions, AARP, or other groups may qualify you for savings on car rentals, plane tickets, hotel rooms, and even meals. Ask about everything; you may be pleasantly surprised.

- ✔ **Ask if your kids can stay in the room with you.** A room with two double beds usually doesn't cost any more than one with a queen-size bed. And many hotels won't charge you the additional person rate if the additional person is pint-size and related to you. Even if you have to pay $10 or $15 extra for a rollaway bed, you'll save hundreds by not taking two rooms.

✔ **Try expensive restaurants at lunch instead of dinner.** Lunch tabs are usually a fraction of what dinner would cost at a top restaurant, and the menu often boasts many of the same specialties.

✔ **Don't rent a gas guzzler.** Renting a smaller car is cheaper, and you save on gas to boot. Unless you're traveling with kids and need lots of space, don't go beyond the economy size.

✔ **Skip the souvenirs.** Your photographs and your memories could be the best mementos of your trip. If you're concerned about money, you can do without the T-shirts, key chains, salt-and-pepper shakers, mouse ears, and other trinkets.

Chapter 5

Planning Ahead for Special Travel Needs

- -

In This Chapter

▶ Taking the kids along

▶ Taking advantage of age: tips for seniors

▶ Dealing with disabilities

▶ Stepping out: resources for gays and lesbians

- -

*I*f you have special needs, interests, or concerns that affect your travel plans — and almost everyone does — this chapter is for you. While I may not be able to answer all your questions on a particular topic, I can point you to some excellent information sources.

Bringing Along the Kids

If you have enough trouble getting the kids out of the house in the morning, dragging them thousands of kilometers away may seem an insurmountable challenge. But family travel can be immensely rewarding, giving you new ways of seeing the world through smaller pairs of eyes. And for kids, travel in the Canadian Rockies can be a whole lot of fun.

Throughout this book, I use the Kid Friendly icon to highlight hotels, eateries, and activities that are especially popular with children. Many restaurants offer kids' menus, and hotels with swimming pools and waterslides are plentiful in areas such as Calgary, Canmore, and Banff.

In Calgary, look for places that get the thumbs-up from **Child and Youth Friendly Calgary.** (Brochures are available at visitor information centers, or go to Internet: www.childfriendly.ab.ca.) The organization operates on the theory that the best judge of whether or not a particular establishment will score with kids is — a kid. Hotels, eateries, attractions, and events earn the "child friendly" designation by meeting certain criteria, such as providing children's programs. Kids do the site inspections. The Child Friendly Web site also recommends a few hotels and events in the Rockies.

Many restaurants and hotel dining rooms in the Rockies offer special menus for children, and in the larger centers fast-food spots and family restaurants aren't hard to find. The most kid-friendly (and walletfriendly) spots to dine are the hundreds of picnic sites inmeadows, beside lakes, and along riverbanks in the Alberta and British Columbia parks. Stock up on healthy food while you're in Calgary, Canmore, Golden, or the town of Banff. Pack your lunch and trek up to a mountain lake or pull off the highway and find a picnic table when you're exploring the Lake Minnewanka Road, Bow Valley Parkway, or the Icefields Parkway.

Chapter 3 offers a Canadian Rockies itinerary that caters specifically to kids. In every region, you find easy walks and interpretive trails that are ideal for younger children. If you're camping, be sure to find out about park interpretive programs. These (usually free) educational talks and shows are designed with youngsters in mind. Visitor centers can direct you to other family-friendly park activities, such as the **junior naturalist program** offered by the Friends of Banff National Park (Internet: www.friendsofbanff.com) in July and August. You find similar programs in other national parks.

If you're ready for a night out without the kids, hotel front desk staff can usually supply names of reliable babysitters. Or, call **KidScenes** at ☎ **403-287-9800** (Calgary) or **403-762-2504** (Banff).

Before you hit the road, you may want to surf around for some sound advice on family travel. You can find good family-oriented vacation advice on such Web sites as the **Family Travel Network** (Internet: www.familytravelnetwork.com) and **Family Travel Files** (Internet: www.thefamilytravelfiles.com), which offers an online magazine and a directory of tour operators and off-the-beaten-path tours for families.

Various books on the market offer tips for vacationing with tots and teens — anywhere. You'll discover plenty of ideas in *How to Take Great Trips with Your Kids* (The Harvard Common Press).

Seeing the Rockies in Senior Style

Many restaurants, attractions, and services in Calgary and the Canadian Rockies offer seniors discounts. Be sure to mention that you're a senior when you make your travel reservations, and while traveling, carry identification showing your date of birth. The definition of a senior varies among establishments but usually applies to people either over the age of 60 or over 65. If you're over 65, you qualify for discounts in the national parks such as park passes, admission to historic sites, and lift tickets at ski hills.

Via Rail offers a 10% discount to people over age 60, and seniors rates for **Greyhound Canada** apply to folks older than 62. **Air Canada** offers a 10% discount on certain fares, and the same reduction for a person traveling with a senior. Some hotel chains cut rates for everyone over the age of 50. Also check for special rates at health and fitness centers, pharmacies, and hair salons.

Many reliable agencies and organizations target the 50-plus market. **Elderhostel** (☎ **877-426-8056;** Internet: www.elderhostel.org) arranges study programs for those aged 55 and over (and a spouse or companion of any age) in more than 90 countries around the world, including Canada. Most courses in the Canadian Rockies last 6 to 12 days and many include airfare, accommodations, meals, and lectures. Active outdoor programs combine learning with cycling, wilderness canoeing, horseback trail riding, and hiking.

Recommended publications offering travel resources and discounts for seniors include the following:

- ✔ *Travel 50 & Beyond* (Internet: www.travel50andbeyond.com)
- ✔ *Travel Unlimited: Uncommon Adventures for the Mature Traveler* (Avalon)
- ✔ *101 Tips for Mature Travelers*, available from Grand Circle Travel (☎ **800-221-2610,** 617-350-7500; Internet: www.gct.com)
- ✔ *The 50+ Traveler's Guidebook* (St. Martin's Press)
- ✔ *Unbelievably Good Deals and Great Adventures That You Absolutely Can't Get Unless You're Over 50* (McGraw-Hill)

Other useful information for traveling seniors can be found at *Arthur Frommer's Budget Travel Online*, starting at the Internet page: www.frommers.com/activities/senior.

Traveling Without Barriers

These days, a disability shouldn't stop anyone from traveling. There are more options and resources than ever before.

The official accommodation guides published by **Travel Alberta** (☎ **800-661-8888**) and **Tourism British Columbia** (☎ **800-435-5622**) provide information about accessibility options at lodgings in each province. **Tourism Calgary**'s vacation planning guide shows which hotels and attractions in that city have wheelchair access. Call ahead (☎ **800-661-1678**) to receive a copy.

In **Calgary**, the **C-Train** (public transit system) stations and platforms are wheelchair accessible, and many routes have low-floor buses that allow convenient access for travelers with wheelchairs and walkers. Priority seats for passengers with disabilities are located at the front of the bus.

At **Stampede Park** all buildings are wheelchair accessible, with elevator access to the Big Four Building and the Grandstand. Telephones for the hearing impaired are available at all telephone booths throughout the park, and TDD telephone service is available in the Stampede Headquarters building at the Olympic Gate.

Checker Cabs (☎ **403-299-9999**) provides wheelchair-accessible taxi service in Calgary.

The national parks in the Canadian Rockies are more wheelchair-friendly than ever before. In Banff, for instance, the visitor information centers, museums, and historic sites are accessible, as are services such as the **Lake Louise Gondola.** The **Miette Hot Springs,** in Jasper, have accessible facilities, as does the **Icefield Centre** on the Icefields Parkway (and Snocoach tours). An all-terrain wheelchair (a companion is required) is available from Jasper National Park or Jasper Park Lodge. Call ☎ **403-852-3301.**

Pick up *The Mountain Guide,* a brochure available throughout the national parks in the Canadian Rockies, to find out which campgrounds offer accessible facilities. **Whistlers,** in Jasper, has two paved sites with adapted picnic tables and wheelchair-accessible showers. In Banff, good choices include **Tunnel Mountain** and **Johnston Canyon** campgrounds.

Numerous scenic trails and interpretive hikes are paved, including the **lakeside trail** at Lake Louise and the **upper canyon trail** at Maligne Canyon in Jasper.

Many travel agencies offer customized tours and itineraries for travelers with disabilities. **Accessible Journeys** (☎ **800-846-4537,** 610-521-0339; Internet: www.disabilitytravel.com) caters specifically to slow walkers and wheelchair travelers and their families and friends. They offer various tours in Canada, including an excursion through the Rockies.

Organizations that offer assistance to disabled travelers include the following:

- ✔ **Moss Rehab Hospital** (Internet: www.mossresourcenet.org), which provides a library of accessible-travel resources online

- ✔ **Society for Accessible Travel and Hospitality** (☎ **212-447-7284;** Internet: www.sath.org; annual membership fees: US$45 adults, US$30 seniors and students), which offers a wealth of travel resources for all types of disabilities and informed recommendations on destinations, access guides, travel agents, tour operators, vehicle rentals, and companion services

- ✔ **American Foundation for the Blind** (☎ **800-232-5463;** Internet: www.afb.org), which provides information on traveling with Seeing Eye dogs.

Also check out these publications:

- ✔ *Emerging Horizons* (US$14.95 per year, US$19.95 outside the U.S.; Internet: www.emerginghorizons.com)

- ✔ **Twin Peaks Press** (☎ **360-694-2462;** Internet: http://disabilitybookshop.virtualave.net/blist84.htm), offering travel-related books for travelers with special needs

- ✔ *Open World Magazine,* published by the Society for Accessible Travel and Hospitality (see above; subscription: $18 per year, $35 outside the U.S.)

Advice for Gay and Lesbian Travelers

In Calgary, pick up a copy of *Outlooks,* a free monthly newspaper published for the gay community (☎ **403-228-1157** or write Box 439, Suite 100, 1039 17th Ave. SW, Calgary, AB T2T 0B2). *Outlooks* is available at many coffee shops and bookstores throughout the city. You can also find it in Vancouver and Edmonton, or online at Internet: www.outlooks.ca.

Gay Calgary (☎ **800-543-6970,** 403-543-6970; Internet: www.gaycalgary.com) can link you up with Calgary and area gay-friendly businesses, including hotels, clubs, and travel agents. The Web site maintains a local events calendar.

The Calgary-based **Alberta Rockies Gay Rodeo Association** (Internet: www.argra.org) hosts the annual **Canadian Rockies International Rodeo** each summer, along with monthly dances throughout the year.

The International Gay & Lesbian Travel Association (IGLTA) (☎ **800-448-8550,** 954-776-2626; Internet: www.iglta.org) is the trade association for the gay and lesbian travel industry, and offers an online directory of gay- and lesbian-friendly travel businesses; go to their Web site and click on "Members."

The following travel guides are available at most travel bookstores and gay and lesbian bookstores, or you can order them from **Giovanni's Room** bookstore, 1145 Pine St., Philadelphia, PA 19107 (☎ **215-923-2960;** Internet: www.giovannisroom.com):

- ✔ *Out and About* (☎ **800-929-2268,** 415-644-8044; Internet: www.outandabout.com), which offers guidebooks and a newsletter 10 times a year packed with solid information on the global gay and lesbian scene

- ✔ *Spartacus International Gay Guide* and *Odysseus,* both good, annual English-language guidebooks focused on gay men

- ✔ *Damron* guides, with separate, annual books for gay men and lesbians

- ✔ *Gay Travel A to Z: The World of Gay & Lesbian Travel Options at Your Fingertips* by Marianne Ferrari (Ferrari Publications, Box 35575, Phoenix, AZ 85069), an excellent gay and lesbian guidebook series

Part II
Ironing Out the Details

The 5th Wave   By Rich Tennant

"The guests are getting hungry. You'd better push over another garbage dumpster."

In this part...

If you've perused Part I, you probably have a particular destination — or several — in mind. This part helps you decide how to get there. In addition to providing information on modes of transport (car, bus, plane), I cover the practicalities of arranging transportation — such as finding group tours, packaged deals, and bargains on the Web. I fill you in on car rentals, and also discuss travel options for those who prefer to let somebody else do the driving. There's a chapter on lodging, so you can sort out the pros and cons (and the impact on your budget) of staying in chain hotels, historic lodges, B&Bs, or tent sites. This part also anticipates some of the questions that first-time visitors to Banff National Park — or to Canada — may be pondering, such as: What's a loonie? Where do I find cash machines in the mountains? and Do I need polypropylene underwear?

Chapter 6

Getting to the Canadian Rockies

In This Chapter

▶ Finding a perfect package

▶ Surfing for deals

▶ Choosing among plane, train, automobile, and bus

*F*iguring out how to plan your visit to the Canadian Rockies is one of the toughest — and earliest — decisions you need to make about your trip. For starters, you have to decide whether you want to tackle trip planning alone (relatively speaking, that is; you do have me to give you advice), let somebody else call the shots, or opt for a combination strategy.

Consulting a Travel Agent

A good travel agent is like a good mechanic or good plumber: hard to find, but invaluable when you locate the right one. And the best way to find a good travel agent is the same way you find a good plumber or mechanic or doctor — word of mouth. Ask friends who travel often whom they use.

To get the most out of a travel agent, do a little homework. Read up on your destination (you've already made a sound decision by buying this book) and pick out some accommodations and attractions that appeal to you. If you have online access, check prices on the Web yourself to get a sense of ballpark figures. Then take your guidebook and Web information to the travel agent and ask him or her to make the arrangements for you. Because they have access to more resources than even the most complete travel Web site, travel agents can generally get you a better price than you can get by yourself. And they can issue your tickets and vouchers right in the agency. If they can't get you into the hotel of your choice, they can recommend an alternative, and you can look for an objective review in your guidebook.

Many travel agents work on commission. The good news is that you don't pay the commission — the airlines, accommodations, and tour companies do. The bad news is that unscrupulous travel agents will try to persuade you to book the vacations that nab them the most money in commissions. Over the past few years, many airlines and resorts have begun to limit or eliminate these commissions altogether. The immediate result has been that travel agents don't bother booking certain services unless the customer specifically requests them. (And some travel agents have started charging customers for their services.) To find a trustworthy agent, ask around.

Choosing Escorted and Packaged Tours

An escorted tour does, in fact, involve an escort, but that doesn't mean it has to be dull — or even tame. Escorted tours range from cushy bus trips where you sit back and let the driver worry about the traffic, to adventures that include river rafting, horseback trips, and backcountry hikes — activities with which most of us can use a bit of guidance. You do, however, travel with a group, which may be just the ticket if you're single and want company. In general, your costs are taken care of after you arrive at your destination, but you still have to cover the airfare.

Which brings us to package tours. Unlike escorted tours, these generally package costs rather than people. While some companies bundle every aspect of your trip, including tours to various sights, most deal just with selected aspects, allowing you to get good deals by putting together, say, an airfare and hotel arrangement, or an airfare and greens fee package. Most packages tend to leave you a lot of leeway while saving you money.

How do you find these deals? I suggest some strategies in the next two sections.

Join an escorted tour

You may be one of the many people who love escorted tours. The tour company takes care of all the details and tells you what to expect at each leg of your journey. You know your costs up front and, in the case of the tame ones, you don't get many surprises. Escorted tours can take you to the maximum number of sights in the minimum amount of time with the least amount of hassle.

When choosing an escorted tour, along with finding out whether you have to put down a deposit and when final payment is due, ask a few simple questions before you buy:

- ✔ **What is the cancellation policy?** Can they cancel the trip if they don't get enough people? How late can you cancel if you're unable to go? Do you get a refund if you cancel? If they cancel?

- ✔ **How jam-packed is the schedule?** Does the tour schedule try to fit 25 hours into a 24-hour day, or does it give you ample time to stroll around town or relax by the fireplace? If getting up at 7 a.m. every day and not returning to your hotel until 6 or 7 p.m. sounds like a grind, certain escorted tours may not be for you.

- ✔ **How large is the group?** The smaller the group, the less time you spend waiting for people to get on and off the bus. Tour operators may be evasive about this, because they may not know the exact size of the group until everybody has made reservations, but they should be able to give you a rough estimate.

- ✔ **Is there a minimum group size?** Some tours have a minimum group size, and may cancel the tour if they don't book enough people. If a quota exists, find out what it is and how close they are to reaching it. Again, tour operators may be evasive in their answers, but the information may help you select a tour that's sure to happen.

- ✔ **What exactly is included?** Don't assume anything. You may have to pay to get yourself to and from the airport. A box lunch may be included in an excursion but drinks may be extra. Beer may be included but not wine. How much flexibility do you have? Can you opt out of certain activities, or does the bus leave once a day, with no exceptions? Are all your meals planned in advance? Can you choose your entree at dinner, or does everybody get the same chicken cutlet?

Here are some reliable companies to contact for escorted tours in the Canadian Rockies:

Brewster: The most prominent name in the tour business in Banff is Brewster (☎ **877-791-5500;** Internet: www.brewster.ca), a company that has been guiding visitors through the Canadian Rockies for over 100 years. Brewster runs escorted trips through the Rockies by bus, train, and car, along with a range of guided day trips from Calgary, Banff, Lake Louise, and Jasper. The cost of a typical five-day bus tour from Calgary to Banff and Jasper National Parks, including accommodation, meals, transportation with a guide, and admission to attractions, ranges from about C$895 to C$1,839 (US$626.50 to US$1,287) per person, depending on where you stay and the time of year you travel.

If you like the idea of having somebody else handle the details, but want more control over your agenda than what you have with a typical escorted tour, check into independent travel packages, such as Brewster's self-drive tours. They include a rental car, accommodation, maps, itinerary, and admission to parks and attractions.

Collette Tours (☎ **800-340-5158;** Internet: www.collettevacations. com) offers a range of escorted trips by bus and train through the Canadian Rockies, starting from either Calgary or Vancouver.

John Steel Rail Tours (☎ **800-988-5778;** Internet: www.johnsteel.com) runs train excursions from Vancouver to Jasper National Park.

Rocky Mountaineer Railtours (☎ **800-665-7245;** Internet: www.rockymountaineer.com), also based in Vancouver, offers numerous train trips through the mountains, including tours to Calgary, Banff, and Jasper.

Numerous firms run guided outdoor adventure trips throughout the Rockies. You can hike, ski, fish, raft, or watch wildlife. For hikers, **Yamnuska Inc.** (☎ **403-678-4164;** Internet: www.yamnuska.com), based in Canmore, offers a variety of backpacking adventures, including hikes to Mount Assiniboine and Mount Robson. The trips run about 6 to 8 days and you can expect to pay between C$1,100 and C$1,300 (US$770 and US$910). The company provides accommodation and food, in Canmore and on the trail, and supplies tents and cooking gear. You carry your personal gear and sleeping bag. If you wish, you can hire a porter for around C$200 (US$140) per day.

Choose a package tour

For lots of destinations, package tours can be a smart way to go. In many cases, a package tour that includes airfare, hotel, and transportation to and from the airport costs less than the hotel alone on a tour you book yourself. That's because packages are sold in bulk to tour operators, who resell them to the public. It's kind of like buying your vacation at a buy-in-bulk store — except the tour operator is the one who buys the 1,000-count box of garbage bags and resells them 10 at a time at a cost that undercuts the local supermarket.

Package tours can vary as much as those garbage bags, too. Some offer a better class of hotels; others provide the same class of hotels for lower prices. Some book flights on scheduled airlines; others sell charters. In some packages, your choice of accommodations and travel days may be limited. Some let you choose between escorted vacations and independent vacations; others allow you to add on just a few excursions or escorted day trips (also at discounted prices) without booking an entirely escorted tour.

To find package tours, check out the travel section of your local Sunday newspaper or the ads in the back of national travel magazines such as *Travel & Leisure, National Geographic Traveler,* and *Condé Nast Traveler.*

Another good source of package deals is the airlines themselves. Most major airlines offer air/land packages, including **American Airlines Vacations** (☎ **800-321-2121;** Internet: www.aavacations.com), **Delta Vacations** (☎ **800-221-6666;** Internet: www.deltavacations.com), **Continental Airlines Vacations** (☎ **800-301-3800;** Internet: www. coolvacations.com), and **United Vacations** (☎ **888-854-3899;** Internet: www.unitedvacations.com). Several big **online travel agencies** — Expedia, Travelocity, Orbitz, Site59, and Lastminute.com — also do a brisk business in packages.

Both **Brewster** and **Collette Tours** (see "Join an escorted tour," above) also offer a variety of packaged deals.

Banff Accommodation Reservations (☎ **877-226-3348;** Internet: www.banffinfo.com) will book your hotels along with bus transportation, train trips, tours, skiing, golf, and other activities throughout the Rockies. If you're willing to ski in early December and sleep in a hostel, you can buy three days on the slopes and three nights accommodation for C$255/US$178.50 (per person). You pay more than twice that rate if you opt for a luxury hotel and travel in peak ski season.

You can book hotel/lift-ticket packages at a range of hotels in the Rockies through Ski Rockies (☎ **888-401-6802;** Internet: www.skirockie.ca). If you already know where you want to stay, check with the hotel or resort — many places in the Rockies offer ski and golf packages.

You can also find deals by contacting the ski hills directly. **Resorts of the Canadian Rockies** (☎ **800-258-7669;** Internet: www.skicr.com), which owns seven ski resorts including Lake Louise in Banff National Park, and Fortress Mountain and Nakiska in Kananaskis Country, offers airfare, lodging, and lift-ticket packages from various cities, including Toronto, Boston, Houston, and New York. Summer holiday packages are also available. Check the Web site for last-minute specials. To book flight/accommodation/lift-ticket packages to ski the three resorts in Banff National Park (Lake Louise, Mount Norquay, and Sunshine Village), call **Ski Big 3** at ☎ **877-754-7080** or go to Internet: www.skibig3.com.

If you're heading to the slopes in Banff, you can buy one pass that lets you ski or snowboard at any of the three park resorts. The Tri-Area Pass also covers transportation from your hotel (in Banff or Lake Louise) to the ski hills. Decide how long you want to stay, then go to Internet: www.skibig3.com to check prices.

Getting the Best Deal on Your Airfare

Competition among the major U.S. airlines is unlike that of any other industry. Every airline offers virtually the same product, yet prices can vary by hundreds of dollars.

If you need the flexibility to buy your ticket at the last minute and change your itinerary at a moment's notice — or if you're traveling for business and want to get home before the weekend — you pay (or perhaps your company pays) the premium rate, known as the *full fare*. But if you can book your ticket far in advance, stay over Saturday night, and are willing to travel midweek (Tuesday, Wednesday, or Thursday), you can qualify for the least expensive price — usually a fraction of the full fare. On many flights, a 7- or 14-day advance purchase ticket costs less than half of the full-fare amount. Obviously, it pays to plan ahead.

The airlines also periodically hold sales, in which they lower the prices on their most popular routes. These fares have advance purchase requirements and date-of-travel restrictions, but you can't beat the prices. As you plan your vacation, keep your eyes open for sales, especially in the off-peak travel periods of early spring and late fall. You almost never see a sale during the summer vacation months of July and August, or around Thanksgiving or Christmas, when many people fly regardless of the fare they have to pay.

Book your travel online

The "big three" online travel agencies, **Expedia** (Internet: www.expedia.com), **Travelocity** (Internet: www.travelocity.com), and **Orbitz** (Internet: www.orbitz.com), sell most of the air tickets bought on the Internet. (Canadian travelers should try Internet: www.expedia.ca and Internet: www.travelocity.ca; U.K. residents can go for Internet: expedia.co.uk and opodo.co.uk.) Each has different business deals with the airlines and may offer different fares on the same flights, so shopping around is wise. Expedia and Travelocity will also send you an **e-mail notification** when a cheap fare becomes available to your favorite destination. Of the smaller travel agency Web sites, **SideStep** (Internet: www.sidestep.com) receives good reviews from users. It's a browser add-on that purports to "search 140 sites at once," but in reality beats competitors' fares only as often as other sites do.

Great **last-minute deals** are available through free weekly e-mail services provided directly by the airlines. Air Canada (Internet: www.aircanada.ca), for instance, will e-mail you each Wednesday with specials for the upcoming weekend. Sign up for weekly e-mail alerts at individual airline Web sites or check mega-sites that compile comprehensive lists of last-minute specials, such as **Smarter Living** (Internet: www.smarterliving.com). For last-minute trips, Internet: www.site59.com in the U.S. and Internet: www.lastminute.com in Europe often have better deals than the major-label sites.

Arriving by Plane

The most convenient international airport to fly to for a trip to the Canadian Rockies is in Calgary, about a 90-minute drive from Banff. **Air Canada** (☎ **888-247-2262;** Internet: www.aircanada.ca) operates nonstop flights to Calgary from many cities in Canada and the U.S. as well as from London and Frankfurt. **WestJet** (☎ **888-937-8538;** Internet: www.westjet.ca) flies direct to Calgary from various places in western Canada and offers flights from Atlantic Canada to Calgary via Hamilton, Ontario. Other major carriers serving Calgary include **Continental Airlines** (☎ **800-231-0856;** Internet: www.continental.com); **Northwest Airlines** (☎ **800-447-4747;** Internet: www.nwa.com); and **United Airlines** (☎ **800-241-6522;** www.ual.com).

Major car rental companies are located at the Calgary Airport. **Airport Shuttle Express** (☎ **403-509-4799;** Internet: www.airportshuttleexpress.com) operates a ride-share service with regular trips to many hotels in Calgary and the bus station. The **Airporter** bus (☎ **403-531-3909**) goes to 10 hotels in the downtown area. **Banff Airporter** (☎ **888-449-2901;** Internet: www.banffairporter.com) runs a shuttle bus service from the Calgary airport to Canmore, Banff, and Lake Louise.

Aside from Calgary, the handiest major airports in western Canada are in **Edmonton** (401km/249 miles from Banff) — a good choice if you're staying in Jasper National Park (362km/224 miles from Edmonton) — and **Vancouver** (848km/530 miles from Banff).

Driving to the Canadian Rockies

Driving to the Canadian Rockies makes a lot of sense, if you live reasonably close and you have the time. It's easy to get there. The Trans-Canada Highway runs right through the park, connecting Banff with Calgary to the east, and Vancouver to the west. If you're coming from the U.S., Highway 2 runs north to Calgary from the Alberta–Montana border, and farther west, highways 93 and 95 (from Montana and Idaho) lead to Kootenay National Park through southern British Columbia.

Arriving by Bus

Greyhound (☎ **800-661-8747;** Internet: www.greyhound.ca) offers bus service to Calgary, Canmore, Banff, Jasper, and other communities in the Canadian Rockies from many parts of Canada and the U.S. (Check on passes that allow you to travel throughout North America for periods of between 4 and 60 days.)

Taking the Train

No companies offer regular scheduled passenger rail service to Calgary or Banff, but **Via Rail** (☎ **888-VIA-RAIL;** Internet: www.viarail.ca) stops at Edmonton and Jasper on its Toronto–Vancouver route. The train departs from Toronto on Tuesday, Thursday, and Saturday, and from Vancouver on Friday, Sunday, and Tuesday. **Amtrak** (☎ **800-USA-RAIL;** Internet: www.amtrack.com) connects with Via Rail trains at several border points.

You can also arrange a guided tour of the Rockies by train. See "Taking the Train," in Chapter 7.

Chapter 7

Getting Around the Canadian Rockies

- -

In This Chapter

▶ Exploring the Canadian Rockies by car

▶ Traveling by train or bus

▶ Getting around safely

- -

*D*riving is definitely the most popular way to see the Rockies. Whether you hop in the car and head directly for the mountains, or fly to Calgary and rent a car when you arrive, you can see and do more — and set your own agenda — if you're behind the wheel. Having said that, traveling by bus or train may be feasible, too, especially for certain itineraries, such as ski trips in Banff and sight-seeing excursions to Jasper.

Getting Around by Car or RV

You can get by without a car in Calgary (see Chapter 11 for tips on cycling around the city or taking the C-Train or bus), but when you head west to the mountains, you'll probably want the convenience and flexibility of a vehicle.

Getting the best deal on a rental car

Rental car agencies with outlets at the Calgary International Airport include **Avis** (☎ 800-230-4898), **Hertz** (☎ 800-263-0600), **Thrifty** (☎ 800-847-4389), **National** (☎ 800-227-7368), **Budget** (☎ 800-268-8900), and **Alamo** (☎ 800-327-9633).

Rental costs vary widely, depending on the type of vehicle you choose, when you rent it, and where you pick it up. You can usually get a better deal if you book at least seven days in advance. Asking a few questions may save even more dollars:

- ✔ Weekend rates may be lower than weekday rates. If you're keeping the car five or more days, a weekly rate may be cheaper than the daily rate. Ask if the rate is the same for pickup Friday morning as for pickup Thursday night.

- ✔ Some companies may assess a drop-off charge if you don't return the car to the same rental location; others, notably National, don't.

- ✔ Check whether the rate is cheaper if you pick up the car at a location in town rather than at the airport.

- ✔ Find out whether age is an issue. Many car rental companies add a fee for drivers under age 25, whereas some don't rent to them at all.

- ✔ If you see an advertised price in your local newspaper, be sure to ask for that specific rate; otherwise you may be charged the standard (higher) rate. Don't forget to mention membership in CAA, AAA, AARP, and trade unions, which may entitle you to discounts ranging from 5% to 30%.

- ✔ Check your frequent-flier accounts. Not only are your favorite (or at least most-used) airlines likely to have sent you discount coupons, but most car rentals also add at least 500 travel miles to your account.

- ✔ As with other aspects of planning your trip, using the Internet can make comparison shopping for a car rental much easier. You can check rates at most of the major agencies' Web sites. Plus, all the major travel sites — **Travelocity** (www.travelocity.com), **Expedia** (www.expedia.com), **Orbitz** (www.orbitz.com), and **Smarter Living** (www.smarterliving.com), for example — have search engines that can dig up discounted car rental rates. Just enter the car size you want, the pickup and return dates, and location — and the server returns a price. You can even make the reservation through any of these sites.

Adding up the charges

In addition to the standard rental prices, other optional charges apply to most car rentals (and some not-so-optional charges, such as taxes). The *collision damage waiver* (**CDW**), which requires you to pay for damage to the car in a collision, is covered by many credit card companies. Check with your credit card company before you go so you can avoid paying this hefty fee (as much as C$20 [US$14] a day).

The car rental companies also offer additional *liability insurance* (if you harm others in an accident), *personal accident insurance* (if you harm yourself or your passengers), and *personal effects insurance* (if your luggage is stolen from your car). Your insurance policy on your car at home probably covers most of these unlikely occurrences. However, if your own insurance doesn't cover you for rentals or if you don't have auto insurance, definitely consider the additional coverage (ask your car rental agent for more information). Unless you're toting around the Hope diamond (and you don't want to leave that in your car trunk anyway) you can probably skip the personal effects insurance, but driving around without liability or personal accident coverage is never a good idea. Even if you're a good driver, other people may not be, and liability claims can be complicated.

Some companies also offer *refueling packages,* in which you pay for your initial full tank of gas up front and can return the car with an empty gas tank. The prices can be competitive with local gas prices, but you don't get credit for any gas remaining in the tank. If you reject this option, you pay only for the gas you use, but you have to return the car with a full tank or pay a per liter refueling surcharge, at a premium to local gas prices. If you usually run late and a fueling stop may make you miss your plane, you're a perfect candidate for the fuel-purchase option.

And don't forget about sales taxes. If you're renting your car in Alberta, you pay the 7% Goods and Services Tax (GST). In British Columbia, you're charged the GST in addition to a provincial sales tax of 7.5%.

RVing around the Rockies

From a budget angle, the cost of renting an RV is quite comparable to what it costs you to rent a car and stay in hotels. For a standard-size motorhome that sleeps five people, high-season rates typically start at C$1,400 to C$1,500 (US$980 to US$1,050) a week (with 1,000km). Rates usually peak in July and August and drop considerably in spring and fall. As with car rentals, you often get a better rate by booking in advance.

Numerous companies rent motorhomes in Calgary, including **Canadian Mobile Holidays** (☎ 866-569-9303; Internet: www. canadianmobile holidays.com), **Canadream** (☎ 800-461-7368; Internet: www.canadream.com), and **Cruise America Calgary** (☎ 800-327-7799; Internet: www.cruiseamerica.com).

Remember that campgrounds operated by Parks Canada (in Banff, Jasper, Yoho, Kootenay, and Waterton national parks) are first-come, first-served. You should arrive before 4 p.m., especially if you're heading for one of the more popular sites.

Facilities at campgrounds in the national parks vary. Some are quite rustic, while others have laundry, showers, stores, and other amenities. Full hookups (power, water, and sewage) are available at the Tunnel Mountain Trailer Court in Banff, Whistlers in Jasper, Redstreak in Kootenay, and the Townsite Campground in Waterton Lakes.

Motoring through the mountains

The main highways through the national parks in the Canadian Rockies are well maintained and open year-round. You don't need four-wheel drive, but winter in the mountains does present some challenges for travelers, particularly if you're not used to coping with ice and snow.

Here are a few tips for navigating the roads in wintry weather. (And keep in mind that at higher elevations, snow can fall any time of the year.)

- Snow tires, all-season radials, or chains are required on most roads in the national parks, including the access roads to all ski areas.

- Slow down when you drive on ice or snow, and leave plenty of room between your vehicle and the one in front of you, to stop and start.

- Don't stop in posted avalanche zones.

- Watch out for black ice, especially around bridges (you may not be able to see it, but if the pavement looks shiny and black, be careful.)

- If the roads are slippery, don't use cruise control. Snow and ice can cause wheel spin, and you need to be able to reduce power, immediately, if necessary to maintain control.

- Keep in mind that on ice, a four-wheel drive vehicle has no more traction than any other type of vehicle.

- Make sure your windows and mirrors are well cleared of snow and that your brakes, wipers, defroster, and heater are working.

- As well as having a snow scraper and a shovel, it's a good idea to equip your car with a few emergency supplies, such as a warm blanket, a flashlight, and a first aid kit. Don't rely on your cell phone: You can't count on good reception outside of the main towns.

Give yourself more time for travel in winter. Keep an eye on the weather and find out what shape the highways are in before you strike out. Dial ☎ **403-762-2088** to hear a **weather forecast** for the **Banff/Kootenay/Yoho** region; call ☎ **780-852-3185** if you're heading north to **Jasper.**

You can check **road conditions** in Banff, Jasper, Kootenay, and Yoho national parks by dialing ☎ **403-762-1450**. For travel outside the national parks, call ☎ **800-550-4997** to inquire about highways in **British Columbia** and ☎ **403-246-5853** (Calgary area) or ☎ **780-471-6056** (Edmonton area) for roads in **Alberta**.

Keeping an eye out for critters

Aside from slippery roads and poor visibility in winter, the main hazard you need to be prepared for in the Canadian Rockies — any time of year — is wild animals (and tourists who stop unexpectedly to see them) along the side of the road. Be on guard all the time, but especially at dawn and dusk, when deer, elk, bears, and other wildlife are most active. Drive slowly, and be prepared for the animal (or animals — where there's one, there are usually more) to run across the highway. Give other drivers the heads-up by flashing your headlights.

Taking the Train

Aside from **Via Rail** (☎ **888-VIA-RAIL;** Internet: www.viarail.ca), which runs regular passenger service to Jasper from Edmonton and Vancouver, **Rocky Mountaineer Railtours** (☎ **800-665-7245;** Internet: www.rockymountaineer.com) offers various scenic tours through the Canadian Rockies, including trips to Jasper and Banff. **Royal Canadian Pacific Luxury Rail Tours** (☎ **877-665-3044;** Internet: www.cprtours.com) runs high-end excursions on refurbished heritage rail cars, including a six-day loop through the Rockies that starts in Calgary, crosses the Crowsnest Pass in southern Alberta, and journeys through Yoho and Banff national parks.

Getting Around by Bus

In addition to **Greyhound** (☎ **800-661-8747;** Internet: www.greyhound.ca), which offers regular service between the main towns in the Rockies, various shuttle services run from Calgary and Edmonton to Banff, Lake Louise, and Jasper. Call **Brewster** (☎ **877-791-5500;** Internet: www.brewster.ca) or **SunDog Tours** (☎ **888-786-3641;** Internet: www.sundogtours.com).

In summer, SunDog also runs a daily shuttle service between the hostels in Banff, Lake Louise, and Jasper. Reserve through your hostel or by calling ☎ 888-786-3641.

If you're staying in Banff, check with your hotel. Many offer shuttle services to popular destinations in the townsite and to ski hills. Banff's public transit system will also get you around town, from the Fairmont Banff Springs Hotel to Tunnel Mountain. In summer, you can hop on a bus in the village of Lake Louise to get to Lake Louise or Moraine Lake.

Chapter 8

Booking Your Accommodation

· ·

In This Chapter

▶ Deciding where to sleep

▶ Avoiding the rack rates

▶ Booking the best room

· ·

*T*he Canadian Rockies offer an enormous range of lodging choices, all the way from C$6-a-night tent sites in the backcountry to C$600 rooms in luxury hotels. On the whole, if you want to be centrally situated and surrounded by luxury with loads of conveniences, you pay the top rates. But certain styles of accommodation may appeal to you (or not) for reasons that have nothing to do with price. If you like the opportunity to meet local people (who are usually knowledgeable about neighborhood restaurants, shops, and attractions), for instance, you can often save dollars by choosing a bed-and-breakfast — and be perfectly happy, too. This chapter sums up your lodging options and provides tips on booking the room (or site) of your choice at the best price.

Finding the Place That's Right for You

These are the main types of accommodation available to visitors in the Canadian Rockies.

Bed down in a B&B

B&Bs can be a great alternative to hotels, especially for couples or people traveling solo, and you have many to choose from throughout the Rockies, particularly when you stay in Calgary or the towns of Banff or Jasper. Options range from simple rooms with shared baths to luxuriously appointed getaways with Jacuzzis and fireplaces, and cost anywhere from about C$50 (US$35) per night to as much as or more than area hotels. Most B&Bs have a no-smoking policy and some don't accept kids, so find out what the restrictions are before you book. Many bed-and-breakfasts are located in restored historic homes, and you can often expect a full breakfast.

Check the accommodation guides published by the tourism bureaus in Alberta and British Columbia or get in touch with groups such as the **Bed and Breakfast Association of Calgary** (☎ **403-277-0023;** Internet: `www.bbcalgary.com`) or the **Alberta Bed and Breakfast Association;** Internet: `www.bbalberta.com`). Many establishments have Web sites where you can see photos. In the town of Jasper, lots of families rent rooms only (no breakfast), a practice that stems from regulations that used to prevent homeowners from serving breakfast. The rules have changed, and you do see some B&Bs in Jasper today, but many places still offer just a room. You can locate them through the **Jasper Home Accommodation Association** (Internet: `www.stayinjasper.com`). Pick up a brochure at the Information Centre. Or, just look for the small green-and-white signs on houses around town.

Motoring up to a motel or hotel

If you're like most people, you probably have your favorite chain hotel — a place where you pull into the parking lot knowing what to expect. If you've stayed there often enough, you may even know the color scheme in your room! The major chains are well represented along the Trans-Canada Highway through Calgary, Canmore, Banff, and Golden. See the Appendix for telephone numbers. As you get away from the main centers, you're more apt to find privately owned lodgings, which may be less predictable than the big guys, but are generally clean, comfortable, and reasonably priced. You see lots of family-run motels in the Radium and Invermere area, just outside Kootenay National Park.

Staying at historic and luxury hotels

The Canadian Rockies have some wonderful historic hotels, many of which were built by the Canadian Pacific Railway around a century ago to pamper well-heeled visitors riding the rails through the Rockies. (Canadian Pacific Limited owns Fairmont hotels — a name you see throughout the parks.) The Fairmont Banff Springs and the Fairmont Chateau Lake Louise are known around the world. You can soak up some history (and also soak in a saltwater pool) in the Fairmont Palliser hotel in downtown Calgary. The Fairmont Jasper Park Lodge offers accommodation in posh chalets and cabins. Waterton's Prince of Wales hotel is a little more rustic. Naturally, beds in these hotels don't come cheap, but if there's room in your budget for luxury, you can find it in a handful of illustrious old hotels throughout the Rockies. (And in some spanking new places, too.)

Choosing a cabin

With a few exceptions, if you opt for a log cabin, cottage, or chalet, you'll be a bit removed from the nearest town. If you're the type that likes to stroll to shops and restaurants, this may be inconvenient, but if you appreciate a wilderness setting this kind of accommodation is worth considering. Costs are usually fairly comparable to what you pay to stay in a moderately priced hotel. Some cabin resorts in the Rockies have their own restaurants and many cabins are equipped with kitchens or at least microwaves and small fridges. Cabins can also be a great option for families. You usually have more space and privacy than you would in a hotel, not to mention handy picnic tables and playground areas right outside your door. And you save money by fixing some of your meals yourself.

Discovering backcountry comfort

Hot showers and gourmet meals don't usually go hand in hand with wilderness accommodation. But exceptions exist. Throughout the Canadian Rockies, for instance, a handful of lodges cater to folks who prefer cushy digs in the backcountry and are thus willing to ski or hike for kilometers (or pay for a helicopter) to get there. For backcountry lodge locations, refer to Chapters 12 and 9, on Banff and Yoho national parks; Chapter 21 on British Columbia provincial parks; and Chapter 18 on Golden. Backcountry lodges generally require a minimum stay and are often booked up well in advance, especially for long weekends in prime hiking or ski season. Prices are steep but usually include memorable food. Meals are generally served in a communal setting, so count on getting to know your fellow guests.

Pitching a tent (or parking a camper)

Camping can be a great way to go, especially if you're on a tight budget. Campgrounds in the national and provincial parks in Alberta and British Columbia range from basic spots where you can pitch your tent, to fully serviced (power, water, and sewage) sites with stores, showers, laundry facilities, playgrounds, and even interpretive programs. You pay about C$20 to C$26 (US$14 to US$18) per night. Campgrounds within the national parks don't accept reservations, but many others do.

Travel Alberta publishes a directory of campgrounds in the province. Call ☎ **800-661-8888** or order over the Internet: www.explorealberta.com. Information is also available from the **Alberta Resort and Campground Association** (☎ **403-742-4060**; Internet: www.camping.ab.ca). The accommodation guide published by **Tourism British Columbia** includes information on campsites in that province. Call ☎ **800-435-5622** to request a copy or order at Internet: www.hellobc.com. You reserve campsites by calling ☎ **800-689-9025** or online at Internet: www. camping.bc.ca or www.discovercamping.ca. For some campsites in B.C. you can book up to three months in advance (☎ **800-689-9025**) by paying a reservation fee of C$6.42 (US$44.50) per night.

Finding a bed in a hostel

Hostels are popular with budget-conscious travelers of all ages. You usually sleep in dorm rooms (although increasingly, hostels are also offering private rooms) and have the use of shared kitchen and laundry facilities. Other amenities vary widely from hostel to hostel. The average cost is C$22 (US$15) per night. The Alpine Centre hostels in Banff and Lake Louise are rated among the top in the world, and feature licensed restaurants. Hostelling International has locations in Calgary and throughout the mountain parks. I include information on some hostels in Parts III and IV of this book. For a complete list, along with details on facilities and rates, go to Internet: www.hihostels.ca.

Uncovering the Truth About Rack Rates

The *rack rate* is the maximum rate a hotel charges for a room. It's the rate you get if you walk in off the street and ask for a room for the night. You sometimes see these rates printed on the fire/emergency exit diagrams posted on the back of your door.

Hotels are happy to charge you the rack rate, but you can almost always do better. Perhaps the best way to avoid paying the rack rate is surprisingly simple: Just ask for a cheaper or discounted rate. You may be pleasantly surprised.

You also save dollars if you avoid traveling when everybody else does. Unless you plan to take in the Calgary Stampede, don't head for Calgary during Stampede Week (July 9 to 18, 2004; July 8 to 17, 2005; July 7 to 16, 2006) when hotels are priciest and heavily booked. In Banff, lodging rates peak between June and September, especially in July and August, and again in ski season, particularly through February and March.

Depending on your holiday itinerary, you may do better with a package deal that covers lodging, transportation, and green fees, lift tickets, or group tours (see Chapter 6).

A travel agent may be able to negotiate a better price with certain hotels than you can get by yourself. (That's because the hotel often gives the agent a discount in exchange for steering his business toward that hotel.)

Reserving a room through the hotel's toll-free number may also result in a lower rate than calling the hotel directly. On the other hand, the central reservations number may not know about discount rates at specific locations. For example, local franchises may offer a special group rate for a wedding or family reunion, but they may neglect to tell the central booking line. Your best bet is to call both the local number and the toll-free number and see which one gives you a better deal. Also check the hotel's Web site for discounts and packages only available online.

Room rates change with the season, as occupancy rates rise and fall. Even within a given season, room prices are subject to change without notice, so the rates quoted in this book may be different from the actual rate you receive when you make your reservation. Be sure to mention your membership in AAA, AARP, frequent-flier programs, any other corporate rewards programs — even your Uncle Joe's Elks lodge in which you're an honorary inductee — when you call to book. You never know when the affiliation may be worth a few dollars off your room rate.

Surfing the Web for Hotel Deals

Although major travel booking sites such as **Travelocity** (Internet: www.travelocity.com), **Expedia** (Internet: www.expedia.com), and **Orbitz** (Internet: www.orbitz.com) (see Chapter 6) offer hotel booking, you may be better off using a site devoted primarily to lodging. You can often find properties that are not listed with more general online travel agencies. Some lodging sites specialize in a particular type of accommodation, such as B&Bs, which you won't find on the more mainstream booking services. Others, such as TravelWeb in the following list, offer weekend deals on major chain properties, which cater to business travelers and have more empty rooms on weekends. Here are a few of the sites worth checking:

- ✔ **All Hotels on the Web** (Internet: www.all-hotels.com): Although the name is something of a misnomer, the site does have tens of thousands of listings throughout the world. Bear in mind that each hotel has paid a small fee ($25 and up) to be listed, so it's less an objective list and more like a book of online brochures.

- ✔ **hoteldiscount!com** (Internet: www.hoteldiscount.com): This site lists bargain room rates at hotels in more than 50 Canadian, U.S., and international cities. Because these folks prebook blocks of rooms, you can sometimes reserve rooms at hotels that otherwise appear to be sold out. Select a city, input your dates, and you get a list of the best prices for a selection of hotels. The site often delivers deep discounts in cities where hotel rooms are expensive. The toll-free number (☎ **800-364-0801**) is available on the Web site; call if you want more options than those listed online.

✔ **InnSite** (Internet: www.innsite.com): InnSite has B&B listings across Canada and around the globe. Find an inn at your destination, see pictures of the rooms, and check prices and availability. This extensive directory of B&Bs includes listings only if the proprietor submitted one (it's free to get an inn listed). The descriptions are written by the innkeepers and many listings link to the inn's own Web sites.

✔ **TravelWeb** (Internet: www.travelweb.com): Listing more than 26,000 hotels in 170 countries, TravelWeb focuses mostly on chains (both upper and lower end), and you can book almost 90% of these online. TravelWeb's Click-It Weekends, updated each Monday, offers weekend deals at many leading hotel chains.

These and similar accommodation booking sites don't rate oor review the properties they list. For suggestions on where to stay in the Canadian Rockies, check out Parts III, IV, and V of this book.

Getting the Most for Your Money

After you make your reservation, asking one or two more pointed questions can go a long way toward making sure you get the best room in the house:

✔ **Always ask for a corner room.** They're usually larger, quieter, and have more windows and light than standard rooms, and they don't always cost more.

✔ **Find out if the hotel is renovating.** If it is, request a room away from the renovation work. Inquire, too, about the location of the restaurants, bars, and discos in the hotel — all sources of annoying noise.

✔ **If you want a nonsmoking room, specifically request one.** While many B&Bs and small inns have no-smoking policies, most large hotels reserve a certain number of rooms for smokers.

✔ **If you aren't happy with your room, talk to the front desk.** If you do this when you arrive, and the hotel has another another room available, they should be happy to accommodate you, within reason.

Chapter 9

Money Matters

. . . .

In This Chapter

▶ Making the best use of traveler's checks, credit cards, and ATMs

▶ Taking action if your wallet is stolen

. . . .

*N*ow that you have a good idea about how much your adventure in
the Canadian Rockies is going to cost, you need to figure out how
to pay for it. Not how you're going to come up with the money — I can't
help you with that — but how (in what form) you're going to carry it.

Making Sense of the "Loonie"

Canadians use dollars and cents, similar to the U.S. currency system.
Recently, the Canadian dollar has been fluctuating around 70 cents in U.S.
dollars, so your C$150 hotel room costs you only US$105 and your C$20
lunch sets you back US$14. Since prices in Canada are roughly on par
with those in the U.S., the favorable exchange makes travel in the
Canadian Rockies a good deal (although you do have to figure in sales
taxes: the 7% GST across Canada in addition to a 7.5% provincial sales
tax in B.C.).

Many stores and restaurants will take U.S. currency, but remember, you
get a better exchange rate at a bank or currency exchange. If you do
spend American money at Canadian establishments, you should
understand how the conversion is done. You may see a sign reading
U.S. currency: __ %, with a percentage, say 25%, in the blank. That
figure is the "premium," meaning that for every U.S. greenback you
hand over, the cashier will see it as $1.25 Canadian.

Traveler's Checks, Credit Cards, ATMs, or Cash?

How much cash you feel comfortable carrying is really a personal preference — and that's true whether or not you're on vacation. Of course, while on holiday you'll probably be moving around more and incurring more expenses than you generally do (unless you happen to eat out every meal when you're at home). Moreover, the odds of leaving your wallet on the bus, in a café, or by a swimming pool are undoubtedly higher when you slip into vacation gear. But, those factors aside, the only type of payment that won't be quite as available to you away from home is your personal checkbook.

Toting traveler's checks

Traveler's checks are kind of a throwback to the days before ATMs gave people quick access to their bank accounts. Although I haven't used them in ages, even during travels to foreign countries, if traveler's checks make you feel more secure about your funds, by all means buy some. Every institution that offers traveler's checks also offers replacements if they're lost or stolen, and the service charges are fairly low, or even nonexistent if you know where to go.

You can get traveler's checks at almost any bank, most often in denominations of $20, $50, $100, $500, and $1,000. If you buy your checks in Canadian Dollars, you know up front what exchange rate you're paying and you won't have to bother exchanging money on your travels.

For **American Express** traveler's checks, you pay a service charge ranging from 1% to 4%, unless you're an Amex gold or platinum card-holder, in which case the fee is waived. You can also get American Express traveler's checks over the phone by calling ☎ **800-221-7282.** AAA members can get checks without a fee at most AAA offices. For details, contact your local office or go to Internet: www.aaa.com.

Visa (☎ **800-732-1322**) also offers traveler's checks, available at Citibank locations across the country and at several other banks. The service charge ranges between 1.5% and 2%. **MasterCard** has its hand in the traveler's check market, too; call ☎ **800-223-9920** for details.

Charging ahead with credit cards

Credit cards offer some real advantages for travelers: They're a safe way to carry your money and they provide a convenient record of all your travel expenses when you arrive home. Of course, the disadvantage is that they're not only easy to use, they're easy to *overuse*. Unlike ATM or debit cards, which are directly connected to the money you have in your checking account, credit cards can take you as far as your credit limit — which may not bear much relation to your actual financial resources — can go. Credit cards let you indulge in a lot more impulse buying than any other form of payment.

You can also get cash advances off your credit card at any ATM if you know your *Personal Identification Number* (PIN). If you've forgotten it or didn't even know you had a PIN, call the phone number on the back of your credit card and ask the bank to send the number to you. You'll then have the number in about five to seven business days. Some banks can give you your PIN over the phone if you tell them your mother's maiden name or provide some other proof of identity.

While being able to get a cash advance from a credit card is handy in emergencies, you pay dearly. Interest rates for cash advances are often significantly higher than rates for credit card purchases. More important, you start paying interest on the advance *the moment you receive the cash.* Keep in mind that on airline-affiliated credit cards, a cash advance doesn't earn frequent-flier miles.

Using ATMs and carrying cash

Wherever you travel in Banff National Park and the Canadian Rockies, you're never very far from an ATM: handy 24-hour cash machines linked to an international network that most likely includes your bank at home. Both the **Cirrus** (☎ **800-424-7787;** Internet: www.mastercard.com) and **Plus** (☎ **800-843-7587;** Internet: www.visa.com) networks have ATM locations listing the banks throughout Canada that accept your card. Check the back of your ATM card to see which network your bank belongs to. Or just look for an ATM with your network's symbol emblazoned on it.

Withdraw just the money you need every couple of days. That way, you don't have to worry about carrying around a large stash (and the threat of having your pocket picked).

One important reminder before you go ATM crazy, however. Many banks now charge a fee ranging from 50¢ to C$3 whenever a nonaccount holder uses their ATMs. Your own bank may also assess a fee for using an ATM that's not one of their branch locations. In some cases you get charged twice just for using your bankcard when you're on vacation. Reverting to traveler's checks may be cheaper (although certainly less convenient to obtain and use).

Paying by debit card

Another way of working with money you have — as opposed to the theoretical money of credit cards (the money you *wish* you had!) — is to use a debit card (an ATM card with a credit card logo). In many cases, your debit and ATM card are the same piece of plastic. Instead of giving you cash, however, the debit card pays for purchases directly from your checking account. The advantage? You're using the money in your account, rather than bumping up against your credit card limit. Plus, you never pay an additional fee to use it, and you have less cash to carry around. Debit cards can usually be used anywhere a credit card is accepted.

What to Do If Your Wallet Is Stolen

Be sure to contact all your credit card companies the minute you discover your wallet has been lost or stolen. You'll also want to file a report with the police. The police are unlikely to be able to recover your wallet for you, but your credit card company or insurer may require a police report number or record of the loss.

Never leave your wallet or valuables in your parked car when you head off for a day hike or ski tour. If you have to leave gear behind, lock it in the trunk.

Almost every credit company has an emergency toll-free number to call if your card is lost or stolen. They may be able to wire you a cash advance immediately or deliver an emergency credit card in a day or two. Call the following emergency numbers in Canada:

- ✔ **American Express** ☎ **800-268-9824** (for cardholders and traveler's check holders)
- ✔ **MasterCard** ☎ **800-307-7309**
- ✔ **Visa** ☎ **800-847-2911**

If you need emergency cash over the weekend when all banks and American Express offices are closed, you can have money wired to you via **Western Union** (☎ **800-325-6000;** Internet: www.westernunion.com).

Chapter 10

Tying Up Loose Ends

· ·

In This Chapter

▶ Considering insurance

▶ Staying healthy on the road

▶ Packing your bags

· ·

*T*his chapter helps you pull together a few picky details that sometimes get left until the last minute. I cover the paperwork you need
for travel to Canada, discuss how to be prepared for medical emergencies
(and how to avoid them), and help you organize your gear.

Getting Passports and Visas

Visitors to Canada must be able to provide proof of citizenship. If
you're a U.S. citizen or permanent resident of the U.S., you aren't
required to have a passport (although a passport is the easiest method
of proving citizenship). If you don't have one, make sure you carry
other proof of citizenship, such as a certificate of naturalization, a
certificate of citizenship, or a birth certificate with photo ID. Some type
of photo ID is definitely a good idea. Permanent residents of the U.S.
who are not U.S. citizens must have their Alien Registration Cards
(green cards).

Applying for a U.S. passport

If you're applying for a first-time passport, follow these steps:

1. Complete a **passport application** in person at a U.S. passport office;
   a federal, state, or probate court; or a major post office. To find your
   regional passport office, either check the **U.S. State Department**
   Web site, Internet: `http://travel.state.gov`, or call the **National
   Passport Information Center** at ☎ **900-225-5674;** the fee is 55¢ per
   minute for automated information and US$1.50 per minute for
   operator-assisted calls.

2. Present a **certified birth certificate** as proof of citizenship. (Bringing along your driver's license, state or military ID, or social security card is also a good idea.)

3. Submit **two identical passport-size photos,** measuring 2×2 inches in size. You often find businesses that take these photos near a passport office. *Note:* You can't use a strip from a photo-vending machine because the pictures aren't identical.

4. Pay a **fee.** For people 16 and over, a passport is valid for ten years and costs US$85. For those 15 and under, a passport is valid for five years and costs US$70.

Allow plenty of time before your trip to apply for a passport; processing normally takes three weeks but can take longer during busy periods (especially spring).

If you have a passport in your current name that was issued within the past 15 years (and you were over age 16 when it was issued), you can renew the passport by mail for US$55. Whether you're applying in person or by mail, you can download passport applications from the U.S. State Department at Internet: http://travel.state.gov. For general information, call the **National Passport Agency** (☎ **202-647-0518**).

American Passport Express (☎ **800-841-6778;** Internet: www. americanpassport.com) can process your first-time passport application in five to eight business days for US$145, plus a US$60 service fee; for renewals, the cost is US$115 plus a US$60 service fee. If you need the passport in three to five business days, the service fee is US$100, and for a US$150 service fee you can receive your passport in 24 hours.

Applying for other passports

If you're visiting Canada from a country other than the U.S., you require a passport and possibly a visa. Visitors from most European countries and of former British colonies do not need visas, but citizens of many other countries do. You can find more information by visiting Internet: www.canadainternational.gc.ca. Apply for a visa at the Canadian embassy in your home country.

Here's additional information for citizens of Australia, New Zealand, and the United Kingdom.

✔ Australians can visit a local post office or passport office, call the Australia Passport Information Service (☎ **131-232** toll-free from Australia), or log on to Internet: www.passports.gov.au for details on how and where to apply. Passports cost A$136 for adults and A$68 for those under age 18.

✔ New Zealanders can pick up a passport application at any travel agency or Link Centre. For information, contact the Passport Office, Department of Internal Affairs, P.O. Box 10 – 526, Wellington (☎ **0800/225-050;** Internet: www.passports.govt.nz). Passports are NZ$80 for adults and NZ$40 for those under age 16.

✔ United Kingdom residents can pick up applications for a standard 10-year passport (5-year passport for children under age 16) at passport offices, major post offices, or a travel agency. For information, contact the United Kingdom Passport Service (☎ **0870-521-0410**; Internet: www.ukpa.gov.uk).

Buying Travel and Medical Insurance

Three kinds of travel insurance are available: trip-cancellation insurance, medical insurance, and lost luggage insurance. Here's the low-down on each:

✔ **Trip-cancellation insurance** is a good idea if you signed up for an escorted tour and paid a large portion of your vacation expenses up front. This type of insurance covers you if a death or sickness prevents you from traveling, if a tour operator or airline goes out of business, or if some kind of disaster prevents you from getting to your destination.

✔ **Medical insurance** probably isn't necessary, since your existing health insurance should cover you if you get sick while on vacation.

✔ **Lost luggage insurance** is not required for most travelers. Your homeowner's or renter's insurance should cover stolen luggage if you have off-premises theft coverage. Check your existing policies before you buy any additional coverage. If an airline loses your luggage, you're compensated up to a maximum amount, which varies from one carrier to another. Canadian airlines usually pay a maximum of C$1,500 (US$1,050) on domestic flights. In the U.S., the airline is responsible for paying US$2,500 per bag on domestic flights. On international flights originating in the U.S. (including U.S. portions of international trips), baggage is limited to approximately US$9.07 per pound (or US$20 per kilogram), up to approximately US$635 per checked bag.

Some credit cards (American Express and certain gold and platinum Visa and MasterCards, for example) offer automatic flight insurance against death or dismemberment in case of an airplane crash if you charged the cost of your ticket to your credit card.

If you're interested in purchasing travel insurance, try one of the following companies:

- ✔ **Access America** (☎ **866-807-3982;** Internet: www.accessamerica.com)

- ✔ **Travel Guard International** (☎ **800-826-4919;** Internet: www.travelguard.com)

- ✔ **Travel Insured International** (☎ **800-243-3174;** Internet: www.travelinsured.com)

- ✔ **Travelex Insurance Services** (☎ **800-457-4602;** Internet: www.travelex-insurance.com)

Don't pay for more insurance than you need. For example, if you need only trip-cancellation insurance, don't buy coverage for lost or stolen property. Trip-cancellation insurance costs about 6% to 8% of the total value of your vacation.

Staying Healthy While You Travel

Getting sick on the road is no picnic — it will ruin your vacation. Here are some tips to help you cope with (or avoid) a medical emergency during your trip.

- ✔ If you have health insurance, be sure to carry your insurance card in your wallet. Most U.S. health insurance plans and HMOs cover at least part of the out-of-country hospital visits and procedures if insurees become ill or are injured while out of the country. Most require that you pay the bills up front at the time of care, and issue a refund after you return and file all the paperwork. (*Note:* Ask for copies of all paperwork.) For information on purchasing additional medical insurance for your trip, see the previous section.

- ✔ Talk to your doctor before leaving on a trip if you have a serious and/or chronic illness. For conditions such as epilepsy, diabetes, or heart problems, wear a **Medic Alert Identification Tag** (☎ **800-825-3785;** Internet: www.medicalert.org), which immediately alerts doctors to your condition and gives them access to your records through Medic Alert's 24-hour hotline.

- ✔ Bring any medications you require with you, preferably in their original labeled containers, along with your prescriptions if you think you'll run out during your trip.

- ✔ Carry an extra set of contact lenses or glasses in case you lose one pair.

If you've read the first few chapters in this section, you've probably already figured out that you're heading to a region that's very beautiful — and wild. Travel in the mountains involves some risks, mainly related to the landscape (such as avalanches and rockslides), the weather (sunburn or hypothermia), and wildlife (bug bites and bigger problems). Knowing what to expect (and how to react) is the key to ensuring that you spend your time trekking down the trails — rather than tracking down a doctor . . . or waiting to be rescued.

Watch where you walk

Even if you don't tackle any long-distance backcountry trips, when you're exploring the mountain parks, visiting waterfalls, and meandering along interpretive trails, you're bound to end up on some steep slopes and slippery terrain. Slips and falls are among the most common injuries suffered by travelers to the Canadian Rockies. Wear sturdy shoes or hiking boots with good soles and ankle support. Take your time. Stay on designated trails and behind safety fences. Keep away from the edge. Loose rock near steep drops is especially hazardous. And when you're walking below steep ridges, stay alert for falling rock from above. Be extra careful in slippery areas near waterfalls and streams.

Be avalanche aware

Avalanches, or snow slides, can happen whenever there's snow on a slope, and not just in winter. If you plan to head into the backcountry on a ski trip or snowshoe expedition, you need to learn how to recognize and avoid avalanche terrain and be familiar with rescue techniques and equipment. Read up on avalanche safety and consider a seminar or course, such as those offered by Yamnuska (Internet: www.yamnuska.ca) or the Canadian Avalanche Association (Internet: www.avalanche.ca). Before your trip, it's critical to get up-to-date news about avalanche hazards in the area you're traveling through. Check with park visitor centers or dial ☎ 403-762-1460 (for the Banff/Kootenay/Yoho area) or ☎ 780-852-6176 for Jasper. You can get avalanche situation updates online by visiting Internet: www.avalanche.ca/weather/bulletins.

Keep cool (and stay warm)

The key thing to remember about weather in the mountains is that you have to be prepared for anything, any time of the year. It's especially important to think ahead if you're setting out for the day, or even for a few hours. It may be clear and sunny when you leave your hotel or campsite in the morning, but raining or snowing a few kilometers up the trail. Pack raingear and something warm for your hike.

In hot weather, wear light clothing and a wide-brimmed hat for sun protection. Take lots of water breaks. (Drinking water regularly is important in cool weather, too.) Eat healthy snacks throughout the day. Don't overdo it during the hottest part of the day. It's wise to avoid hiking at midday. How do you recognize **heat exhaustion?** The symptoms are pale skin, sweating, thirst, nausea, and dizziness. Victims may also get headaches or muscle cramps. You need to drink water and find a place to rest and cool down.

Don't forget sunglasses and sunscreen, even on cloudy days.

In winter, to avoid overheating and sweating, dress in layers (polypropylene, Gore-Tex, and fleece are good materials) instead of wearing one heavy garment. Make sure you have something dry to change into in case you get wet. If you do get soaked and cold, you're at risk for **hypothermia.** You're particularly susceptible when you're exhausted. Symptoms include uncontrollable shivering, lack of coordination, and slow or slurred speech. You treat hypothermia by sheltering the victim from the weather, getting them into dry clothes (or sharing a sleeping bag with them, to share body heat), and having them drink warm, nonalcoholic liquids.

If a thunderstorm comes up when you're hiking, try to get to a low, wooded area to minimize your chances of getting hit by lightning. Stay away from tall, single trees, especially in open areas. Get off peaks, ridges, and ledges and keep away from open water. Don't hold onto anything metal, such as a hiking pole.

Evade bugs and critters

In the spring and early summer, be on the lookout for **wood ticks** — small, flat, spider-like animal parasites that can cause diseases in people. They're most active in April and June. Check yourself over carefully when you've been walking in areas that may be tick-infested (dry, grassy slopes). Ticks usually head for the back of your neck, around your ears, or other hairy areas. Often, you can remove ticks before they attach themselves. If a tick proves hard to remove, or if you get a rash, see a doctor. Insect repellent that contains DEET will discourage ticks. Wearing long pants tucked into your socks or pants with tight cuffs also helps.

The other nasty bug you need to be careful about is a waterborne parasite called **Giardia lamblia,** from which you can contact giardiasis (known as "beaver fever," because the parasite is carried in water polluted by the feces of beavers and other animals). Giardiasis causes diarrhea, cramps, and nausea. To avoid it, don't drink water from lakes, streams, or rivers. When you hike, carry water with you, or boil and filter untreated water.

Packing for the Canadian Rockies

Before a backcountry trip, read up on the area you intend to visit. Excellent hiking guides are available in major bookstores and in hiking and outdoor gear shops and many park visitor centers in Alberta and British Columbia. You'll also want good maps, preferably 1:50,000-scale topographic maps. The *Gem Trek* map series is a good bet, and it's widely available. Here's an equipment checklist suggested by Parks Canada:

Backpacking checklist

Clothing

- ❑ Long underwear
- ❑ Wool sweater, down vest, or fleece jacket
- ❑ Rain-proof pants and jacket
- ❑ Hat and gloves
- ❑ Shorts, pants, and shirt
- ❑ Extra socks
- ❑ Boots with good support
- ❑ Sandals or runners for fording streams and wearing at camp

Shelter

- ❑ Tent with waterproof fly
- ❑ Backpack, sleeping bag, sleeping pad
- ❑ Stove, fuel, pot, dishes, utensils
- ❑ Enough food for an extra day
- ❑ Water filter or purification tablets

Other Necessities

- ❑ Wilderness Pass
- ❑ Topographic map and compass
- ❑ Waterproof matches, candle, flashlight, and extra battery
- ❑ First aid kit, repair kit
- ❑ Signaling device (whistle, mirror)
- ❑ Emergency blanket
- ❑ Sunglasses, hat, sunscreen, lip balm
- ❑ Garbage bags, toilet paper
- ❑ Rope, knife, and water bottle

Things are pretty casual in the mountains. Concentrate on clothing that's comfortable and warm. Because weather in the Rockies is so unpredictable, it's best to pack gear you can layer: a shirt layer, a fleece layer, and a windproof layer.

In summer, you'll want a couple of pairs of shorts, some lightweight pants, and a few T-shirts (quick-drying synthetic beats cotton, especially for hiking and other outdoor activities). Add a fleece jacket or sweatshirt for cooler evenings, a rain jacket or waterproof shell, and comfortable walking shoes or hiking boots. Don't forget sunglasses and a hat. For dining out, the tone is usually casual: nice jeans or casual slacks and shirts.

In winter, too, the layering principle works best. For really cold spells, polypropylene underwear is ideal: it's warm, it wicks moisture away from your skin, and it dries fast. Add wool or fleece shirts and a water-repellent or waterproof outer layer. Of course, you'll need a warm hat and gloves or mittens and some weather-resistant boots.

Getting Through Customs

Basically, you can bring into Canada goods for your own personal use. That means you can pack along your skis, snowmobile, boat, fishing tackle, and, if you wish, your television and your clarinet. When you arrive at Customs, if you aren't sure whether you should declare something, declare it first and then discuss it with the Customs officer.

You can bring, duty-free, up to 200 cigarettes, 50 cigars, and 200 grams (7 ounces) of tobacco, as long as you're of age in the province you're visiting (18 in Alberta). You're also allowed 1.14 liters (40 ounces) of liquor or 1.5 liters (52 ounces) of wine or 24 containers (355 milliliters, or 12 ounces, each) of beer.

Rules on bringing firearms into Canada are strict. You can't bring hand-guns without a special permit, and then only under certain conditions. Rifles are allowed only for specific purposes, such as hunting in season or for use in competition. You have to declare all guns at Customs or they will be seized.

There are also certain restrictions on meat, plants, and vegetables.

Here are a few other things you should keep in mind:

- ✔ If you're carrying prescription drugs they should be in their original containers and clearly labeled. It's smart to bring a copy of your prescription.

- ✔ If you're bringing a dog or cat, you need proof that it's had a rabies vaccination during the previous 36 months. (There are no restrictions on Seeing Eye dogs.)

- ✔ You can bring gifts, duty-free, as long as they don't exceed C$60 (US$42) each in value and don't contain alcohol or tobacco. It's best not to wrap them until after you've cleared Customs.

For more information about items you may wish to bring in or take out of Canada, visit Internet: www.ccra.gc.ca. The site also posts estimated wait times for land border crossings.

Part III

Exploring Banff and Jasper National Parks

The 5th Wave   By Rich Tennant

GOLFING BANFF

In this part...

You may be sneaking a look at this part before you read anything else. That's okay. As I mentioned in the beginning, this book wasn't intended to be read from front to back, like a novel. If you've never been to Banff, you're no doubt excited about your first visit to this famous park. If you're already acquainted with the region, you may be thrilled to be heading back. In any case, I can appreciate why you may be dipping into this part of the book first.

This section gives you the scoop on the city of Calgary, which you may pass through on your way to Banff, or maybe even visit for a few days with a side trip to Banff. I guide you through Calgary's downtown and point out parks, shopping districts, and bike trails. I let you know where to find the top hotels, the best restaurants, and the most worthwhile attractions. I also throw in a handful of my favorite Calgary shops and mention a couple of reliable spots to enjoy beer . . . and meet cowboys.

Then, we travel west to Banff. You find plenty of advice on visiting the town of Banff — I deal with everything from bed-and-breakfasts to Rocky Mountain cuisine. Once you've explored the town, you'll want to investigate the rest of the park. This part helps you get your bearings and lays out top driving tours and hikes. Finally, I escort you north along the Icefields Parkway, to Jasper National Park. You probably won't have time to visit *all* the alpine lakes, rugged peaks, and waterfalls in Jasper. It's the biggest park in the Canadian Rockies. This part guides you to the must-see attractions.

Chapter 11

Calgary: Gateway to the Rockies

*I*f you're looking for cowboys, Stetsons, and rodeos, you won't be disappointed. Calgary is the undisputed Texas of Canada. Kick up your boots in a country bar, dine on buffalo burgers, or saddle up and head out on a trail ride. But Calgary is also a modern city of 1 million people: a high-tech, high-energy urban center that starts early, works hard, and moves fast.

As the energy capital of Canada, home to 90% of the country's oil and gas producers, Calgary is a city of risk-takers. It's a think-on-your feet, give-it-a-whirl, anything's possible kind of town. Calgarians are a work-hard, play-hard lot, and for many, of course, the playground of choice is the Canadian Rockies. You can linger over a latte in a Calgary cafe at breakfast and hike to a mountain summit for lunch.

You can also get close to nature in the city itself. Explore two of North America's largest urban parks and cycle the most extensive urban pathway system in North America. (Calgary city planners seem to love superlatives: They've also built the biggest skateboard park on the continent and they're busy expanding the largest indoor walkway system in the world.)

If you haven't visited Calgary for a while, you may not recognize this city — more than 18 new hotels have sprung up in the past few years, and the downtown core is bustling with new bars, restaurants, and clubs.

Getting There

Getting to Calgary is a breeze, unless you plan to travel by train. VIA Rail Canada's closest stop is Edmonton, about 300km (186 miles) north of Calgary.

Arriving by air

Calgary International Airport is in the northeast corner of the city, 17km (11 miles) from downtown. To get downtown, take Barlow Trail south and follow the city center signs. It's about a 20-minute trip, longer during rush hours. A taxi costs roughly C$25 (US$18). Car rental companies at the airport include Avis, Hertz, Thrifty, National, Budget, and Alamo.

Airport Shuttle Express (% 403-509-4799) will get you downtown for about C$12 (US$8). The ride-share service stops at many downtown hotels, as well as the bus station and the youth hostel. Passenger vans leave the airport about every 20 minutes, 22 hours a day. Book ahead or just buy your ticket at the airport (Main Terminal, arrivals level). The Airporter bus (% 403-531-3909) goes to ten hotels in the downtown area. Buy a ticket (C$12/US$8) across from the international arrivals.

The cheapest way to get into the city center (C$2/US$1.40) is by bus. Catch bus 57 on the airport arrivals level and transfer to the Light Rail Transit (C-Train) system at the Whitehorn Station.

Driving in

The main routes through Calgary are the Trans-Canada Highway (Highway 1) — which links Alberta with Saskatchewan to the east, and with Banff National Park and British Columbia to the west — and Highway 2, which runs north–south from the Alberta–Montana border through Calgary and Edmonton. If you're driving, Calgary is about 3 hours from Edmonton, 11 hours from Vancouver, B.C., and 8 hours from Regina, Saskatchewan. If you're coming through Montana, allow about 5.5 hours to reach Calgary from Great Falls.

Taking the bus

Greyhound (☎ **800-661-8747**) provides bus service to Calgary from many parts of Canada and the U.S. The Calgary bus station is just west of the city center at 850 16th St. SW (☎ **403-265-9111**).

Orienting Yourself in Calgary

Calgary is laid out in four quadrants: southwest (SW), northwest (NW), southeast (SE), and northeast (NE); to find an address, you need the suffix indicating in which quadrant of the city it's located.

Avenues run east–west and streets run north–south. Centre Street separates the east and west quadrants of the city, while Centre Avenue is the divider between north and south. If you're getting disoriented just reading this, steer clear of the suburbs, where the neighboring streets are not numbered but similarly — and frustratingly — named (Oakfern, Oakfield, Oaktree, Oakwood).

Downtown

Downtown Calgary spreads from the south bank of the Bow River to about 10th Avenue SW, between 4th Street SE and 10th Street SW. Explore it on foot or hop on the C-Train (see "Getting Around" below) to get from the east end to the west.

If the weather turns nasty, you can travel just about anywhere downtown without venturing outside. Office buildings, stores, and restaurants are linked by an above-the-street, enclosed walkway system called the **Plus 15** (you guessed it, it's about 15 feet [4.5 meters] off the ground). Just don't get lost in there.

The **Calgary Tower** is on Centre Street at 9th Avenue. To the east, around 1st and 2nd streets SE, is Calgary's arts and cultural district. Here's where you'll find the **Glenbow Museum** and the **EPCOR Centre for Performing Arts. Stephen Avenue Walk** (8th Avenue) is a pedestrian-only street lined with historical buildings, shops, galleries, and restaurants. Follow Stephen Avenue into the downtown retail core where you find a five-block shopping complex with over 400 stores. If you head north toward the Bow River, you'll pass the **business district,** dominated by energy company head offices. (Calgary is the second largest head-office city in Canada, after Toronto.) Continuing north, **Chinatown** is on your right (look for the bright blue cone on top of the Chinese Cultural Centre) and the **Eau Claire district** is along the river beside **Prince's Island Park.** Eau Claire is teeming with people year-round, especially in summer: runners, cyclists, skateboarders, dog walkers, office workers, buskers, and jugglers. The **Eau Claire Market** has food stalls, shops, and restaurants, along with an IMAX theater.

Calgary Accommodations/Dining

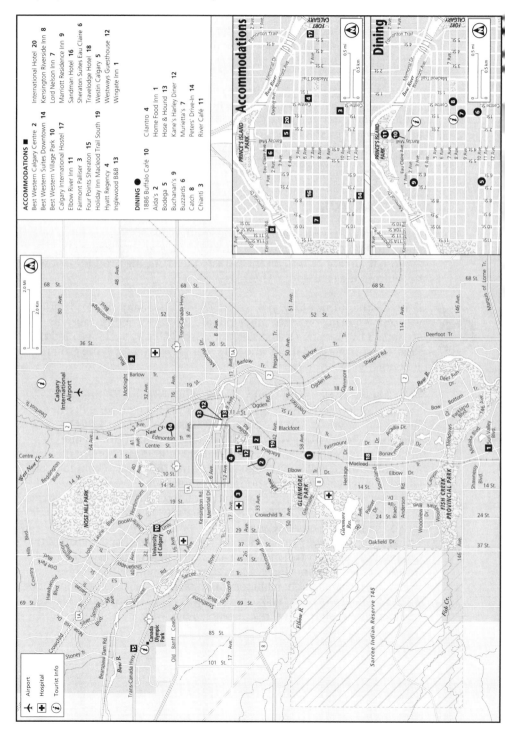

ACCOMMODATIONS ■
Best Western Calgary Centre **2**
Best Western Suites Downtown **14**
Best Western Village Park **10**
Calgary International Hostel **17**
Elbow River Inn **11**
Fairmont Palliser **3**
Four Points Sheraton **15**
Holiday Inn Macleod Trail South **19**
Hyatt Regency **4**
Inglewood B&B **13**

International Hotel **20**
Kensington Riverside Inn **8**
Lord Nelson Inn **7**
Marriott Residence Inn **9**
Sandman Hotel **16**
Sheraton Suites Eau Claire **6**
Travelodge Hotel **18**
Westin Calgary **5**
Westways Guesthouse **12**
Wingate Inn **1**

DINING ●
1886 Buffalo Café **10**
Aïda's **2**
Bodega **5**
Buchanan's **9**
Buzzards **6**
Catch **8**
Chianti **3**

Cilantro **4**
Home Food Inn **1**
Hose & Hound **13**
Kane's Harley Diner **12**
Murrieta's **7**
Peters' Drive-In **14**
River Café **11**

Near the heart of the city

These nearly downtown neighborhoods (see map, page 90) are fun places to shop or grab a bite to eat:

- ✔ Head to **4th Street SW** for maximum eateries per block: restaurants dishing up the hottest culinary trends, little ethnic spots, coffee shops, juice bars, and pubs.

- ✔ Bordered by the Bow River to the north and the Elbow River to the west, **Inglewood** is where the city of Calgary was born. Shop here for antiques and second-hand stuff.

- ✔ On **17th Avenue SW,** you find a diverse mix of apartments, businesses, and shops selling everything from flowers and candles to furniture and shoes. Most shops and restaurants are concentrated in the area between 10th and 4th streets.

- ✔ Craving a cappuccino? Wander over to **Kensington,** a trendy little district at the junction of Kensington Road and 10th Street NW (just across the Bow River from downtown). A handful of coffee shops share the streets with stores selling wine, pottery, chocolate, and used books.

Getting Information After You Arrive

Tourism Calgary visitor centers are located at the airport on the arrivals level and downtown in the Riley & McCormick Western Stores at 220–8th Ave. SW and Eau Claire Market. Call ☎ **800-661-1678** or 403-263-8510 or visit Internet: www.tourismcalgary.com.

Getting Around

Many of Calgary's top attractions are located in or near downtown and it's easy to get from one to the other on foot or by public transit. A great pathway network runs through downtown (along the Bow River) to nearby parks and neighborhoods. To venture farther from the city center (to see Canada Olympic Park, for instance, or Heritage Park), you need a car, bike, or bus schedule.

By public transit

In Calgary, mass transit consists of the Light Rail Transit (LRT) system, also called the **C-Train**, and buses. You can transfer between trains and buses and from one bus to another. If you ride the train first, keep your ticket to show the bus driver. If you start your trip on a bus, ask the driver for a transfer. The transit fare (adult) is C$2 (US$1.40), for both the bus and the C-Train. A day pass costs C$5.60 (US$3.92). Transit tickets and passes are sold at many convenience stores, grocery stores, drugstores, and Calgary Transit's customer service center downtown at 224–7th Ave. SW. The C-Train works on an honor system. Be sure to have your pass or ticket with you at all times. For help planning your trip, call **Calgary Transit** (☎ **403-262-1000;** Internet: www.calgarytransit.com).

When you're exploring downtown Calgary, take advantage of Calgary Transit's no-fare zone. Along 7th Avenue, between 10th Street SW and City Hall, you can ride the C-Train for free.

By taxi

Hail a cab on the street or head for a taxi stand near a major hotel, theater, or museum. Taxis in Calgary offering 24-hour city-wide service include **Advance** (☎ **403-777-1111**), **Associated** (☎ **403-299-1111**), **Red Top** (☎ **403-974-4444**), and **Mayfair** (☎ **403-255-6555**). For a taxi from the airport to downtown you'll pay about C$25 (US$18); from downtown to the University of Calgary, about C$12 (US$8); from downtown to Stampede Park, about C$7 (US$5).

By car

Calgary isn't a particularly tough city to navigate (streets run north–south, avenues east–west, remember?), especially if you can steer clear of the main routes into downtown during weekday rush hours.

In and around the city center, watch for one-way streets and streets closed to vehicles, such as the C-Train route along 7th Avenue and the pedestrian-only (Stephen Avenue) walkway on 8th Avenue.

Parking costs in lots and at meters vary, but in general, the closer you park to city center, the more you pay. On average, lots charge C$2 to C$3 per half-hour or C$10 to C$15 (US$7 to US$11) a day. Meter rates are in effect from 9 a.m. to 6 p.m., weekdays. On Saturdays you pay 50¢ an hour, and Sundays and holidays are free.

Meters on some streets in the downtown area become no-stopping zones at 3:30 p.m. Check the signs where you park. If you forget to move your car, somebody will remove it for you: to the impound lot. You must pay a hefty fee to retrieve it.

By bicycle

With 550km (340 miles) of off-road pathways and 260km (160 miles) of on-street bike routes, Calgary is a great city for cyclists. Get a copy of the excellent **pathway and bikeway map** (C$2/US$1.40) from the City of Calgary Planning Information Centre, 4th floor, Municipal Building, 800 Macleod Trail SE. Many Calgary Co-op grocery stores also sell the map. It's online at Internet: www.calgaryemaps.com.

 More than 100,000 Calgarians work downtown, and if you're traveling the bike paths near the city center at rush hour, you may suspect that all of them commute by bike or on foot. Pathway traffic gets a little hectic, especially around Eau Claire in summer. Expect to dodge runners, kids, dogs, tourists, and sun-lovers, along with geese and ducks. Stay in your lane, use your bell, and hey, take it slow.

Stop in at the **Pathway Hub** on Memorial Drive (it's in a former fire station on the southwest corner of 10th Street NW and Memorial) to get information on bike routes or trip ideas. The **Pathway Hotline**, for safety tips, bylaws, detours, and path closures, is ☎ **403-268-2300.**

Need a bike? Visit **Sports Rent,** 4424 16th Ave. NW (☎ **403-292-0077**), or the **University of Calgary's Outdoor Program Centre,** 2500 University Dr. NW (☎ **403-220-5038**). Rentals start at C$20 (US$14) a day.

Where to Stay

If you opt for a hotel downtown, attractions such as the Calgary Tower, Glenbow Museum, and EPCOR Centre for Performing Arts are right on your doorstep, as are the districts of Chinatown and Eau Claire. You're not far from Stampede Park, and you can walk to many of the city's top restaurants. That said, downtown hotels, in general, are the priciest and you can also count on at least C$12 (US$8) a day for parking.

You can save money by booking into a spot south of downtown along Macleod Trail, the main route into Calgary from the south. Macleod Trail is packed with restaurants, bars, and shopping malls. Hop on the C-Train to get to Stampede Park or downtown. Macleod Trail is also a convenient location if you plan to spend time at Spruce Meadows or Heritage Park.

North of downtown, the Motel Village area (in the northwest) is a good bet for sports-minded travelers who may want to take in a football game at nearby McMahon Stadium, check out the Olympic Oval at the University of Calgary, or visit Canada Olympic Park. If you're heading off to Banff, the airport area (northeast) affords quick access to the Trans-Canada Highway.

The top hotels

Fairmont Palliser

$$$–$$$$ **Downtown**

The Palliser was a grand hotel when the Canadian Pacific Railway opened it in 1914, and it's a grand hotel today. Rooms are reasonably large, with lots of natural light, heaps of atmosphere, and numerous conveniences. Rooms on the south side overlook the railway, so you'll hear the train — not necessarily objectionable. The in-room video games will impress the kids. Children also get a special menu. If the Palliser isn't in your budget, soak up its ambience with a stroll through the marble-floored lobby, a martini in the elegant lounge, or dinner in the stately Rimrock Restaurant.

133–9th Ave. SW. ☎ ***800-441-1414,*** *403-262-1234. Fax: 403-260-1260. E-mail:* palliser@fairmont.com. *Internet:* www.fairmont.com/palliser. *Rack rates: C$179–C$329 (US$125–US$230) double. Valet parking C$21 (US$15), self-parking C$18 (US$13). AE, DC, DISC, MC, V.*

Hyatt Regency

$$–$$$$ **Downtown**

This downtown newcomer scores top points for its "wow" factor. Located on Stephen Avenue alongside some of Calgary's hottest restaurants, the Hyatt is built into a redeveloped city block that includes several restored heritage buildings. The lobby boasts 20-meter (65-foot) pillars and a 15-meter (50-foot) mahogany canoe. (Look up, it's inverted on the ceiling.) If you stay here, you also get to ogle a 500-piece art collection and soak in an 18th-floor Jacuzzi with a dreamy mountain view. Indulge in a jet-lag treatment at the hotel's Stillwater Spa.

Check for weekend specials at the Hyatt for as little as C$129 (US$90) a night.

700 Centre St. S. ☎ ***800-233-1234,*** *403-717-1234. Fax: 403-537-4444. E-mail:* sales@calrcpo.hyatt.com. *Internet:* www.calgaryhyatt.com. *Rack rates: C$144–C$304 (US$101–US$213) double. Valet parking $C26 (US$18), self-parking C$16 (US$11). AE, DC, DISC, MC, V.*

Kensington Riverside Inn

$$$$ **Kensington**

This little inn is one-of-a-kind in Calgary: part neighborhood B&B, part first-class hotel. It has a fresh, traditional look, 3-meter (10-foot) high ceilings, chunky columns, and lots of French doors. The owners pride themselves on attention to detail, from Egyptian cotton towels and heated towel bars in the bathrooms to a 24-hour cookie jar in the lobby. The 19 rooms, some of which have private garden patios, are all stunning and each unique. A 10- or 15-minute walk along the Bow River will put you in the city center.

Those who like to "light up" should look elsewhere. The whole inn is nonsmoking.

1126 Memorial Dr. NW. ☎ *877-313-3733, 403-228-4442. Fax: 403-228-9608. E-mail:* krinn@telusplanet.net. *Internet:* www.kensingtonriversideinn.com. *Rack rates: C$249–C$309 (US$174–US$216) double. AE, DC, DISC, MC, V.*

Sheraton Suites Calgary Eau Claire

$$–$$$$ **Downtown**

You can't beat the location. This luxuriously appointed all-suite hotel is next door to the Eau Claire Market, surrounded by restaurants, and a few steps from Prince's Island Park, a downtown green area that's a favorite site for summer festivals. The typical suite features a living and work area with pullout sofa, separate bedroom, and a wet bar. Suites are tastefully furnished in mahogany and cherry. Kids love the pool and waterslide, not to mention the in-suite Sony PlayStations.

If you start your day with a jog, ask the concierge for a running route map. The riverfront pathway is just steps away.

255 Barclay Parade SW. ☎ *888-784-8370, 403-266-7200. Fax: 403-266-1300. E-mail:* hotelinfo@sheratonsuites.com. *Internet:* www.sheratonsuites.com. *Rack rates: C$145–C$489 (US$102–US$242) double. AE, DISC, MC, V.*

Westin Calgary

$$–$$$$ **Downtown**

Expect a casually comfortable brand of first class. Newly renovated guest rooms are bright and spacious, with beds dressed in luxurious cream-colored duvets. And the Westin seems to think of everything: Beds, for example, have both feather and foam pillows, in case you're allergy-prone. Ask about a kid's program that includes a gift package geared to your child's age, and order-ahead express service in Westin restaurants. (So the food's ready when you get there.) If you're planning a romantic weekend, the Westin's posh Owl's Nest dining room may be just the ticket: roses on arrival and matches engraved with your name.

320–4th Ave. SW. ☎ ***800-937-8461,*** *403-266-1611. Fax: 403-233-7471. E-mail:* calga@westin.com. *Internet:* www.westin.com/calgary. *Rack rates: C$99–C$299 (US$69–US$209) double. Sun–Thurs valet parking C$13 (US$9), self-parking C$9 (US$6); Fri & Sat valet parking C$9 (US$6), self-parking C$5 (US$3.50). AE, DC, DISC, MC, V.*

Runner-up hotels

Best Western Calgary Centre

$–$$ **South of Downtown**

If you're driving into Calgary from the south, this is one of the last hotels you'll pass before the city center. It's also one of the nicest in the area.

3630 Macleod Trail S. ☎ ***877-287-3900,*** *403-287-3900. Internet:* www.bestwestern. com/ca/calgarycentreinn.

Best Western Village Park

$$ **North of Downtown**

Who knows, maybe you'll see your favorite football player here. This hotel is 20 years old but in splendid shape, and it has a family-friendly atmosphere.

1804 Crowchild Trail NW. ☎ ***888-774-7716,*** *403-289-0241. Internet:* www. villageparkinn.com.

Lord Nelson Inn

$ **Downtown**

Just a little removed from the downtown core, this small hotel is still centrally located, and it's bargain priced. Rooms are basic, and if you're not old enough to remember pink toilets, rather funky.

1020–8th Ave. SW. ☎ ***800-661-6017,*** *403-269-8262.*

Marriott Residence Inn

$$–$$$ **Airport**

In keeping with the "home away from home" focus, this all-suite hotel looks like a condominium complex. Kitchens are fully equipped. These folks will even do your grocery shopping.

2622–39th Ave. NE. ☎ ***800-331-3131,*** *403-735-3336. Internet:* www. residenceinncalgary.ca.

Wingate Inn

$$–$$$ South of Downtown

The Wingate is a posh version of the Super 8 across the highway. The concept's the same: free breakfast, efficient service, and you're on your way.

400 Midpark Way SE. ☎ *800-228-1000, 403-514-0099. Internet:* www. wingateinns.com.

Where to Eat

Welcome to gourmet Cowtown. Here in the heart of cattle country, you can certainly count on finding a top-notch steak. But steakhouses are just one component of a restaurant scene that also includes bistros, noodle shops, curry houses, sushi bars, diners, tavernas, and trattorias. The trendiest (and priciest) restaurants, for the most part, are downtown, particularly in the Stephen Avenue area.

For less costly fare, try the neighborhoods near the heart of the city (17th Avenue SW, 4th Street SW, Inglewood, and Kensington). At many restaurants, bars, cafes, and ethnic spots in these districts, dinner entrees go for between C$9 (US$6) and C$15 (US$9).

Aida's

$–$$ Near the Heart of the City   MEDITERRANEAN

This low-key little bistro serves fresh, flavorful, and reasonably priced food that always earns high praise. While you can spend C$9 to C$12 (US$6 to US$8) on a platter or main course, pitas stuffed with marinated chicken, falafel, or kafta go for about C$5 (US$3.50). Or share a few dishes from the wide-ranging appetizer list. If you like Mediterranean food, you'll love Aida's.

2208 4th St. SW. ☎ *403-541-1189. Main courses: C$9–C$12 (US$6–US$8). AE, DC, MC, V. Mon 11 a.m.–9 p.m., Tues–Thurs 11 a.m.–10 p.m., Fri & Sat 11 a.m.–11 p.m., Sun 4–9 p.m.*

Bodega

$$$ Downtown   SPANISH

If the tapas menu doesn't put you in a Mediterranean frame of mind, perhaps the Flamenco guitarist will. This cozy, candlelit restaurant is a wonderful place to spend an evening. The menu, which concentrates on dishes sized for sampling and sharing, features traditional Spanish fare alongside a lineup of contemporary meat, fish, and vegetable dishes. Pair them up with perfect wines: many are available by the glass.

720–11th Ave. SW. ☎ *403-262-8966. Reservations recommended. Tapas C$8–C$12 (US$6–US$8) main courses C$15–C$25 (US$11–US$18). AE, MC, V. Mon–Fri 11:30 a.m.–11 p.m. Sat 5–11 p.m.*

Buchanan's
$$$–$$$$ **Downtown** **CHOPHOUSE**

If you want to impress Scotch lovers, this restaurant and bar, just a few blocks west of the Eau Claire district, is the place to head for — the menu here features more than 130 varieties of Scotch. Buchanan's is a favorite with Calgary's after-work crowd, and a great place for dinner, too. The menu, which emphasizes steak and chops, includes an inspired assortment of starter-size salads (such as Savoy spinach with black mission figs or English Stilton with walnuts, bacon, and curly endive) and appetizers.

738–3rd Ave. SW. ☎ *403-261-4646. Reservations recommended. Main courses: C$25–C$35 (US$18–US$25). AE, DC, MC, V. Mon–Wed 11:30 a.m.–10:30 p.m., Thurs & Fri 11:30 a.m.–11:00 p.m., Sat 5–11 p.m.*

1886 Buffalo Café
$ **Downtown** **CAFE**

If you like a hearty breakfast, wander down to Eau Claire and head for the tiny white wooden cafe behind the Barley Mill restaurant. The kitchen turns out fluffy omelettes filled with choice of cheese, onion, bacon, peaches, salsa, pineapple, or mushroom, delivered with a side of thick toast. Add grilled tomatoes if you wish. Expect lengthy lineups on weekends.

187 Barclay Parade SW. ☎ *403-269-9255. Reservations not accepted. Most items under C$10 (US$7). Mon–Fri 6 a.m.–3 p.m., Sat & Sun 7 a.m.–3 p.m.*

Buzzard's Cowboy Cuisine
$$ **Downtown** **WESTERN**

Buzzard's is unabashedly ranch-hand style, with walls and ceilings bedecked in cowboy hats, lanterns, western art, and hokey signs. ("Cowboy parking only. Violators will be castrated.") If it sounds like a tourist attraction, it is, but count on seeing plenty of local folks here too. Try the house brew, Buzzard Breath Ale. The pub next door, which boasts one of the biggest beer menus in the city, hosts a unique culinary event each June where you can sample prairie oysters (cooked calf testicles).

140–10th Ave. SW. ☎ *403-264-6959. Reservations recommended. Main courses: C$12–C$15 (US$8–US$11). AE, DC, MC, V. Mon–Sat 11 a.m.–10 p.m., Sun 4–10 p.m.*

Catch

$$$$ Downtown   SEAFOOD

The developers of this posh three-level seafood spot spent a whopping $5.6 million to renovate a former Imperial Bank building next to the Hyatt hotel, and lured award-winning chef Michael Nobel from the West Coast. The main-floor oyster bar is casual and relaxed, with live seafood tanks, big wooden booths, and a pounded-tin ceiling. Dining on the second floor is a more sophisticated affair. The wine list is mammoth, and the menu offers wine suggestions for every dish.

100–8th Ave. SE. ☎ 403-206-0000. Reservations recommended. Main courses: C$20–C$42 (US$14–US$30). AE, DC, MC, V. Oyster bar: daily 11:30 a.m.–2:00 p.m., Sun–Thurs 5–11 p.m., Fri & Sat 5 p.m.–1 a.m. Dining room: Mon–Sat 11:30 a.m.– 2:00 p.m., 5–9 p.m.

Chianti

$ Near the Heart of the City   ITALIAN

Generous portions, quickly served and priced right are a formula for success, judging by the popularity of this casual Italian eatery. Chianti has been around forever, and it's still packing in the crowds. The wide-ranging menu will appeal to both traditionalists and those who like to experiment. Look for midweek special prices on pastas. Chianti is generally noisy and boisterous. Families and large groups are easily accommodated. *Hint:* Avoid the patio: it's next to a noisy bus stop.

1438–17th Ave. SW (near the northwest corner of 17th Ave. & 14th St.). ☎ 403-229-1600. Most pastas under C$10 (US$7). AE, DC, MC, V. Mon–Thurs 11 a.m.–11 p.m., Fri & Sat 11 a.m. to midnight, Sun 4–11 p.m.

Cilantro

$$$–$$$ Near the Heart of the City   CALIFORNIA

Cilantro is pure antidote for stress. It's cool and calm with hardwood floors and a rustic elegance. The sheltered courtyard, with its wall of Virginia creeper, is my top choice for dining alfresco on 17th Avenue. In the evenings, heat lamps take the chill off the air. Chocolate lovers take note: Cilantro's signature dessert, a warm fallen chocolate soufflé, will leave you swooning.

338–17th Ave. SW. ☎ 403-229-1177. Reservations recommended. Main courses: C$29 (US$20); pizzas, pastas C$12–C$16 (US$8–US$11). AE, DC, MC, V. Mon–Fri 11 a.m.–10 p.m., Sat & Sun 5–11 p.m.

Home Food Inn

$ North of Downtown   CHINESE

This friendly Peking/Cantonese restaurant — look for the big pink building on the east side of Macleod Trail — offers a wide-ranging menu and puts on popular lunch and dinner buffets. Share a chicken or seafood hot pot or try crispy, sizzling rice. Fans of salt-and-pepper–style seafood can try shrimp, squid, and scallops.

5222 Macleod Trail. ☎ *403-259-8585. Most items under C$10 (US$7). AE, MC, V. Sun–Thurs 11 a.m.–10 p.m., Fri & Sat 11 a.m.–11 p.m.*

Hose & Hound

$ Near the Heart of the City   PUB

Providing you can order "rescue boats," "fire blanket brie," or "nozzleman's nachos" with a straight face, you'll find plenty to choose from at this neighborhood pub in the Inglewood district, located, if you haven't guessed, in a renovated fire hall. A neighborly spot it is, too, so drop by for a beer (14 draughts on tap). For a hearty dinner, steak-and-sausage pie is a good bet. Portions are pub-size. In nice weather, nab a spot outdoors.

1030–9th Ave. SE. ☎ *403-234-0508. Most items under C$10 (US$7). AE, DC, MC, V. Mon 11:30 a.m.–11:00 p.m., Tues–Thurs 11:30 a.m. to midnight, Fri & Sat 11:30– 2:00 a.m., Sun noon to 11 p.m.*

Kane's Harley Diner

$–$$ Near the Heart of the City   DINER

Parents and kids lunch alongside tough guys in leather in this 1950s-style diner, located in a former Harley-Davidson shop in Inglewood. The decor, predictably, is black and orange and chrome. Kane's is known for big hearty breakfasts. At lunch, opt for meat loaf or macaroni-and-cheese. To really enjoy the food here, forget about your cholesterol level.

1209–9th Ave. SE. ☎ *403-269-7311. Main courses: C$9–C$13 (US$6–US$9). AE, MC, V. Daily 7 a.m.–10 p.m.*

Murietta's West Coast Bar and Grill
$$$–$$$$ **Downtown   WEST COAST**

Everybody loves Murietta's. Located in the splendidly refurbished Alberta Hotel building on Stephen Avenue, this restaurant is worth a visit just to check out the decor. Luckily, the food is equally outstanding. Murietta's caters to seafood lovers. Select a sauce (herb aioli, vanilla saffron butter, or spicy Szechuan) to pair with Arctic char, Ahi tuna, salmon, or grilled scallops. Other main courses of note include beef tenderloin and rack of lamb.

#200, 808–1st St. SW. ☎ 403-269-7707. Reservations recommended. Main courses: C$20–C$30 (US$14–US$21). AE, DC, MC, V. Mon–Wed 11 a.m. to midnight, Thurs & Fri 11 a.m–1 a.m., Sat 11 a.m.–2 a.m., Sun 4–10 p.m.

Peters' Drive-In
$ **North of Downtown   BURGERS**

This independent burger joint has been pulling in the crowds for decades with a menu that's stayed pretty much the same. Peters' is a local institution, known for big, juicy hamburgers topped with a special secret sauce and thick, creamy shakes in a multitude of flavors. Portions are generous and service is swift. Drive up to the window, order at the speaker, and find a picnic table or chow down in your car.

219–16th Ave. NE. ☎ 403-277-2747. Most items under C$10 (US$7). No credit cards. Daily 9 a.m. to midnight.

River Café
$$$$ **Downtown   REGIONAL**

With an inspiring downtown island park location and a menu to match, River Café is on many lists of favorite Calgary restaurants. The restaurant has a Rocky Mountain fishing lodge feel, with an open-hearth fieldstone fireplace, tall windows, and a sprawling deck. While you admire the view, savor a meal that features the best of what's fresh and in season. The menu showcases Canadian ingredients with a focus on local organic produce.

Prince's Island Park. (Leave your car at Eau Claire.) ☎ 403-261-7670. Reservations recommended. Main courses: C$25–C$40 (US$14–US$28). AE, DC, MC, V. Mon–Fri 11 a.m.–11 p.m., Sat & Sun 10 a.m.–11 p.m. Closed Jan 2–31.

Calgary Attractions

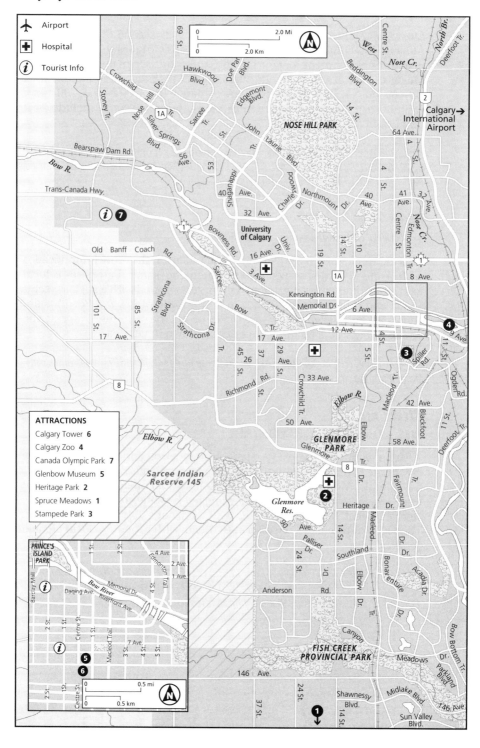

✈ Airport
✚ Hospital
(i) Tourist Info

NOSE HILL PARK

University of Calgary

GLENMORE PARK

Sarcee Indian Reserve 145

ATTRACTIONS
Calgary Tower 6
Calgary Zoo 4
Canada Olympic Park 7
Glenbow Museum 5
Heritage Park 2
Spruce Meadows 1
Stampede Park 3

PRINCE'S ISLAND PARK

FISH CREEK PROVINCIAL PARK

Calgary → International Airport

Exploring Calgary: The Top Attractions

These attractions are all easy to get to. From downtown hotels, some are within walking distance. If you're riding the C-Train, this section tells you where to hop off.

Calgary Tower
Downtown

High-speed elevators whisk you to the top in 62 seconds. And on a clear day, you have a superb perspective on downtown and outlying areas, the foothills, and the Rocky Mountains. Built in 1967, the Calgary Tower is 190 meters (625 feet) tall, with an observation terrace at 158 meters (525 feet). The revolving restaurant at the top offers up the entire 360-degree view in the span of one hour.

101–9th Ave. SW. ☎ 403-266-7171. C-Train: Centre Street. Admission: C$9.95 (US$7) adults, C$7 (US$5) seniors & youth, C$5 (US$3.50) children 3–12. Mid-May to 1st Sunday in Oct, daily 7:30 a.m. to midnight. All other months, daily 8 a.m.–11 p.m.

Calgary Zoo, Botanical Garden and Prehistoric Park
East of Downtown

With its trails and pathways, bridges across the Bow River, and distinctly un-zoo-like enclosures, this place is a treat for both adults and kids. The complex offers more than many typical city zoos. In summer, peacocks strut through dazzling gardens of red marigolds, pale snapdragons, and purple petunias. The latest addition is Destination Africa, with underwater viewing of the river hippopotamus.

You find food stalls and snack bars throughout the zoo. The nicest spot for lunch is the Kitamba Café, a cafeteria-style restaurant that opened in 2002.

1300 Zoo Rd. NE (east of downtown at the Memorial Dr./Deerfoot Trail Interchange). ☎ 403-232-9300. C-Train: Zoo. Admission: C$15 (US$11) adults, C$13 (US$9) seniors, C$9 (US$6) youth 13–17, $C6.50 (US$4.55) children 3–12. Daily 9 a.m.–5 p.m.

Canada Olympic Park
West of Downtown

Ski-jumping, freestyle skiing, bobsleigh, and luge events were held here during the 1988 Winter Olympics. Known to Calgarians as COP, the park lives on as a year-round recreation and training center. Take a tour and check out the view from the observation deck of the 90-meter (295-foot) ski jump tower. In the mountainbike park, two-wheelers can blast down 25km (15.5 miles) of groomed trails and ride a chairlift (equipped with bike carriers) back to the top.

88 Olympic Rd. SW (on Hwy. 1 [Trans-Canada] about 15 minutes' drive west of downtown). ☎ *403-247-5452. Self-guided tours C$10 (US$7) per person, C$35 (US$24) families. Guided bus tours C$15 (US$11). Mid-May to early Sept 9 a.m.–8 p.m. Off-season 9 a.m.–4 p.m. Tours run hourly in summer, several times daily in off-season.*

Glenbow Museum
Downtown

Spend a few hours in Western Canada's largest museum and you come away with a new appreciation for the cultural diversity of the Canadian West. Stories of immigrants who journeyed to the Prairies from Europe, Asia, the United States, and other parts of Canada come to life as you tour the art and artifacts in the museum's permanent collection on the third floor. Call before your visit to check on temporary exhibits.

If you're traveling with kids, drop by the Discovery Room on the second floor, a hands-on, arts-and-crafts oriented area where visitors create their own souvenirs.

130–9th Ave. SE. ☎ *403-268-4100. C-Train: Centre Street. Admission: C$11 (US$8) adults, C$8.50 (US$5.95) seniors, C$7 (US$4.90) students & youth. Free for children under 6. Tues–Sat 9 a.m.–5 p.m., Sun noon to 5 p.m.*

Captivating collections

For museum lovers visiting Calgary, the Glenbow's the top draw. Some smaller collections around the city are also worth a look. Most impressive is the little-known **Cantos Music Museum** at 134–11th Ave. SE (☎ 403-261-7790), which houses one of the finest collections of keyboard instruments in the world. Tours cost only $2, but you have to make an appointment. If you're interested in aviation, the **Aero Space Museum** near the Calgary International Airport (at 4629 McCall Way NE, near the intersection of McKnight Boulevard and 19th Street NE) has one of the best aero engine collections around. Call ☎ 403-250-3752. Admission is $6 for adults, $3.50 seniors and students, $2 children 2 to 12. At the **Calgary Police Interpretative Centre,** 316–7th Ave. SE (☎ 403-268-4566), kids get to play detective. Visitors solve crimes and learn about forensic science using interactive video and computer exhibits. Admission is $2 for adults, free for children under 18.

Heritage Park
South of Downtown

Women in floor-length dresses stroll the streets, roosters crow beside the ranch house, and a smell of cinnamon drifts from the bakery. Canada's largest living historical village definitely has a lived-in feel. It's all about life in Canada, pre-1914. Kids like to catch a ride on the steam locomotive and visit the amusement park, which features a Ferris wheel.

Calgary Transit runs a shuttle service between the C-Train station and the park. Call ☎ **403-262-1000** to check schedules.

1900 Heritage Dr. SW. ☎ **403-268-8500.** *C-Train: Heritage. Admission: $11 adults, C$8 (US$6) children 3–17, C$45 (US$32) families. Admission includes Stampede-style breakfast served 9–10 a.m. Mid-May to early Sept, daily 9 a.m.–5 p.m.; early Sept to mid-Oct, weekends only 9 a.m.–5 p.m.*

Spruce Meadows
South of Downtown

Whether or not you're a horse lover, this world-class show-jumping facility on Calgary's southwest city limits is fun to see. Several major tournaments are held throughout the year, including the Masters (in September), where the world's best athletes compete for the largest purse of any show-jumping competition. Visitors are welcome to drop by and take a look at the facility any time of year.

18011 Spruce Meadows Way SW (on the southern city limits about 40 minutes' drive from downtown). ☎ **403-974-4200.** *C-Train: Fish Creek Lacombe (during tournaments, Spruce Meadows runs a free shuttle bus from the C-Train station). Gate admission during tournaments (first-come, first-served seating): C$5 (US$4.90) adults, free for seniors & children under 12.*

The Calgary Stampede

If you've always wanted to get in touch with your inner cowboy, here's your chance: a ten-day tribute to all things western. But plan ahead. Many hotels in and around the city are booked well in advance, and popular bars and restaurants are packed.

The Calgary Stampede attracts thousands of visitors, but it's a home-town show at heart. About a week before the festivities kick off, hay bales and barn boards surface everywhere, from shops and restaurants to hospitals and office towers. Queues form at western-wear stores. (If you think you'd feel silly in tight jeans and pointy-toed boots, try showing up at a Stampede breakfast dressed like a city slicker.)

You see cooking contests, wagon rides, western exhibits, and square dancing throughout the city, but the big events take place at **Stampede Park** ("the grounds"), just southeast of the city center. Cowboys do battle with bulls and bucking broncs at the **rodeo,** held every afternoon. In the evening, **chuckwagons** thunder around a track known as "a half-mile of hell," and singers, dancers, and acrobats entertain visitors at an outdoor **grandstand show.** For amusement park ride fans, the **midway** seems to have something new every year: on the Skyscraper, get tossed 48 meters (160 feet) into the air at 96 kmh (60 mph). If you prefer to keep your feet on the ground, try your luck at the casino or visit the agricultural exhibits.

Traffic gets hectic during Stampede and it's a hassle finding parking close to the grounds. You're better off riding the C-Train, which runs 24 hours a day during Stampede. Many transit routes also run extra buses for the week.

If you're driving, you may find a spot in the lot on 14th Avenue between Macleod Trail and 1st Street SE (C$10/US$7 per day). In the Victoria Park area on the west side of Macleod Trail, local residents sell parking spots in their yards, but they fill up early. If you don't mind walking for 20 minutes, you can usually find a spot farther west in the 17th Avenue area.

Stampede parade

On the first Friday of Stampede week, the parade sets the festivities in motion, with bands, floats, horses, First Nations people in traditional dress, chuckwagons, and outriders. The parade gets under way at 9 a.m., traveling down 6th Avenue from Macleod Trail SE to 10th Street, then turning south to 9th Avenue, and returning east on 9th Avenue to Fort Calgary. It takes about two hours to pass any one point. You'll have to set your morning alarm in order to get a good view; spectators stake out spots on the street as early as 6 a.m.

That's a BIG breakfast

If you have an appetite for flapjacks, you can feast your way through Stampede week. Just show up and get in line. The famed — and free — pancake breakfasts started in 1923, when a cowboy named Wildhorse Jack raced his chuckwagon into downtown Calgary, fired up his stove, and offered pancakes and bacon to everyone who passed by. Today, complimentary breakfasts are a Stampede tradition. Chinook Centre on Macleod Trail just south of downtown puts on one of the most popular events, cooking up pancakes, beans, and bratwurst for 60,000 to 70,000 people. (Chinook set a Guinness World Record for the biggest cooked breakfast.)

During the ten days of Stampede, the Stampede Caravan travels to major shopping centers around the city serving pancakes, sausages, juice, coffee, music, and entertainment from 9 to 11 a.m. Check local papers for daily schedules.

Or head downtown any morning and follow the smell of coffee to the nearest chuckwagon. Best bets are Rope Square (in Olympic Plaza on the corner of 7th Avenue and Macleod Trail SE) or Stephen Avenue (8th Avenue).

If you have young children, try for a spot on 6th Avenue near the parade start. The kids won't have as long to wait. For photography, the best spot is 9th Avenue. (You have the sun at your back.) *Another tip:* Stand close to a TV camera; the bands will always be playing when they pass by.

Stampede tickets

Admission to Stampede Park costs C$11 (US$8) for adults, C$6 (US$4.20) for children and seniors. For midway rides, coupons are sold separately or in packages.

When you buy advance tickets to the rodeo or chuckwagon races/ grandstand show, which are held at the Stampede Grandstand, admission to Stampede Park is included. Call ☎ **800-661-1767** or 403-269-9822 or order online at Internet: www.calgarystampede.com. Tickets are also available from any Ticketmaster outlet. Call ☎ **403-777-0000**. You pay C$22 to C$46 (US$15 to US$32) for tickets to the rodeo and C$27 to C$63 (US$19 to US$44) for the chuckwagons/ grandstand show. Priciest seats are in the air-conditioned clubhouse section and on the main level, just above the center of the arena. Rush seating tickets for the rodeo and chuckwagon races (you're on the main level but farthest from the center field) go on sale at the Grandstand rush admission booth 90 minutes before these events begin: C$12 (US$8) for adults, C$6 (US$4.20) for seniors and children. (You pay the park admission separately.)

If you're flexible about when you go to Stampede Park, there's a deal to be found on the first Sunday of Stampede week, **Family Day:** admission is free between 7 and 9 a.m. On Wednesday, **Kids' Day,** children under 12 and the adults accompanying them get in free between 7 and 9 a.m. You should arrive by 8:30 a.m. at the latest. While the gate admission is free for these two days, you still have to pay for rides and events. You find a few freebies on the grounds, though: a pancake breakfast (the queue is usually long) and a grandstand show that's a hit with younger kids. If you're 65 or older, head for the grounds on Tuesday, when **seniors get in free all day** and can take advantage of other seniors' deals.

Suggested Itineraries

If you have only one day to explore Calgary, you may want to concentrate on seeing the sights in and around downtown. From the city center, most attractions I suggest in the one-day itinerary, below, are easy to get to on foot. For the two-day itinerary, you'll need a car, bicycle, or bus schedule.

Calgary in one day

If the weather's fine, start the day with a visit to the **Calgary Tower.** You can spot attractions that you want to check out later and enjoy a great panorama of downtown and outlying areas in the bargain. Then, stroll over to Stephen Avenue (8th Avenue) and spend an hour exploring the restored sandstone buildings on this pedestrian-only street. If you're a shopper, go hunting. **Stephen Avenue** runs through the heart of the downtown shopping district.

Find a spot along Stephen Avenue for lunch, then wander over to **Olympic Plaza,** where in summer, you may catch a concert or a festival. (Medal ceremonies were held here during the 1988 Olympic Winter Games.) Set aside most of the afternoon to explore an attraction in or near downtown. For Western Canadian history buffs and art enthusiasts, the best bet is the **Glenbow Museum.** Families may want to head for the **Calgary Zoo.** In the evening, you're off to the Eau Claire district for dinner. Casual restaurants and pubs are located both in the **Eau Claire Market** and adjacent pedestrian plaza. Or splurge on dinner at the River Café (remember to make a reservation), next door on **Prince's Island Park.** The park, connected with the Eau Claire district by a footbridge, hosts various cultural events and music festivals throughout the summer and is a fine spot for an after-dinner stroll any time of year.

Calgary in two days

If you've followed the one-day itinerary on your first day, spend your second morning exploring neighborhoods in and around downtown. Start with breakfast at Nellie's on **4th Street SW,** then wander down to **17th Avenue SW.** Shops here sell everything from shoes and CDs to used books. Next, head for **Chinatown** and see the Chinese Cultural Centre, or visit **Inglewood** to hunt for antiques. You usually have no trouble finding a lunch spot in either district.

In the afternoon, drive west of downtown to **Canada Olympic Park,** where you can watch bobsleigh athletes in training. If you prefer to spend a few hours on foot, head south to **Heritage Park** historical village to take a stroll through the past. Horse lovers may prefer to wander around the show-jumping facilities at **Spruce Meadows.** For dinner, pay a visit to **Kensington,** just northwest of downtown.

Shopping

If you have your heart set on a pair of bull-hide ropers or a Stetson, you won't be disappointed. Calgary has western wear, and lots of it. But the shopping scene here goes beyond boots and hats and belt buckles. Calgary's also a good spot to pick up sports clothes and outdoor gear. The city has a great selection of wine shops, fine bookstores — and fabulous chocolates.

 Most stores open at about 9:30 or 10 a.m., Monday through Saturday, and close at around 6 p.m., with longer hours on some evenings, generally Thursday and Friday. Many shops are open on Sunday afternoon. In major malls, you can usually shop until about 9 p.m., Monday through Saturday, and until 6 p.m. on Sunday.

Shopping districts

If you have serious buying to do, head for downtown or a major mall elsewhere in the city. **Downtown,** a five-block complex along 8th Avenue SW between 1st and 5th streets that's linked by indoor walkways, houses hundreds of stores and restaurants. Among the malls, **Chinook Centre** is the largest. It's just south of downtown (Macleod Trail at Glenmore Trail) and offers 200 stores along with a food court and theaters.

If you're just exploring, or traveling with a companion who doesn't share your passion for shopping, skip the mega-malls. You'll have more fun browsing through the mix of second-hand and antique shops along 9th Avenue SE in **Inglewood,** or exploring **Kensington,** just north of downtown, or **17th Avenue SW** between 4th Street and about 10th Street.

Offbeat finds in Inglewood

If your taste in fashion runs to military paraphernalia, you won't want to miss Inglewood's big army surplus store: **Crown Surplus** (1005–11th St. SE; ☎ **403-265-1754**). Even pop-star Cher shopped here (for Bundeswehr German Army T-shirts) when she came to Calgary. If vinyl's your passion, stop by **Recordland** (1208–9th Ave. SE; ☎ **403-262-3839**). It's been called the best used-record store in Canada.

Great stores

Here are some top shops to check out downtown and in nearby neighborhoods:

- ✔ Western boot manufacturer **Alberta Boot,** 614–10th Ave. SW (☎ **403-263-4605**), will outfit you whether you plan to spend $200 or $2,000. If you don't fancy one of the 12,000 pairs in stock, you can always have your boots custom-made.

- ✔ **Arnold Churgin Shoes,** 227–8th Ave. SW (☎ **403-262-3366**), is an upscale women's shoe shop with a big local following. Don't miss the affiliated discount store two doors down.

- ✔ **Bernard Callebaut,** 1313–1st St. SE (☎ **403-266-4300**), is synonymous with chocolate in Calgary. The award-winning Belgian chocolatier's 4,830-sq.-meter (52,000-sq.-foot) factory and flagship store has the look and feel of an exclusive jewelry house. Choose from dozens of varieties of decadent treats or stock up on quality baking chocolate.

- ✔ **Bin 905,** 2311–4th St. SW (☎ **403-261-1600**), has a knowledgeable staff to help you find your way around 1,500 products, including wines, specialty spirits, and beers from around the world. It's a great place to shop for Canadian wines.

- ✔ **The Cookbook Company,** 722–11th Ave. SW (☎ **403-265-6066**), isn't just a bookstore; it's the heart of the local culinary scene. You will find 3,000 cookbooks, alongside an impressive array of specialty items and hard-to-find ingredients.

✔ **Mountain Equipment Co-op,** 830–10th Ave. SW (☎403-269-2420), is the place in Calgary to shop for serious outdoor gear. MEC is known for tough, durable basics at reasonable prices — boots, hats, gloves, shorts, and raingear, including an impressive selection in kids' sizes. You need a membership to shop here, and can buy one in the store for C$5 (US$3.50).

✔ **Pages Books** on Kensington, 1135 Kensington Rd. NW (☎ 403-283-6655), carries books by many local and regional authors and is a favorite of Calgary readers and writers.

Nightlife

The latest hot spot for the dance crowd is 1st Street SW, where you find a strip of clubs in the 12th Avenue area. Stephen Avenue also boasts a handful of trendy dance floors, as does Macleod Trail in the south. Quieter watering holes, some with live entertainment, are scattered around the fringes of downtown and in nearby neighborhoods. Some spots you may enjoy:

✔ **Ceili's Irish Pub & Restaurant,** #126, 513–8th Ave. SW (☎ 403-508-9999), a trendy three-level pub, is popular with the after-office crowd.

✔ **Kaos Jazz and Blues Bistro,** 718–17th Ave. SW (☎ 403-228-9997), is a great place to hear top-flight jazz and blues entertainment.

✔ **The Mercury,** 801B–17th Ave. SW (☎ 403-541-1175), is part martini bar, part neighborhood pub.

✔ **Outlaws Niteclub,** #24, 7400 Macleod Trail (☎ 403-255-4646), boasts a big dance floor and a mostly student crowd. There are only so many places where you can take a wild ride on a mechanical bull.

✔ **The Ranchman's,** 9615 Macleod Trail S (☎ 403-253-1100), is the real McCoy: an authentic honky-tonk restaurant and nightclub. Learn how to two-step and maybe even meet a cowboy.

Fast Facts: Calgary

Area Code

Calgary's area code is **403**. You don't need to dial it if you're calling local numbers.

American Express

An American Express Travel Service office is located at 421–7th Ave. SW. (☎ **403-261-5982**). For card member services, including lost or stolen cards, call ☎ **800-668-2639**.

Emergencies

Dial **911**.

Hospitals

Emergency care is available at Alberta Children's Hospital, 1820 Richmond Road SW, ☎ **403-229-7211**; Foothills Hospital, 1403–29th St. NW, ☎ **403-670-1110**; Peter Lougheed General Hospital, 3500–26th Ave. NE, ☎ **403-291-8555**; and Rockyview General Hospital, 7007–14th St. SW, ☎ **403-541-3000**.

Internet Access and Cybercafes

Many downtown hotels offer Internet access from guest rooms. You can get online at **Cinescape,** in Eau Claire Market (200 Barclay Parade, 2nd level; ☎ **403-265-4511**), or **Wired,** 1032–17th Ave. SW. (☎ **403-244-7070**).

Maps

Maps of Calgary are widely available in convenience stores and bookshops or from Tourism Calgary. Many sports shops and Calgary Co-op grocery stores sell an excellent pathway and bikeway map. **Map Town,** 100, 400–5th Ave. SW (☎ **403-266-2241**), has outdoor recreation maps, atlases, and guidebooks.

Newspapers

Calgary's daily newspapers are the *Calgary Herald* and the *Calgary Sun.* The national *Globe and Mail* and *National Post* are also widely available.

Police

In a life-threatening emergency, call ☎ **911**. For other matters, ☎ **403-266-1234**.

Smoking

Bars and restaurants that allow children under age 18 are all nonsmoking.

Weather

Call Environment Canada's 24-hour line (☎ **403-299-7878**) for current conditions and storm warnings around the province

Chapter 12

Banff National Park

. . . .

In This Chapter

▶ Discovering Canada's best-loved park

▶ Planning your stay in Banff National Park

▶ Finding famous lakes and viewing stellar peaks

▶ Locating the best beds and meals

. . . .

*W*elcome to Canada's most popular park. To many people, Banff National Park *is* the Canadian Rockies. It's also where Canada's national system of protected areas, which now includes 39 parks, got off the ground more than a century ago. Banff has more historic sites within its boundaries than any other national park in the country.

All this notoriety generates a lot of traffic; millions of tourists visit Banff each year. Many don't venture all that far from the main highways, however. That leaves about 6,000 sq. km (2,340 sq. miles) for those who do. How you explore this vast region really depends on your interests. Hiking is the big draw. But Banff also has some of the world's best downhill skiing and snowboarding. It's easy to arrange a journey through the backcountry on a mountain bike, on horseback, in a canoe or raft. Like to golf? On the Fairmont Banff Springs Hotel course, you hit the links in the shadow of two majestic peaks, Mount Rundle and Sulphur Mountain.

Photographers, birders, and wildlife enthusiasts have the chance to spot bears, elk, deer, and moose, among other animals, not to mention more than 200 species of birds.

If your notion of a vacation has more to do with being pampered than getting active, you'll be interested to know that Banff National Park has some of the top restaurants in the Canadian Rockies, along with a handful of very cushy resorts, hot springs, health clubs, and spas.

Banff National Park

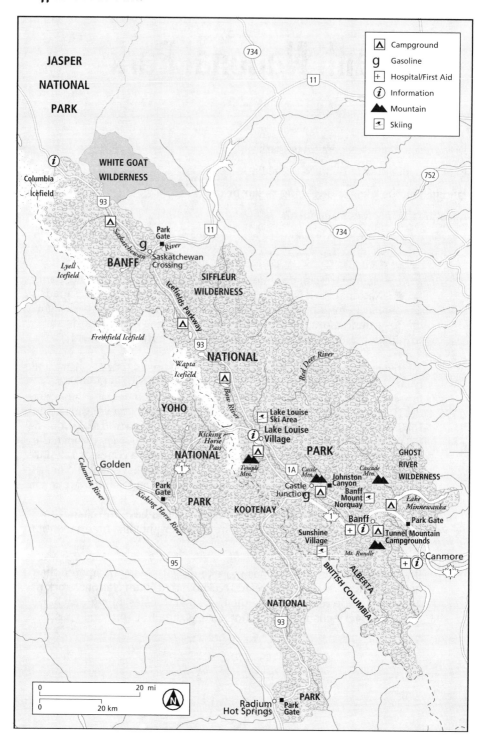

JASPER
NATIONAL
PARK

Campground

Gasoline

Hospital/First Aid

Information

Mountain

Skiing

734

11

752

WHITE GOAT
WILDERNESS

Columbia
Icefield

93

Park
Gate

Saskatchewan River

Saskatchewan
Crossing

11

734

BANFF

Lyell
Icefield

Freshfield Icefield

SIFFLEUR
WILDERNESS

Icefields Parkway

93

NATIONAL

Wapta
Icefield

Red Deer River

YOHO

Bow River

Lake Louise
Ski Area

Lake Louise
Village

Kicking
Horse
Pass

NATIONAL

Golden

1

Temple
Mtn.

PARK

Castle
Mtn.

Cascade
Mtn.

GHOST
RIVER
WILDERNESS

Columbia River

Park
Gate

Kicking Horse River

1A

Johnston
Canyon

Castle
Junction

Banff
Mount
Norquay

Lake
Minnewanka

PARK

KOOTENAY

1

Banff

Park Gate

Tunnel Mountain
Campgrounds

95

Sunshine
Village

Mt. Rundle

Canmore

1

ALBERTA

BRITISH COLUMBIA

NATIONAL

93

0   20 mi

0   20 km

N

PARK

Radium
Hot Springs

Park
Gate

Must-See Attractions

Many of the most popular sites in the Canadian Rockies, including museums and cultural attractions, are located in or near the town of Banff. For details, refer to Chapter 13. This chapter offers suggestions on what to see and do elsewhere in the park.

- ✔ **Lake Louise:** When you think of a lake in the Rockies, you're probably picturing Lake Louise: A castle-like resort (**Fairmont Chateau Lake Louise**) perches above its shores and a glacier-topped peak (**Mount Victoria**) is reflected in its waters.

- ✔ **The Village of Lake Louise:** Situated below the famous lake, this picturesque village is near Canada's biggest ski resort and close to some of the greatest hikes in the Rockies. In summer, survey the scene from a height of 2,088 meters (6,850 feet). Ride the **Lake Louise Gondola.**

- ✔ **Moraine Lake:** In the Valley of the Ten Peaks, this lake rivals Lake Louise for scenic splendor. It's a little quieter, however, especially in winter when the road to the lake is converted to a ski trail.

- ✔ **The Bow Valley Parkway** (Highway 1A): Joining the communities of Banff and Lake Louise, this highway is a spectacular route for a scenic drive.

Getting There

Notwithstanding the Canadian Pacific Railway's historic importance in the development of Banff as a major tourist attraction, you can't ride the rails to Banff today. That is, you can't just hop on a regular passenger train. You can, though, take a luxury tour through the Rockies; contact **Rocky Mountaineer Railtours** (☎ **800-665-7245;** Internet: rockymountaineer.com).

Flying in

The closest major airport is in Calgary, about a 90-minute drive from Banff. **Air Canada** (☎ **888-247-2262;** Internet: www.aircanada.ca) and **WestJet** (☎ **888-937-8538;** Internet: www.westjet.ca) operate nonstop flights from many Canadian cities. From the U.S., Air Canada flies direct to Calgary from Los Angeles, San Francisco, Las Vegas, Spokane, Phoenix, Houston, and Chicago. **Continental Airlines** (☎ **800-231-0856;** Internet: www.continental.com), **Northwest Airlines** (☎ **800-447-4747;** Internet: www.nwa.com), and **United Airlines** (☎ **800-241-6522;** Internet: www.ual.com) also offer nonstop flights from various U.S. centers.

Driving in

Major car rental companies are represented at the Calgary International Airport, including **Avis** (☎ **800-230-4898**), **Alamo** (☎ **800-327-9633**), **Budget** (☎ **800-268-8900**), and **Hertz** (☎ **800-263-0600**). Banff is 128km (79 miles) west of Calgary on the four-lane Trans-Canada Highway.

From British Columbia, you travel either the Trans-Canada Highway, through Field, or Highway 93, through Radium. From Jasper, follow the Icefields Parkway (Highway 93).

As you motor through the park, be sure to keep an eye out for the locals. They include about 3,200 elk, 2,000 bighorn sheep, 800 mountain goats, 1,000 deer, and more than 50 grizzlies, along with black bears, wolves, and coyotes. It's a thrill to spot one of these creatures by the road. But keep your cool. If you decide to pause for a better look, pull over safely, stay in your car, and move on shortly to avoid creating an "animal jam."

Planning Ahead

Most of the 4 million and some odd visitors that come to Banff each year descend on the park in July and August. This is when highways are busiest and hotels priciest. The ski season runs from late November to early May. Spring and fall are the quietest times in the park, great for bird-watching, wildlife viewing, and photography. You also get the best rates on hotels.

The average summer high temperature is a balmy 18 to 22° Celsius (64 to 72° Fahrenheit), while winter highs average only –7 to 0° Celsius (19 to 32° Fahrenheit). When you pack, keep in mind that mountain weather is notoriously unpredictable. It can snow any time of year. The best advice is to take clothes you can layer.

For advance information about the park, write or call the **Banff Information Centre**, Box 900, Banff, AB T1L 1K2; ☎ **403-762-1550;** Fax: 403-762-1551. On the Web, visit Parks Canada at Internet: www. parkscanada.gc.ca/banff. You may also want to get in touch with the **Banff/Lake Louise Tourism Bureau**, P.O. Box 1298, Banff, AB T0L 0C0; ☎ **403-762-8421;** Internet: www.banfflakelouise.com. To book hotels, tours, and ski packages, call ☎ **877-226-3348,** 403-762-0260 or visit Internet: www.banffaccommodations.com.

Figuring Out the Lay of the Land

Banff National Park is 6,641 sq. km (2,564 sq. miles) of wilderness. The Trans-Canada Highway cuts through the park, east–west, past the town of Banff and the village of Lake Louise. Banff is the main center in the park. Lake Louise consists mainly of a small shopping area, service stations, and a handful of hotels. Lake Louise is the name of both the village and the world-famous lake, about five minutes' drive away. Also in the Lake Louise area (about 14km/8.4 miles from the village) is Moraine Lake.

The most scenic route between Banff and Lake Louise is Highway 1A, called the Bow Valley Parkway. The Trans-Canada Highway connects with Highway 93, which heads north to Jasper National Park (this stretch is known as the Icefields Parkway) and south to Kootenay National Park.

Arriving in the Park

Arriving from Calgary, the Banff National Park gate is 114km (71 miles) west, just past the town of Canmore. If you don't have a park pass, you must purchase one at the park gate. Visitors traveling from British Columbia enter the park via the Trans-Canada Highway through Yoho National Park or along Highway 93 from Kootenay National Park. Buy your park pass in one of the B.C. national parks or from information centers in Banff and Lake Louise. From the north, Banff is 287km (178 miles) from Jasper along the Icefields Parkway.

Finding information

Two large visitor centers in the park provide advice on accommodations and attractions as well as information for hikers and skiers (maps, trail reports, weather outlooks, avalanche warnings, wildlife sightings).

In the town of Banff, the **Banff Information Centre** is on the main street, 224 Banff Avenue (☎ **403-762-1550**). It's open daily from 8 a.m. to 8 p.m. in summer (mid-June to September 1), 8 a.m. to 6 p.m. in spring and fall (mid-May to mid-June/early to late September), and 9 a.m. to 5 p.m. from late September to mid-May.

The **Lake Louise Visitor Centre** is next to the Samson Mall in the village of Lake Louise (☎ **403-522-3833**). Hours here are from 9 a.m. to 7 p.m. in summer (late June to early September), 9 a.m. to 5 p.m. in spring and fall (May 1 to late June/early September to mid-October), and 9 a.m. to 4 p.m. (mid-October to the end of April).

Friends of the mountains

You find Friends of Banff National Park shops in the information centers in both Banff and Lake Louise. Friends of Banff is a not-for-profit group that focuses on helping people better understand and appreciate the park. Similar "friends" organizations operate in other parks, such as Jasper and Kananaskis. Proceeds raised by these groups go toward education and research. Besides selling books and maps, Friends of Banff run the Banff radio station (FM 101.1), which carries programs about park history and culture, and operates the Bear and the Butterfly, a gift shop with a nature theme at 214 Banff Avenue in the town of Banff. The group rents out discovery kits (C$10/US$7 a day) for exploring the park. The pack includes binoculars, field guides, and maps. Call ☎ 403-762-2933 or visit Internet: www.friends-ofbanff.com.

Paying fees

You need a **National Parks Pass** to visit Banff National Park. If you plan to stay in the park for only a day, the cost is C$7 (US$4.90) for adults; C$6 (US$4.20) for seniors; C$3.50 (US$2.45) for youth 6 to 16; and C$14 (US$9) for groups of between two and seven people in the same vehicle. Your other option is to purchase an annual pass, which also gets you through the gates at other national parks in Canada. It sells for C$45 (US$32), adults; C$38 (US$27), seniors; C$22 (US$14) youth 6 to 16; and C$89 (US$63) for a group pass.

Hiking is free, unless you plan to stay in the backcountry overnight, in which case you require a Wilderness Pass. These cost C$8 (US$6) per person a night, or C$56 (US$39)for an annual pass, good for backcountry camping in the Canadian national parks of Banff, Jasper, and Waterton Lakes in Alberta, and Mount Revelstoke, Kootenay, and Yoho in B.C.

Fees in the park's road-accessible campgrounds, range from C$19 to C$26 (US$13 to US$18) a night.

For information on ski passes and costs to visit the top attractions, see "Enjoying the Park" later in this chapter.

Anglers need to buy a fishing license: C$7 (US$4.90) a day or C$20 (US$14) for the year.

Getting around

Having your own car is the easiest way to see the park, but you do have some alternatives, at least on the most heavily traveled routes.

In Banff Townsite, local buses run from the Tunnel Mountain area, through the town center, and up to the Fairmont Banff Springs Hotel. Bus fare is C$1 (US$0.70).

In summer, shuttle buses travel from the town center to the Banff Gondola and to the Upper Hot Springs, and in Lake Louise, you can take the bus (C$1/US$0.70) from the village to Lake Louise or Moraine Lake. In winter, many hotels in the park provide shuttle service to area ski hills.

Numerous buses and tours travel from Banff to Lake Louise and from Banff to Jasper, with stops at popular sites along the way. Check in with Brewster (☎ **403-762-6700;** Internet: www.brewster.ca) or Sundog Tours (☎ **780-852-4056;** Internet: www.sundogtours.com) for a look at your options.

Car rental agencies in Banff Townsite include Avis (☎ **800-879-2847,** 403-762-3222) and **Banff Rent-A-Car (☎ 403-762-3352).**

Enjoying the Park

Most visitors head for the town of Banff, which is the park's main commercial center. See Chapter 13 for advice on what to see in and near the townsite. Beyond Banff, the national park is thousands of square kilometers of opportunity for outdoor adventure.

Exploring the top attractions

This section introduces you to some of Banff's best views and vistas. Don't forget your camera.

Seeing Louise: The lake and the village

The village of Lake Louise, about a 40-minute drive from Banff on the Trans-Canada Highway and home to about 1,200 people, is essentially a small shopping center (Samson Mall) and a couple of gas stations. Above the town, at an elevation of 1,731 meters (5,680 feet), the world-famous lake by the same name reflects the Victoria Glacier in its blue-green waters. There's nothing quite like it.

Consequently, tour buses deliver hordes of visitors up here, year-round, to stroll the lakeshore and ogle the majestic **Fairmont Chateau Lake Louise.** In the height of summer, this makes for a fair amount of congestion. Dodge some of the crowds by visiting in early morning or evening. To spare yourself the hassle of finding a spot in the parking lot, leave your car in the village and ride a shuttle bus to the lake.

While you have your camera handy, pay a visit to the enchanting **Moraine Lake** in the Valley of the Ten Peaks. It's about 15km (9 miles) from the village, and also accessible by shuttle bus. In winter, the winding road to Moraine Lake is closed, but you can ski in.

Besides enchanting scenery, Lake Louise boasts 75km (47 miles) of hiking trails and Canada's biggest ski resort.

Lake Louise Gondola

In summer (June to September) enjoy an awesome perspective on the Rockies from the Lake Louise ski hill. In 14 minutes, a gondola whisks sightseers to an elevation of 2,088 meters (6,850 feet) on Mount Whitehorn (you can also ride in an open chairlift) to gaze out on Lake Louise, the Victoria Glacier, and neighboring peaks. Grizzly bears are often seen on the slopes below. If by chance you plan to tie the knot, the lodge on the face of Mount Whitehorn is a dazzling spot for a wedding. (You will, of course, need to arrange this in advance.)

The Gondola is five minutes from Lake Louise village. ☎ **403-522-3555.** *Admission: C$19.95 (US$14) adults, C$17.95 (US$13) seniors & students, C$9.95 (US$7) children 6–12. May, 9 a.m.–4 p.m., June & Sept, 8:30 a.m.–6:00 p.m., July & Aug, 8 a.m.–6 p.m.*

Are we there yet? Beautiful brief drives

On these short trips, you have numerous reasons to hop out of your car and admire the surroundings. Odds are high, as well, of seeing wildlife.

Lake Minnewanka Loop

Watch for bighorn sheep on the 15-minute drive from Banff Townsite to Lake Minnewanka, the largest lake in the park and a favorite boating, fishing, picnicking, and hiking destination. Scuba divers come here to explore the remains of a flooded town. En route to the lake, you visit the Cascade Pond picnic area and an abandoned coal mine, at Bankhead.

Tour boats cruise Lake Minnewanka several times a day in summer. The 48-passenger, glass-enclosed boats escort passengers through marvelous Rocky Mountain scenery, including Devil's Gap, a glacial path from where you can look out to the foothills of the Rockies. Boats leave at 10:30 a.m., 12:30 p.m., 5:00 p.m., and 7:00 p.m. You don't need a reservation, but get there 30 minutes before departure. Cost: C$30 (US$21) adults, C$13 (US$9) children 5 to 11, free for children under 5.

To reach Lake Minnewanka, take the Lake Minnewanka Interchange from the Trans-Canada Hwy.

Bow Valley Parkway

The fastest way to get from Banff to Lake Louise is the Trans-Canada Highway (Highway 1). But why rush? The original road between the two communities, Highway 1A, or the Bow Valley Parkway, meanders through meadows and forests past scenic viewpoints and picnic areas. About 18km (11 miles) west of Banff Townsite, you reach the turnoff to **Johnston Canyon,** where you may want to stop for a hike. An interpretive trail escorts you past waterfalls to the canyon. Back on the parkway, take a break at Moose Meadows, where you enjoy impressive views of **Castle Mountain** (2,766 meters/9,073 feet). Set aside an hour to travel between Banff and Lake Louise via this route — more if you picnic along the way.

Park officials ask travelers to stay off a stretch of the Bow Valley Parkway between Banff and Johnston Canyon from March 1 to June 25, from 6 p.m. until 9 a.m. The restriction is intended to help protect area wildlife. During these times, take the Trans-Canada Highway instead.

Access to the Bow Valley Parkway is 5km (3 miles) west of Banff at Castle Junction.

Taking a hike

If you think the peaks and valleys of Banff National Park look impressive from the Trans-Canada Highway, wait until you venture into the wilderness on foot. You can scale mountain slopes to reach panoramas that inspire you to ponder the meaning of life. You don't have to, of course. You can also be awestruck by the beauty of Banff on trails that involve considerably less exertion. The tough part, actually, is deciding which hike to try.

The hikes in this section are favorites because they lead to some of the best viewpoints. But these suggestions are just a taste of a smorgasbord of possibilities: Banff National Park boasts 1,600km (1,000 miles) of trails.

If you have more time, or want to venture onto lesser-traveled paths, get your hands on a trail guide. Bookstores and outdoor gear shops in Calgary and Banff carry many excellent titles. Parks Canada staff at the information centers in Banff Townsite (224 Banff Ave.; ☎ **403-762-1550**) and Lake Louise (Samson Mall, ☎ **403-522-3833**) can also help you plan a hike.

Throughout the park, you find many short walks and interpretive trails (see "Tamer treks" below) that are well marked, easy to follow, and perfect for families. Half-day hikes (one to four hours) and day hikes (five hours or more) call for more planning. At the very least, carry extra clothing, food, and water (one to two liters/quarts per person). Running shoes are fine for interpretive trails, but for longer trips on more rugged terrain, sturdy hiking boots provide better support. Before heading out, check in with the nearest visitor information center to get the latest news on trail conditions and find out about wildlife sightings or temporary trail closures.

Half-day hikes

Larch Valley
Lake Louise area

Larch Valley is spectacular in mid-September when the larch trees turn golden, and many Calgary hikers make an annual pilgrimage to this trail. Moraine Lake, where the trail begins, is encircled by towering peaks. (This scene used to be on the back of the Canadian $20 bill.) Larch Valley and the Minnestimma Lakes are only 4km (2.5 miles) away, but you climb more than 500 meters (1,640 feet) to reach them. Strong and fit hikers can continue on to Sentinel Pass.

Another top spot in the Lake Louise area from which to admire larches in autumn is the Boulder Pass trail, which begins in the Lake Louise ski area.

Distance: 11.6km (7.2 miles) round-trip to Sentinal Pass. Level: Moderate to Strenuous. Access: In front of Moraine Lake Lodge.

Plain of the Six Glaciers
Lake Louise area

This is a Canadian Rockies favorite, so it's wise to get an early start. The hike begins on a well-traveled trail (and hugely popular tourist stroll) around the shores of Lake Louise (in front of the Fairmont Chateau Lake Louise). You climb up a valley to splendid views of the lake and — you guessed it — six glaciers. Mountain goats are often spotted from the trail. About 5km (3 miles) from the trailhead, the Plain of Six Glaciers Teahouse sells tea and scones. The best views await you at the top of the trail, about 1km farther on.

Distance: 11km (7 miles) round-trip. Level: Moderate. Access: Lake Louise Shoreline Trail.

Sulphur Mountain
Near Banff Townsite

You have two options for getting to the summit of Sulphur Mountain, which is the highest peak in the Banff area, at 2,282 meters (7,486 feet): Pay your C$25.50 (US$17.85), hop on the gondola, and you're there in eight minutes. Or grab your hiking boots, throw a day pack over your shoulder, and follow the switchbacks. The top section of the trail to the gondola terminal is quite steep. From the terminal, follow a boardwalk to an old weather observatory with great views of the surrounding peaks. Have your jacket handy. Once you're up here, there's no charge to ride the gondola down, but if you intend to do this, check the schedule before you head out.

11km (6.8 miles) round-trip. Level: Moderate. Access: Upper Hot Springs parking lot.

Tunnel Mountain
Near Banff Townsite

You too can bag a peak. Follow the well-marked trail that winds to the summit of Tunnel Mountain (about 2km/1.2 miles) and pat yourself on the back while you gaze down on the town of Banff, Vermilion Lakes, and the Bow Valley.

Distance: 4.6km (2.9 miles) round-trip. Level: Easy to moderate. Access: Follow Wolf St. to St. Julien Rd. The parking lot is 0.3km up Julien Rd. on the left side.

Day hikes

Aylmer Lookout
Near Banff Townsite

This popular trail leads you through a forested area along the north shore of Lake Minnewanka before climbing about 4km (2.5 miles) to the site of a former fire lookout, where you enjoy a sweeping panorama of the lake. Bighorn sheep are often seen on this hike.

Distance: 23.2km (14 miles) roundtrip. Level: Moderate. Access: Lake Minnewanka day-use area.

Bourgeau Lake
Castle Junction Area/Sunshine Meadows region

It's a bit of a grind through the forest, but totally worth it to visit this alpine lake named for Eugene Bourgeau, a botanist with the Palliser Expedition. The expedition explored the southern passes through the Canadian Rockies in the mid-1800s. You gain about 700 meters (2,300 feet) over 7.4km (4.6 miles).

Distance: 15km (9 miles) round-trip. Level: Moderate. Access: 13km (8 miles) west of Banff Townsite on the Trans-Canada Hwy. Watch for a parking lot on the south side of the highway.

Cory Pass Loop
Near Banff Townsite

Only experienced hikers should tackle this tough trail: It's rated one of the most difficult in the park and features a 915-meter (3,001-foot) elevation gain. Be ready for a long day of steep climbing. The first leg of the journey, up to Cory Pass between Mount Cory and Mount Edith, is spectacular in itself. You could call it a day and head back the way you came, but if your knees can take it, carry on down into the Gargoyle Valley and follow the loop through Edith Pass. A highlight of this hike is an unparalleled perspective on Mount Louis, which rises up out of the valley below. You're also apt to spot bighorn sheep and elk.

13-km (8-mile) loop. Level: Strenuous. Access: Fireside Picnic Area at the east end of Bow Valley Parkway.

Healy Pass
Castle Junction Area/Sunshine Meadows

Healy Pass is known for striking views of Egypt Lake and Scarab Lake. You have to climb through some forest to reach the viewpoint, but you also get to wander through alpine meadows, which in early August are littered with wildflowers. The trail gains 655 meters (2,148 feet). Give yourself about five hours, return.

Distance: 19km (12 miles) round-trip. Level: Moderately difficult. Access: Sunshine Ski Area parking lot, near the gondola terminal.

Tamer treks

The **Fenland Trail,** which starts at the Forty Mile Creek picnic area on the west side of the Mount Norquay Road, is one of the most interesting spots in the **Banff Townsite area** for a short stroll. The trail is also popular with runners and cyclists. A fen, in case you're wondering, is somewhere between a bog and a marsh. Look for beavers and muskrats. In the **Lake Louise area,** stroll along the shores of two of the most picturesque lakes in the Canadian Rockies: **Lake Louise,** in the shadow of snow-topped Mount Victoria, and **Moraine Lake,** in the Valley of the Ten Peaks.

The **Sunshine Meadows ski area** has 12km (7 miles) of easy (and far less congested) trails to explore in summer, ranging from one-hour walks to full-day hikes. Since you're already at an elevation of 2,220 meters (7,283 feet), you're treated to tantalizing views from the get-go. You can't drive up here, but a shuttle bus makes the trip every day. It costs C\$18/US\$13 from the Sunshine parking lot, or C\$35/US\$25 if you're coming from Banff. Your ticket includes a two-hour guided nature hike. To reserve, call **White Mountain Adventures, ☎ 800-408-0005.** Alternatively, you can walk up. It's 6km (3.7 miles).

Backcountry adventures

The top backpacking trails in the park are in the **Egypt Lake** and **Shadow Lake** areas. An overnight trip calls for a little more effort than a day hike, but you can get far enough from civilization to deter most of the crowds. To stay in one of Banff's backcountry campgrounds, you need a permit, called a Wilderness Pass. These cost C\$8 (US\$6) a night, or C\$56 (US\$39) for an annual pass, which you can also use in other national parks in the Canadian Rockies. You should book your campsite in advance — you can reserve up to three months before your trip — by contacting the Banff Information Center ☎ 403-762-1550. The reservation fee is C\$12 (US\$8).

For the latest word on trail conditions, call the park's Trail Report line: ☎ 403-760-1305.

Staying active

If you enjoy an active lifestyle, you can take advantage of numerous opportunities to savor the park's legendary scenery while staying on the go. Besides exploring the hiking trails I've just mentioned and checking out the ski hills in the next section, investigating outdoor activities such as the following.

Biking

Mountain bikers are welcome on nearly 200km (124 miles) of trails in the park. Stop at one of the information centers to pick up a brochure showing designated routes and find out about any closures or warnings. Be prepared to meet hikers and horseback riders on the trails. **Backtrax Bike Shop,** 225 Bear Street in Banff (☎ 403-762-8177), rents bikes. Costs range from C\$8 to C\$12 (US\$5.60 to US\$8)) by the hour or C\$30 to C\$42 (US\$21 to US\$29) per day.

Because they are fast and quiet, cyclists need to be especially cautious in bear country. Make enough noise to let bears know you're coming.

Hey, this is just like the movies

Ever feel like you just want to saddle up your mount and amble off into the Rockies? **Holiday on Horseback** runs wilderness cookouts from its stables in Banff to various spots along the banks of the Bow River, to Sulphur Mountain, and through the Spray River Valley. A typical day-long trail ride costs C$135 (US$95) a person, including lunch (beef and beans). If this sounds a little tame, the same company offers five-day expeditions that take you deeper into the mountains and test your ability to set up camp. Call ☎ **800-661-8352,** 403-762-4551.

Canoeing

You can paddle on both Lake Louise and Moraine Lake. For canoe rental information, contact **Lake Louise: ☎ 403-522-3511, Moraine Lake: ☎ 403-522-3733. Rocky Mountain Raft Tours** at the corner of Wolf Street and Bow Avenue in Banff (☎ **403-762-3632**) rents canoes for trips on the Bow River. A canoe costs about $16 (US$11) an hour or C$40 (US$28) a day.

Golfing

The **Fairmont Banff Springs** 27-hole golf course runs along the Bow River in the shadow of Mount Rundle, Sulphur Mountain, and Tunnel Mountain. The scenery here is legendary. Green fees range from C$75 (US$53) in May and October to C$150 (US$105) July through September. You needn't be a guest at the Banff Springs Hotel to play the course. To book a tee time call ☎ **403-762-6801**.

Letting it snow

Aside from the scenery, the big draw in Banff National Park for downhill skiers and snowboarders is variety. Based in Banff, you can check out three resorts with more than 3,035 hectares (7,500 acres) of trails. **Mount Norquay** is the closest — about a 15-minute drive from the town of Banff; **Lake Louise** is the largest, with 11 lifts to deliver skiers to 100 runs spread across four mountain faces; and **Sunshine Village** gets the most snow: more than 9 meters (30 feet) a year.

Downhill skiing

The locals head for Mount Norquay (☎ **403-762-4421;** Internet: www.banffnorquay.com). The terrain is fairly evenly spread between beginner, intermediate, and expert runs, and a day pass costs C$49 (US$50) for an adult. A plus of skiing here is that you can also buy hourly passes for various durations: two hours, for instance, costs C$26 (US$18) for an adult; three hours C$30 (US$21). On Fridays, Norquay offers night skiing from 4 to 9 p.m. (C$24/US$17 for adults).

Sunshine Village (☎ **403-762-6500;** Internet: www.skibanff.com) boasts all-natural snow and is the only resort in the park with a hotel on the mountain (**Sunshine Inn;** ☎ **403-762-6555**). From the Sunshine parking lot, 8km (5 miles) west of Banff Townsite, a six-person gondola (said to be the world's fastest) whisks skiers to the village, where super-speedy quad chairs distribute them across three mountain faces. There's something here for all abilities. The latest addition, if you enjoy a challenge, is Delirium Dive, a double black–diamond run from the top of the resort's Continental Divide Chair down a shockingly steep cirque. (Avalanche transceivers, rescue shovels, and partners are mandatory.) A lift ticket at Sunshine costs C$59 (US$41) (adult) per day. Half-day and multi-day passes are available.

Lake Louise (☎ **403-522-3555;** Internet: www.skilouise.com), a five-minute drive from the village of Lake Louise, is known for spectacular scenery. It's the biggest ski resort in the Canadian Rockies and one of the largest in North America, with 113 runs, the longest of which is 8km (5 miles). There's a huge range of terrain here, and the resort boasts at least one beginner run from every chair. At the base of the hill, catch your breath in a majestic log lodge with a wraparound deck. Day passes go for C$57 (US$40) for an adult. Half-day and multi-day tickets are also for sale.

As well as lift tickets for individual resorts, you can get a **Tri-Area Pass** that covers lifts at all three resorts along with transportation to the hills from hotels in Banff and Louise. Costs range from C$186 (US$130) (adult) for 4 days to C$828 (US$580) for 18 days. For more information, visit Internet: www.skibig3.com. **Snowboarders** can buy three days of instruction (one day at each resort) for C$214 (US$150).

The ski season in the park runs from November to May.

Cross-country skiing and snowshoeing

Cross-country skiers can zip along 80km (50 miles) of groomed trails, many of which start near Banff Townsite. The **Spray River Trail** is a favorite 12.5-km (8-mile) loop. If you like to snowshoe, the **Stoney Squaw Trail** (2.3km/1.4 miles) from Banff's Mount Norquay ski area parking lot offers great views of the Bow Valley. In the Lake Louise area, follow the trail along the **Bow River.** Access the trail on the south side of the Bow River bridge (turn right).

Rent gear from the ski hills or one of a number of shops in Banff, including **SnowTips,** 225 Bear Street (☎ **403-762-8177**). You can get a cross-country ski package for about C$9 (US$6.30) a day; snowshoes for C$7 (US$4.90) a day.

Motoring through the Rockies in winter

Winter can be a spectacular time to travel through the mountain parks, but take it slow on snowy roads and when visibility is poor. You can check **road conditions** in Banff and other national parks in the Canadian Rockies before you start out by dialing ☎ **403-762-1450**. Here are a few more tips to ensure a safe trip:

- ✔ Watch for black ice, particularly near bridges.

- ✔ Avoid using cruise control.

- ✔ Remember that the law requires snow tires (or all-season radials), except on the Trans-Canada Highway (Highway 1) and the Yellowhead Highway (Highway 16).

- ✔ Be prepared for an emergency by carrying extra warm clothes in your car, along with a flashlight, shovel, blanket, and some food.

- ✔ Don't count on your cell phone. Reception is unreliable outside of Banff Townsite and the village of Lake Louise.

Where to Stay in Banff National Park

Banff Townsite has by far the largest concentration of hotels in the park. For help choosing a hotel in the town, see Chapter 13. You also find a handful of hotels in Lake Louise, about a 40-minute drive from Banff. If you want a cabin or chalet, check out the resorts along the Bow Valley Parkway (Highway 1A) between Banff and Lake Louise. Rooms in the park don't come cheap, although rates drop after the peak summer season. Not surprisingly, you find the best deals from April to mid-May (ahead of the hiking season) and in October and November (before the ski slopes open). In summer, hotels in the park fill up fast, so be sure to call ahead.

Baker Creek Chalets
$$$ **Bow Valley Parkway (between Banff & Lake Louise)**

These cabins aren't all that far from civilization, but they're surrounded by a cushion of wilderness. Stay in one of the 25 bright chalets or book a suite in the main lodge. Either way, you get a kitchen and your own deck. If you're too tired to cook, the Baker Creek Bistro offers an extensive and interesting menu. The best deals here are in spring or fall, when you pay only C$130 (US$91) for the same cabin that costs C$220 (US$154) in summer.

Bow Valley Parkway, 10km (6 miles) east of Lake Louise. ☎ *403-522-3761. Fax: 403-522-2270. E-mail:* bakerinfo@bakercreek.com. *Internet:* www. bakercreek.com. *Rack rates: C$170–C$315 (US$111–US$183) double. MC, V.*

Fairmont Chateau Lake Louise

$$$$ **In Lake Louise**

This grand historic hotel gives new meaning to the term "lakefront room." A room on the lakeside here gets you a front-row view of Lake Louise, whose stunning blue-green waters at the base of glacier-draped Mount Victoria are among the most photographed in the Canadian Rockies. In summer, canoes paddle by. Hiking trails start just steps from the hotel lobby. In winter, an international ice sculpture competition transforms the lakeshore into a gallery of cool, clear art. Secluded it isn't. Lake Louise attracts millions of tourists. It's all very magical, nonetheless. Check the hotel Web site for special rates such as a bed-and-breakfast package, which starts at C$126 (US$88) per person per night in winter.

111 Lake Louise Dr. ☎ *800-441-1414, 403-522-3511. Fax: 403-522-3834. E-mail:* chateaulakelouise@fairmont.com. *Internet:* www.fairmont.com. *Rack rates: C$551–C$656 (US$386–US$459) double. AE, DISC, MC, V.*

Lake Louise Inn

$$$ **In Lake Louise**

This big complex (more than 200 rooms) is a short walk from the few shops and restaurants in the village of Lake Louise. A couple of casual restaurants are on-site. Lake Louise Inn is popular with the ski crowd. The hotel provides a ski storage area, repair service, and shuttle buses to the slopes.

210 Village Rd. ☎ *800-661-9237, 403-522-3791. Fax: 403-522-2018. E-mail:* llinn@telusplanet.com. *Internet:* www.lakelouiseinn.com. *Rack rates: C$159–C$261 (US$111–US$183) double. AE, DISC, MC, V.*

Post Hotel

$$$$ **In Lake Louise**

The Post Hotel opened as a ski lodge 60 years ago and was expanded and renovated to accommodate summer visitors. In the late 1970s, two Swiss brothers, André and George Schwarz, bought the lodge and transformed it into a luxury getaway: down quilts, in-room fireplaces, jetted tubs. You can expect accommodation that's every bit as upscale as that at Chateau Lake Louise (but without all the tourists cruising around). The Post Hotel is part of the prestigious Relais & Châteaux hotel group, and its dining room is considered one of the top spots to eat in Canada.

P.O. Box 69, Lake Louise, AB T0L 1E0. ☎ ***800-661-1586***, *403-522-3989. Fax: 403-522-3966.* E-mail: info@posthotel.com. *Internet:* www.posthotel inn.com. *Rack rates: C$305–C$400 (US$214–US$280) double. AE, MC, V.*

Storm Mountain
$$$ **Highway 93 South (Banff–Radium Highway)**

The 14 cabins on this forested site, about a 25-minute drive from either the town of Banff or the village of Lake Louise, were built by the Canadian Pacific Railway in 1922. After having been closed for years, the cabins re-opened in 2003, sporting hand-crafted log beds and clawfoot tubs. Renovations have respected the resort's historic character. A restaurant in the main lodge serves organic vegetables and free-range meats. The setting is secluded and features impressive views of Storm Mountain, Castle Mountain, and the Sawback Range. The resort closes from October 15 to December 15.

P.O. Box 3249, Banff, AB T1L 1C8. ☎ ***403-762-4155***. *Fax: 403-762-4151. E-mail:* info@stormmountainlodge.com. *Internet:* www.stormmountainlodge. com. *Rack rates: C$195 (US$137) double. MC, V.*

Runner-up lodgings

Paradise Lodge & Bungalows
$$$ **Lake Louise**

Book your own cabin or get a suite in the main lodge. This complex, just down the hill from the lake, is open from mid-May to mid-October.

105 Lake Louise Dr. ☎ ***403-522-3595***. *Internet: www.paradiselodge.com.*

Mountaineer Lodge
$$$ **Lake Louise**

This summer-only hotel (mid-May to mid-October) is centrally located in the village of Lake Louise.

101 Village Rd. ☎ ***403-522-3844***. *Internet:* www.mountaineerlodge.com.

International Hostel
$ **Lake Louise**

Operated by Hostelling International and the Alpine Club of Canada, this popular hostel offers some of the few budget rooms in the park. Check into guided hikes and ski packages.

Village Rd. ☎ ***866-762-4122***, *403-670-7580. Internet:* www.hihostels.ca.

Luxury in the wilderness

Overnight adventures in the backcountry are variations on the following: You disappear into a forest (or up the side of a mountain or through a river valley), hike through some of the most remote and spectacular country imaginable, rehydrate dinner, and crawl into your tent. This can be marvelous. But you also have the option (for a price) of dining like a king — or a queen — and dozing off in a log cabin tucked under a down quilt. If you're already reaching for your credit card, read on to discover Banff's backcountry lodges.

Throughout the Canadian Rockies, a handful of rustic resorts — some even have hot showers — are located in wilderness areas away from the main roads. To get to these places, you hike, ski, ride a horse, or take a helicopter. Note that prices are per person, so rates are steep, but they do include meals. Good ones.

Shadow Lake Lodge (☎ **403-762-0116;** Internet: www.shadowlake lodge.com) has 12 cabins that you can hike or ski to from Red Earth Creek, about 19km (12 miles) west of Banff Townsite. Rates are C$160 (US$112) per person per night. **Skoki Lodge** (☎ **403-522-3555;** Internet: www.skilouise.com/skoki), built by a Banff ski club in 1930, now accommodates 23 people in a lodge and three cabins. Hike or ski an 11-km (7-mile) trail from the Lake Louise ski area. Rates are C$145 to C$180 (US$102 to US$126) per person per night. The trail to **Sundance Lodge** (☎ **403-762-4551;** Internet: www.xcskisundance.com) is about 16km (10 miles) from Banff Townsite. On cross-country skis, you can get there in about 2.5 hours. In summer, you reach Sundance Lodge on horseback. Rates are C$85 (US$60) per person per night, with cheaper rates for the second and third nights.

Campgrounds

Camping amenities in Banff National Park range from basic tent sites to full-service RV parks. But even with 13 campgrounds and more than 2,000 sites, finding a spot can be a challenge. Campgrounds don't take reservations, so your best strategy is to get there early in the day. You can, though, put in a call to the Banff Information Centre (☎ **403-762-1550**) to find out if the campground you have in mind is already full. Rates range from about C$19 (US$13) for tent sites to C$26 (US$18) for full-service sites.

Closest to the town of Banff is the **Tunnel Mountain Campground.** Tunnel Mountain is just northeast of the town center: You can walk to Banff Avenue or take the bus. The campground has three sections with 321 full-service sites, 222 sites with power only, and another 600 tent sites.

For a quieter and more tranquil setting, try for a spot at the **Two Jack Campground** on the Minnewanka Loop Road, 13 km (8 miles) from Banff. The **Two Jack Main Campground,** in a treed area, has kitchen shelters and toilets (but no showers). The scenic **Two Jack Lakeside Campground,** across the road, has showers.

At Lake Louise, you can pitch your tent in the **Lake Louise Campground,** along the Bow River. It's about 1km from the village and has both tent sites and an RV section.

Along the Bow Valley Parkway (Highway 1A), the **Castle Mountain** and the **Johnston Canyon** campgrounds are good choices if you want something more remote and rustic. These sites don't have RV hookups.

Where to Eat in Banff National Park

The town of Banff (see Chapter 13) boasts most of the park's eateries. You also find some reputable spots in the Lake Louise area, including the following:

Baker Creek Bistro
$$$ **CANADIAN**

Whether or not you're staying at Baker Creek Chalets, it's tempting to head here for dinner. The food easily justifies the drive east of Lake Louise along the Bow Valley Parkway. Appetizer dishes feature creative flavor combinations, such as spinach leaves in potato dressing and marinated salmon with a creamy dill sauce. Main courses are equally imaginative, and include trout in a Riesling sauce and pork tenderloin paired with camembert.

Bow Valley Parkway, 10km (6 miles) east of Lake Louise. ☎ *403-522-2182. Reservations recommended. Main courses: C$17–C$29 (US$12–US$20). AE, MC, V. Summer: daily, 8:00 a.m.–9:30 p.m. Winter: Wed–Sun 4:00 p.m.–9:30 p.m. & Sunday brunch 8:00–10:30 a.m.*

Post Hotel Dining Room
$$$–$$$$ **INTERNATIONAL**

Winner of countless awards and accolades for its cuisine and outstanding wine cellar, the upscale rustic dining room in the Post Hotel does everything just right. It's one of the best spots in the park to splurge. Flavorful sauces highlight both fish and meat dishes on the menu. The setting is semi-secluded and the views, any time of year, are superb. A dinner jacket would not be out of place.

In the Post Hotel. ☎ *403-522-3989. Reservations recommended. Main courses: $30–$40 (US$21–US$28). AE, MC, V. Two dinner seatings: before 6:30 p.m., after 8:30 p.m.*

For cheaper food and more casual eats (meals under C$10/US$7), the places to go in Lake Louise are **Laggan's** in the Samson Mall (baked goodies, substantial sandwiches, and good coffee) and **Bill Peyto's Café** in the Lake Louise Hostel on Village Road (try burgers, meat loaf, or chili).

Fast Facts: Banff National Park

Area Code

☎ **403** (You don't need it to dial local numbers.)

ATMs

In banks along Banff Avenue in the town of Banff.

Emergency

Dial 911

Fees

A National Parks Pass costs C$7 (US$4.90) adult; C$14 (US$9) group for a day or C$45 (US$32) adult; C$89 (US$62) group.

Fishing License

Licenses are sold at information centers and fishing supply stores: C$7 (US$4.20) per day or C$20 (US$14) for an annual pass.

Hospitals

Banff Mineral Springs Hospital, 301 Lynx St., ☎ **403-762-2222.**

Information

Banff Information Centre, 224 Banff Ave., ☎ **403-762-1550;** Lake Louise Visitor Centre, next to the Samson Mall in Lake Louise, ☎ **403-522-3833.**

Pharmacies

Cascade Plaza Drug, 317 Banff Ave., ☎ **403-762-2245.**

Post Office

204 Buffalo St., Banff ☎ **403-762-2586.** Samson Mall, Lake Louise ☎ **403-522-3870.**

Road conditions

☎ **403-762-1450.**

Weather

☎ **403-762-2088.**

Taxes

A 7% national Goods and Services tax is charged on most goods and services. Visitors to Canada can apply for a rebate on certain purchases. The hotel tax is 5%. Alberta has no provincial sales tax.

Time Zone

Mountain Standard

Web Site

Internet: www.parkscanada.gc.ca

Chapter 13

The Town of Banff

*T*his is where Canada's national park system all began — in 1883. That's when employees of Canadian Pacific Railway stumbled across hot springs above the Bow River Valley. Two years later, squabbles over ownership prompted the Canadian government to declare a 16-km (10-mile) region around the springs as a natural reserve. The town of Banff has been wowing visitors from Canada and around the world ever since.

Touristy? Definitely. Crowded? Yes. But Banff is also undeniably beautiful. The postcard images that spring to mind when you think of the Canadian Rockies most likely originated here: the castle-like Fairmont Banff Springs Hotel; the panorama from the 2,282-meter (7,486-foot) summit of Sulphur Mountain. Banff has mountain scenery galore, and no end of venues from which to appreciate it: restaurant patios, big-windowed chalets, hotel hot tubs and spas.

Getting There

The closest major airport is in Calgary. The Trans-Canada Highway (Highway 1) runs west from Calgary to Banff National Park, and past the town of Banff and the village of Lake Louise before continuing west to Vancouver, British Columbia. Banff Townsite is 128km (79 miles) west of Calgary, about a 90-minute drive. From Vancouver, it's 850km (595 miles), so you're on the road for 10 to 12 hours. The towns of Banff and Lake Louise are separated by 58km (36 miles).

Banff Townsite

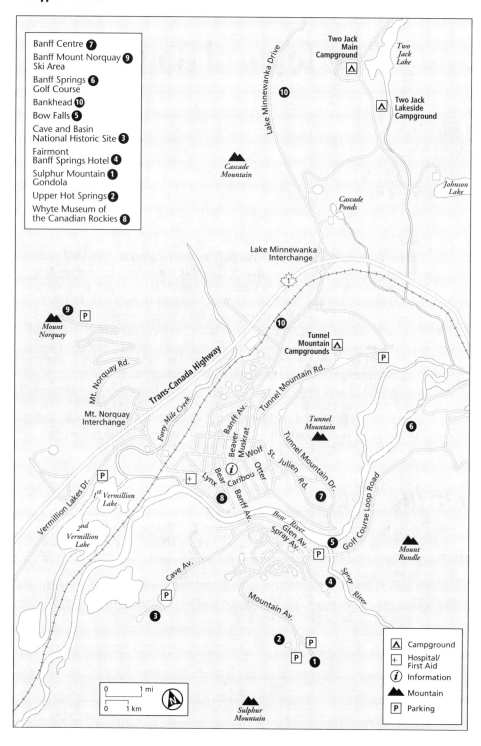

Banff Centre **7**
Banff Mount Norquay **9**
Ski Area
Banff Springs **6**
Golf Course
Bankhead **10**
Bow Falls **5**
Cave and Basin
National Historic Site **3**
Fairmont
Banff Springs Hotel **4**
Sulphur Mountain **1**
Gondola
Upper Hot Springs **2**
Whyte Museum of
the Canadian Rockies **8**

Two Jack
Main
Campground
Two
Jack
Lake

Two Jack
Lakeside
Campground

10

Lake Minnewanka Drive

Cascade
Mountain

Johnson
Lake

Cascade
Ponds

Lake Minnewanka
Interchange

Mount
Norquay **9** P

10

Tunnel
Mountain
Campgrounds

P

Trans-Canada Highway

Mt. Norquay Rd.

Mt. Norquay
Interchange

Tunnel Mountain Rd.

Tunnel
Mountain

6

Forty Mile Creek

Banff Av.

Beaver
Muskrat
Wolf
Otter
St. Julien Rd.

Tunnel Mountain Dr.

P

Vermillion Lakes Dr.

P

1st Vermillion
Lake

Lynx
Bear
Caribou
Banff Av.

8

7

Golf Course Loop Road

2nd
Vermillion
Lake

Bow River
Glen Av.
Spray Av.

5
P

Mount
Rundle

Cave Av.

P

4

Spray River

3

Mountain Av.

2 P

P **1**

Sulphur
Mountain

0   1 mi
0   1 km

N

◬ Campground
✚ Hospital/
First Aid
ⓘ Information
▲ Mountain
P Parking

Driving in

From Calgary, head west on the four-lane Trans-Canada Highway. If you're coming from British Columbia, you either follow the Trans-Canada east through Field, in Yoho National Park, or take Highway 93 from the south, which runs through Radium Hot Springs in Kootenay National Park. The speed limit on the Trans-Canada is 110 kph (68 mph) outside Banff National Park and 90 kph (56 mph) within the park. From Jasper, Banff is a 287-km (178-mile) trip along the Icefields Parkway (Highway 93).

If you're traveling the Trans-Canada through Banff National Park between May 1 and September 20, watch out for signs near Lake Louise alerting you to slow down to 70 kph (43 mph). In summer, a reduced speed limit is enforced on a 9-km (5.5-mile) stretch here to help protect wildlife, especially bears, which often cross the highway in this area. Obeying this speed limit adds only a few minutes to your travel time, but it helps prevent accidents and could spare a bear's life (and spare you a speeding ticket).

Busing in

Greyhound (☎ **800-661-8747;** Internet: `www.greyhound.ca`) and **Brewster** (☎ **877-791-5500;** Internet: `www.Brewster.ca`) both offer regular service to Banff from Calgary, Edmonton, and Vancouver. The bus station in Banff is at 100 Gopher St. (☎ **403-762-1092**). Various shuttle services operate between the Calgary airport and Banff.

Orienting Yourself and Getting Around Banff

When you head into the townsite along Banff Avenue, you see the **Banff Information Centre** on your left (224 Banff Ave., ☎ **403-762-1550**). Park in one of the lots behind the Information Centre (free for three hours). The center is open daily, except December 25 and January 1. In summer (June 13 to September 1), it's open from 8 a.m. to 8 p.m., in spring (May 16 to June 12) and fall (September 2 to September 21) from 8 a.m. to 6 p.m. Winter (September 22 to May 15) hours are from 9 a.m. to 5 p.m.

In the center, you find a **Banff/Lake Louise Tourism** office, where you can pick up maps and brochures on Banff Townsite attractions, and a **Parks Canada** desk, which has park passes and up-to-date information on trail conditions in the park. The not-for-profit group **Friends of Banff** also has a shop here, with a great selection of hiking guides, maps, and books on Banff.

Most hotels, stores, and restaurants are also located on or close to Banff Avenue, which runs through the heart of the town and across the Bow River.

On the north side of the Bow River, turn right to head for the **Cave and Basin National Historic Site** or left for the **Banff Gondola** and **Fairmont Banff Springs Hotel.**

Banff Transit buses run along Banff Avenue to Tunnel Mountain and the Fairmont Banff Springs Hotel. The fare is C$1 (US$0.70).

Many hotels offer free shuttle service to popular destinations in town, and in winter, to ski hills at Norquay, Sunshine Village, and Lake Louise.

Where to Stay in Banff

Hotels in the town of Banff fill up fast, so it's wise to book in advance. Here are just a few of your options.

Buffalo Mountain Lodge
$$$

You don't have to rough it in this romantic mountain getaway on the slopes of Tunnel Mountain. Throw a log on the fire, kick back, and take in the view. In addition to gorgeous fieldstone wood-burning fireplaces, most rooms in the lodge have balconies or patios. The dining room specializes in Rocky Mountain cuisine, which features game (elk, caribou) and fish with local and regional fruit and vegetables. It always earns rave reviews. Or, dine in the more casual Cilantro Rocky Mountain Café. You can walk to Banff Avenue from here, if you can tear yourself away.

700 Tunnel Mountain Rd. ☎ **800-661-1367**, *403-762-2400. Fax: 403-760-4495. E-mail:* info@crmr.com. *Internet:* www.crmr.com. *Rack rates: C$215–C$245 (US$151–US$171) double. AE, MC, V.*

Bumper's Inn
$$

Book a room around the central courtyard and you can step out your door onto a shady deck. Bumper's gives you some distance from the crowds on Banff Avenue, yet it's only a block away. It's an older hotel, but well maintained, and rooms are basic but bright. The quietest spots face the courtyard or the parking area, which backs on to a stand of evergreens. You can walk to the town center in less than 15 minutes. A popular steakhouse (also called Bumper's) is next door.

Banff Ave. at Marmot Cres. ☎ ***800-661-3518,*** *403-762-3386. Fax: 403-760-4495. E-mail:* bumpersinn@banff.net. *Internet:* www.bumpersinn.com. *Rack rates: C$125 (US$88) double. AE, MC, V.*

Caribou Lodge

$$$

If you want to stay on Banff's main drag, I highly recommend Caribou Lodge. Stroll out your door and join the parade of shoppers on Banff Avenue. The fieldstone and slate decor makes for a rugged, outdoorsy atmosphere — you certainly won't forget you're in the Rockies. The loft rooms on the fourth floor are particularly nice, and have pull-out sofas so that they can sleep four people. Some have Jacuzzis and two-story views. Standard rooms overlook a courtyard. A popular restaurant, The Keg, is on the main level, and it's a short stroll to more restaurants and shops.

521 Banff Ave. ☎ ***800-563-8764,*** *403-762-5887. Fax: 403-762-5918. E-mail: reservations@bestofbanff.com. Internet:* www.bestofbanff.com *Rack rates: C$220–C$235 (US$154–US$165) double. AE, DISC, MC, V.*

Fairmont Banff Springs

$$$$

Close your eyes and think of Banff. See a castle in the wilderness? It's the Fairmont Banff Springs hotel, a national historic site and the landmark most associated with Banff National Park. The Banff Springs opened in 1888 as an oasis of luxury in the Rockies — at the time, it was the largest hotel in the world. Today, it's even larger. Much larger, especially when you include the ten bars and restaurants, on-site spa, and more than a dozen shops, not to mention the nearby golf course (watch for deer and elk). If you're visiting Banff for the first time, a tour through the lobby of this magnificent stone structure is a must. The hotel offers various packages and specials throughout the year. Check the Web site before your trip. Smaller rooms, for instance, are sometimes available for about C$149/US$104 (double). A bed-and-breakfast package in a standard room goes for C$242/US$170 (double) if you book online.

405 Spray Ave. ☎ ***800-441-1414,*** *403-762-2211. Fax: 403-762-5755. E-mail:* bshres@fairmont.com. *Internet:* www.fairmont.com. *Rack rates: C$476–C$656 (US$333–US$459) double. AE, DISC, MC, V.*

Rimrock Resort Hotel
$$$$

If a first-class resort is in your budget, you won't want for anything here, and a lofty location on the side of Sulphur Mountain guarantees outstanding views everywhere you turn. Guest rooms are spacious and tastefully turned out. After your adventure in the backcountry, take a dip in the saltwater pool or visit the hotel spa to indulge in a Swedish massage (C$58/US$41 for 30 minutes). When you feel like heading downtown, catch the hotel shuttle. (It's free.)

Mountain Ave. ☎ *800-661-1587, 403-762-3356. Fax: 403-762-4132. E-mail:* info@rimrockresort.com. *Internet:* www.rimrockresort.com. *Rack rates: C$280–C$385 (US$196–US$270) double. AE, DISC, MC, V.*

Rundlestone Lodge
$$$

This spiffy new mountain lodge features up-to-date conveniences, such as high-speed Internet access. Many rooms have balconies. For C$195/US$137 (high season) you get a spacious room with two queen beds. If you're after a specific style of accommodation, I can say with confidence that you will find it here. The Rundlestone offers an amazing variety of room configurations, including loft suites with kitchens and fireplaces (C$255/US$179).

537 Banff Ave. ☎ *800-661-8630, 403-762-2201. Fax: 403-762-4501. E-mail:* res@rundlestone.com. *Internet:* www.rundlestone.com. *Rack rates: C$195 (US$137) double. AE, DISC, MC, V.*

Great B&Bs

The Banff Information Centre at 224 Banff Ave. (☎ **403-762-1550**) has a list of bed-and-breakfasts in Banff. Many are booked weeks, if not months, ahead for July and August. If you do arrive without a place to stay, the folks at the information center know which B&Bs have vacancies.

Blue Mountain Lodge
$–$$

This rambling, rustic, gregarious place dates to the early 1900s. It's more akin to a boarding house than a B&B, with ten rooms and a communal kitchen. Rooms are small but bursting with character and all have private baths. Breakfast is buffet-style. In the afternoon, help yourself to chocolate chip cookies.

Muskrat St. at Caribo St. ☎ *403-762-5134. Fax: 403-762-8081. E-mail:* info@bluemtnlodge.com. *Internet:* www.bluemtnlodge.com. *Rack rates: C$49–C$110 (US$34–US$77) double. MC, V.*

Eleanor's House

$$$

This impressive house on a quiet, residential street was built as a B&B, and it's one of the nicest in town. Guests have a separate entrance. Rooms are large with ensuite baths and mountain views. The owners are experts on the national park and its attractions.

125 Kootenay Ave. ☎ **_403-760-2457._** _E-mail:_ info@bbeleanor.com. _Internet:_ www.bbeleanor.com. _Rack rates: C$165 (US$116) double. MC, V._

Mountain Home B&B

$$–$$$

You're treated to a different breakfast each morning: lemon poppyseed pancakes, vegetable frittata, banana bread, and much more. The three upstairs guest rooms in this upscale B&B are spacious and immaculate with large baths that feature pedestal sinks. You even get high-speed Internet.

129 Muskrat St. ☎ **_403-762-3889._** _Fax: 403-762-3254._ _E-mail:_ info@mountain homebb.com. _Internet:_ www.mountainhomebb.com. _Rack rates: C$100–C$165 (US$70–US$116) double. MC, V._

Two-Twenty Beaver Street

$$–$$$

Although it's called a B&B, accommodation here is mostly in quaint little cabins, grouped in a backyard with a garden and gazebo. You feel calm and relaxed here, although you're just a block from Banff's main street. The cabins have either one or two bedrooms, private bath, small fridges, and microwaves, but no stoves.

220 Beaver St. ☎ **_403-762-5077._** _Fax: 403-762-5071._ _Rack rates: C$125–C$165 (US$88–US$116) double. No credit cards._

Thea's House

$$$–$$$$

Thea's House gives new meaning to the term "bed-and-breakfast." This place is more like an elegant private escape. "Elegant alpine," in fact, is how the owners characterize the look here, which is spacious and airy with vaulted ceilings and fir floors. Rooms have fireplaces and entertainment centers. No pets, no kids, no smokers. Thea's House is just three blocks from Banff Avenue.

138 Otter St. ☎ **_403-762-2499._** _Fax: 403-762-2496._ _E-mail:_ theashouse@ telusplanet.net. _Internet:_ www.theashouse.com. _Rack rates: C$245–C$265 (US$172–US$186) double. MC, V._

Runner-up lodging

Dynasty Inn

$$$

Rooms in this spiffy and centrally located hotel are spacious, fresh, and bright. At press time, renovations were in the works, including a new lounge area where complimentary breakfasts are served.

501 Banff Ave. ☎ *800-667-1464, 403-762-8844. Internet:* www.banffdynasty inn.com.

Inns of Banff

$$$

Once you figure out how to navigate your way around, this monstrous place has lots going for it, including a view of Cascade Mountain, Stoney Squaw, and Mount Norquay from the outdoor hot tub.

600 Banff Ave. ☎ *800-661-1272, 403-762-4581. Internet:* www.innsofbanff.com.

International Hostel

$

This hillside hostel has great mountain views. The original building is 20 years old; a newer one next door is C$2 (US$1.40) a night more. Rent a bike and head downtown — it's all downhill from here.

801 Coyote Dr. ☎ *866-762-4122, 403-670-7580. Internet:* www.hihostels.ca.

Red Carpet

$$–$$$

Survey the action on main street from your balcony, or opt for a quieter room at the back.

425 Banff Ave. ☎ *800-563-4609, 403-762-4184.*

Where to Eat in Banff

Banff has by far the biggest concentration of restaurants anywhere in the Canadian Rockies. Here are some of the best.

Wake up and find the coffee

Need a coffee? Many Banff coffee shops (and there are many) are open from 7 a.m. to 11 p.m. A coffee and a muffin or bagel at one of these places will set you back about C$4.50 (US$3.15). I'm partial to the **Jump Start**, on Buffalo Street, which is a bit removed from the Banff Avenue action (and a bit more laid-back). You can get toasted bagels, hearty cookies, and sandwiches to go. **Second Cup** in the Cascade Plaza is a reliable specialty coffee chain, and **The Coffee Bar** on Banff Avenue (join the crowds) offers soups, sandwiches, and croissants. Also on Banff Avenue, you find the long-standing favorite, **Evelyn's Coffee Bar**, and if you just can't get enough of Evelyn, you can wander over to Bear Street and visit **Evelyn's Too.** (And yes, as of 2003, **Starbucks** is here, as well — in the Banff Avenue Mall at 225-A Banff Ave.)

Barpa Bill's Souvlaki

$ GREEK

This small spot (next door to Saltlik) is easy to miss but a genuine find: the food is fresh, fast, and affordable. Souvlaki on pita costs C$5 (US$3.50), or C$10 (US$7) if you add a side of Greek salad. Try other Mediterranean favorites such as hummus, spanikopita, and dolmades. A few stools are available for those who want to dine in, but the concept here is food to go.

*223 Bear St. ☎ **403-762-0377**. Most items under C$10 (US$7). Cash only. 11 a.m.–9 p.m.*

Le Beaujolais

$$$ FRENCH

A landmark on the Banff culinary scene, Le Beaujolais has been garnering rave reviews for more than two decades. It's the perfect spot for a special dinner at a slow pace. The menu features three prix fixe options, including the Beaujolais Classic, for C$75 (US$53): Start with lobster salad or foie gras, move on to roasted Alberta rib-eye steak, and finish with a souffle. For C$90 (US$63) you can feast your way through a six-course "surprise" meal, consisting of whatever creations the chef opts to serve. (Be sure to dress nicely.)

*Banff Ave. at Buffalo St. ☎ **403-762-2712**. Reservations recommended. Three- to six-course dinners C$55–C$90 (US$39–US$63). MC, V. 6 p.m.–10 p.m.*

Buffalo Mountain Lodge

$$–$$$ **REGIONAL**

Dine in a timber-frame lodge with huge windows and stunning views. Roast lamb is served with caramelized carrot and potato; rainbow trout is delivered atop pinenut couscous, and pork is cooked in a hazelnut crust then paired with rhubarb relish. Buffalo Mountain Lodge wins applause for its version of Rocky Mountain cuisine, a cooking style that combines fish and game with the region's freshest fruit and vegetables. For dessert, try a Canadian ice wine.

Tunnel Mountain Rd. ☎ *403-760-4484. Reservations recommended. Main courses: C$22–C$33 (US$15–US$23). AE, DC, MC, V. Daily 6–10 p.m.*

Coyotes

$$–$$$ **SOUTHWESTERN**

This cozy eatery bills itself as Southwestern with a Mediterranean influence: burritos, enchiladas, and quesadillas share a menu with chorizo pizza, and tagliatelle with pancetta and mushrooms. The marriage seems to work. Coyotes is wildly popular with the locals.

206 Caribou St. ☎ *403-762-3963. Reservations recommended. Main courses: C$14–C$24 (US$9–US$17). AE, DC, MC, V. Daily from 5 p.m.*

Georgios Trattoria

$$–$$$ **ITALIAN**

This lively Banff Avenue restaurant is *the* place to head for when you're craving the flavors of Italy. You can nibble on deep-fried calamari while you ponder the pasta menu. Pizzas from the wood-burning oven are great. If you like smoked salmon, you may enjoy it paired with onions, capers, basil, tomatoes, and roasted garlic.

219 Banff Ave. ☎ *403-762-5114. Reservations accepted only for groups of 8 or more. Main courses: C$12–C$26 (US$8–US$18). AE, MC, V. Daily from 5 p.m.*

Joe Btfsplk's

$ **DINER**

Joe who? (It's much easier to find — on Banff Avenue right across from the Banff Information Centre — than to pronounce.) Done up like a 1950s diner, this colorful eatery is a hit with kids (they also get a separate menu). Adults fall for it, too. It's hard to take life too seriously when you're seated on red vinyl, ordering liver and onions.

221 Banff Ave. ☎ *403-762-5529. Reservations not accepted. Most items under C$10 (US$7). AE, MC, V. 8 a.m. – 9 p.m.*

Maple Leaf Grille & Spirits

$$–$$$$ **CANADIAN**

When you dine at a place called the Maple Leaf, you would hope to be served fish and game. The Maple Leaf delivers: smoked salmon, elk burgers, bison stroganoff. A mammoth wine list (400 bottles) includes many wines available by the glass. The Maple Leaf has an open, lodge-like feel. Grab a table by the window and gaze out on Banff Avenue. The bars (one on each floor) are hot spots at night.

137 Banff Ave. ☎ 403-760-7680. Reservations recommended. Main courses: C$15–C$35 (US$11–US$25). AE, MC, V. 11 a.m.–11 p.m.

Saltlik

$$–$$$$ **STEAKHOUSE**

Saltlik is an upscale sidekick of the Earl's restaurant chain, and a relative newcomer to the dining scene in both Calgary and Banff. Although the menu acknowledges that some people prefer fish (you may see tuna or salmon), Saltlik is a steakhouse at heart. The fun part about eating here is that you get to select what appears on your plate (beside the steak). A "this and that" list offers mushrooms, grilled asparagus, wild rice, cream corn, skinny fries, and cheese toast, to mention a few of the possibilities.

221 Bear St. ☎ 403-762-2467. Main courses: C$15–C$30 (US$11–US$21). AE, MC, V. Daily 11 a.m.–2 a.m.

Typhoon

$$ **ASIAN**

This funky Asian eatery swept into town in 2003, and has attracted quite a following. The wide-ranging menu, which takes its inspiration from several Asian cuisines, offers special curries, noodle salads, nasi goreng, and papaya creations. At night, this is quite a cool spot to be seen with a martini in your hand.

211 Caribou St. ☎ 403-762-2000. Reservations recommended. Main courses: C$16–C$20 (US$11–US$14). AE, MC, V. 11:30 a.m.–3:00 p.m., and 6–11 p.m. Bar service and appetizers 11 p.m.–1 a.m.

Exploring Banff Townsite

More than 4 million people visit Banff each year. On Banff Avenue, you feel as though you're bumping into all of them. Prepare for crowds on this strip of hotels, souvenir shops, outdoor stores, restaurants, and bars. And remember, there's plenty to see beyond the main street.

Banff Park Museum

This century-old building is one of Canada's oldest museums and a national historic site. It houses wildlife specimens dating to the 1800s, a reading room, and a discovery room. The museum re-opened in 2003, following a year-long closure for a $500,000 renovation.

91 Banff Ave. (by the Bow River bridge). ☎ *403-762-1558. Admission: C$4 (US$2.80) adults, C$3 (US$2.10) youth 6–18, C$3.50 (US$2.45) seniors. May 15–Sept 30, 10 a.m.–6 p.m., other months, 1–5 p.m.*

Banff Gondola

On a clear day, this is a must. The Gondola whisks you to the top of Sulphur Mountain (2,285 meters/7,500 feet) in eight minutes for a breathtaking view of Banff Townsite, the Bow Valley, Lake Minnewanka, and the surrounding mountain ranges. You find viewing platforms, interpretive trails, and a restaurant at the top. Take warm clothes, because the weather changes unexpectedly and it's usually windy up there. If you're inclined to walk back down rather than ride the Gondola, follow the well-worn trail.

Mountain Ave. ☎ *403-762-5438. Admission: C$21.50 (US$15.05) adults, C$10.75 (US$7.52) youth 6–15. Free for children under 6. June 1–Sept 1, daily 7:30 a.m.– 9:00 p.m. Hours vary in other months. Call ahead.*

Mountain films and festivals

To really immerse yourself in the mountain way of life, see what's happening at the Banff Centre (107 Tunnel Mountain Dr. ☎ 403-762-6100; Internet: www.banffcentre.ca). Launched as a summer theatre in 1933, this place is the cultural heart of Banff and the Canadian Rockies. The two biggest annual events are the Banff Arts Festival, held between June and August, where you can take in theater, opera, dance, and other performances, and the prestigious Banff Festival of Mountain Films, in November, which features hundreds of films from around the world on mountain themes.

Cave and Basin National Historic Site

This site commemorates the birthplace of Banff National Park and Canada's national parks system. You learn about the discovery of the hot springs that led to the establishment of Banff, not to mention interesting facts about the springs themselves — for example, they are home to a special snail found nowhere else in the world. The swimming pool isn't open here: To soak in the mineral waters, head for the Upper Hot Springs.

End of Cave Ave. ☎ *403-762-1566. Admission: C$4 (US$2.80) adults, C$3 (US$2.10) youth 6–16, C$3.50 (US$2.45) seniors. May 15–Sept 30, 9 a.m.–6 p.m., other months: Sat & Sun 9:30 a.m.–5:00 p.m., Mon–Fri 11 a.m.–4 p.m.*

Upper Hot Springs

Visitors have been coming here to soak in hot mineral water and ogle mountain scenery for hundreds of years. Bathe in the outdoor spring-fed hot pool and check out the view of Mount Rundle. Lockers, swimsuits, and towels are available, as is a spa and massage service. You also find a wading pool for kids and a restaurant.

At the end of Mountain Ave. ☎ *403-762-1515. Admission: C$7.50 (US$5.25) adults, C$6.50 (US$4.55) children & seniors. May 9–Oct 13, 9 a.m.– 11 p.m., other months, Sun–Thurs 10 a.m.– 10 p.m., Fri & Sat 10 a.m.– 11 p.m.*

Whyte Museum of the Canadian Rockies

This museum celebrates the Canadian Rockies in four art galleries, a heritage gallery dedicated to the human history of the area, and an archives research library. The newest addition is a theater where you can watch a breathtaking film about Canadian Rockies adventure, exploration, scenery, and wildlife. The grounds include two historic log homes and four cabins.

111 Bear St. ☎ *403-762-2291. Admission: C$6 (US$4.20) adults, C$3.50 (US$2.45) seniors & students. Free for children under 5. Daily 10 a.m.–5 p.m.*

Shopping

You probably didn't come to the Canadian Rockies to shop for French crystal or Italian stemware. But should you find yourself in need of these items, you can pick them up in Banff — along with high-end sunglasses, alpaca sweaters, gourmet kitchen gadgets, and lacy lingerie. Banff Avenue is lined with boutiques and gift shops. And when you tire of these ones, you can go wild on nearby Wolf, Bear, Caribou, or Buffalo streets. **Cascade Plaza**, at 317 Banff Avenue (corner of Banff Avenue and Wolf Street), is a shopping mall with stores and services on three levels. Most stores in Banff are open every day, usually until at least 10 p.m. You were expecting a quaint mountain town? Sorry. (All this commerce does, however, take place in a very pretty setting.)

Nightlife

If you return from your hike with energy to burn, you can party the night away. Favorite dance spots on Banff's main drag include **Aurora,** at 110 Banff Avenue, **Outabounds,** at 137 Banff Avenue, and **Wild Bill's Legendary Saloon,** at 201 Banff Avenue. Or have a beer and mingle at **Maple Leaf Grille & Spirits,** 137 Banff Avenue, or the **Lic Lounge** (in the **Saltlik** restaurant), 221 Bear Street. For a nightcap in a more intimate atmosphere, pop by **Typhoon,** 211 Cariboo Street.

Fast Facts: Town of Banff

Area Code

Banff's area code is **403.** You don't need to dial it if you're calling local numbers.

American Express

101 Gopher St. ☎ **403-760-6900.**

Emergencies

Dial **911.**

Hospitals

Banff's Mineral Springs Hospital, 301 Lynx St. ☎ **403-762-2222.**

Internet Access and Cybercafes

Internet terminals are located in the lower level of Cascade Plaza, 317 Banff Ave. You need Canadian coins or bills. Each C$1 (U.S.$0.70) buys 7.5 minutes of Internet access.

Maps

Visit the **Friends of Banff** shop in the Banff Information Centre, 224 Banff Ave.

Newspapers

The local paper is the *Banff Crag & Canyon.* The *Calgary Herald,* as well as the national *Globe and Mail* and *National Post,* are also widely available.

Police

Banff RCMP ☎ **403-762-2226.**

Weather

Call ☎ **403-762-2088** or tune in to the Banff Park radio station: 101.1 FM.

Chapter 14

Jasper National Park

. . . .

In This Chapter

▶ Getting to know the largest park in the Canadian Rockies

▶ Planning your stay in Jasper National Park

▶ Exploring the park's peaks and valleys

▶ Finding the best beds and meals

. . . .

*J*asper National Park is huge — more than 10,000 sq. km (4,200 sq. miles) of magnificent mountains, dazzling glaciers, rivers, valleys, and meadows. It is, in fact, the largest park in the Canadian Rockies, as well as the most northerly.

Together with Banff National Park to the south, Kootenay and Yoho national parks, and the provincial parks of Hamber, Mount Robson, and Mount Assiniboine, Jasper is part of a UNESCO World Heritage Site that's one of the biggest protected areas in the world. The park preserves habitat for deer, elk, bighorn sheep, black bears, grizzly bears, mountain lions, and wolves. Visitors to Jasper can spot many of these animals without even leaving their cars. Not that you'd want to stay in your car when you can trek through the backcountry, head for the links, try your luck trout fishing, or soak in hot mineral springs.

The main center in the park, also called Jasper, or Jasper Townsite, is a community of fewer than 5,000 people that surges to 30,000 in summer. Situated in the center of the park, the town sports souvenir shops, restaurants, and hotels, but not on the scale of what you find in Banff. The pace here is slower. If you're looking for solitude and wilderness adventure, Jasper's a great spot to head for. Hiking is outstanding, and there's lots of choice: a trail network covers more than 1,200 wild kilometers (744 miles) along with 100 backcountry campsites.

Jasper National Park

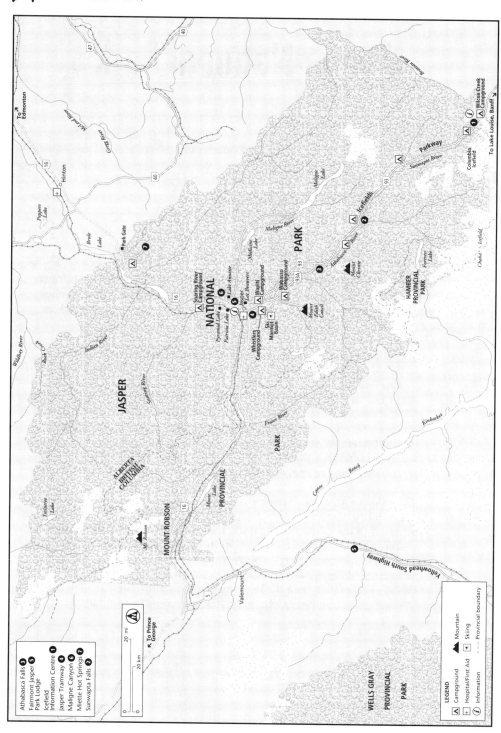

Athabasca Falls ❸
Fairmont Jasper ❺
Park Lodge
Icefield ❹
Information Centre ❶
Jasper Tramway ❹
Maligne Canyon ❻
Miette Hot Springs ❼
Sunwapta Falls ❷

LEGEND
◬ Campground   ▲ Mountain
✚ Hospital/First Aid ⛷ Skiing
ⓘ Information   ‒‒‒ Provincial boundary

Must-See Attractions

Jasper National Park is open year-round, but the weather is nicest in July and August. Unfortunately, this is also when highways and hiking trails are busiest. June and September can also be fine months to visit, with warm daytime temperatures. Some hikes, though, won't be doable until snow melts in July. Between mid-October and early May, you have fewer accommodation choices. Most lodges and cabin resorts throughout the park are closed. Motels in the town of Jasper stay open all winter, as does the Fairmont Jasper Park Lodge.

- ✔ **The Icefields Parkway** (Highway 93): Running between Banff and Jasper parks, this parkway ushers travelers through some of the most spectacular wilderness in the Rockies, if not in the world. Along the route, you can picnic at **Athabasca Falls,** swoon over **Sunwapta Falls,** and marvel at the **Columbia Icefield.** Other park highlights include the following:

- ✔ **Maligne Lake:** An hour's drive outside Jasper Townsite will put you on the shores of this lovely lake. On the way, you can stop at Maligne Canyon, and farther along, visit Medicine Lake. (Bring your fishing rod.)

- ✔ **Miette Hot Springs:** The hottest mineral springs in the Canadian Rockies (40° Celsius/103° Fahrenheit) are located 61km (38 miles) northeast of Jasper.

- ✔ **Mount Edith Cavell:** South of Jasper Townsite, the winding road to Mount Edith Cavell delivers great vistas — and hairpin turns. Watch for wildlife.

- ✔ **The Whistlers:** Ride the Jasper Tramway to the top of this peak. Rather walk? Give yourself at least three hours to climb to the tramway's upper terminal. It's about 7km (4 miles).

Getting There

Jasper National Park is situated in northern Alberta, 370km (230 miles) west of Edmonton, Alberta, 404km (256 miles) northwest of Calgary, Alberta, and 805km (500 miles) northeast of Vancouver, British Columbia.

Flying in

Most visitors fly to Calgary and drive to Jasper through Banff National Park. If you plan to visit only Jasper, you may wish to fly to Edmonton, about a four-hour drive from Jasper. **Air Canada** (☎ **888-247-2262;** Internet: www.aircanada.ca) operates nonstop flights to Calgary and Edmonton from many Canadian and U.S. cities. **WestJet** (☎ **888-937-8538;** Internet: www.westjet.ca) flies direct to both cities from many places in Western Canada.

Driving in

If you're driving to Jasper from Calgary, you travel through Banff and Lake Louise, then north along Highway 93, the Icefields Parkway. In summer, you can get from Lake Louise to Jasper in about three hours, but you'll want to figure in more time to visit the Columbia Icefield and admire other natural wonders along the way.

If you travel the Icefields Parkway in winter, plan for weather-related delays. And be sure to fuel up before you set out. You won't find any service stations open between Lake Louise and Jasper.

From Edmonton, Jasper's a four-hour drive west on Highway 16 (the Yellowhead Highway). You travel the Yellowhead if you're coming from Vancouver — count on at least eight hours for the trip.

Planning Ahead

Call or write the Jasper National Park Information Centre, 500 Connaught Drive, Jasper AB T0E 1E0 (☎ **780-852-6176**) or visit Internet: www.parkscanada.gc.ca. For help booking accommodation, call Rocky Mountain Reservations (☎ **877-902-9455,** 780-852-9455).

You may also want to contact Jasper Tourism, 409 Patricia St., P.O. Box 98, Jasper AB T0E 1E0 (☎ **780-852-3858;** Internet: www.jaspercanadianrockies.com).

For information about backcountry trips or to reserve a campsite in the backcountry, contact Parks Canada's Trail Office (☎ **780-852-6177,** e-mail: jnp_info@pc.gc.ca).

Check the weather outlook for Jasper by dialing ☎ **780-852-3185.** The thing to remember about mountain climate is that it changes quickly and dramatically, not only from one area to another, but from one minute to the next. Usually, the higher you go, the colder it gets. (Expect a dip in the thermometer of about 1.7° Celsius/3° Fahrenheit for every 300 meters/980 feet of elevation you gain.) So in July, you're apt to be comfortable exploring the town of Jasper in shorts and a T-shirt, but when you step out of your car at the Icefield Centre you'll be reaching for your polar fleece and wind pants. Pack clothing that you can layer. Even in summer, if you plan on venturing far from your car, make sure you're prepared for cold temperatures, high winds, rain, and even snow.

Remember that ultraviolet radiation is stronger at higher elevations. You need sunglasses and sunscreen, even for overcast days.

Learning the Lay of the Land

The main route into Jasper is the Yellowhead Highway (Highway 16), which cuts across the park from east to west and passes through Jasper Townsite. Heading east out of the park, the Yellowhead runs to Edmonton, Alberta. On the west side, you drive through the Yellowhead Pass and the town of Tete Jaune Cache toward Prince George and Prince Rupert, B.C. (The highway, the pass, and the town, by the way, were named for Pierre Bostonais, an Iroquois Métis guide whom the French voyageurs called "Tête Jaune" or Yellowhead" because of his light-colored hair.)

The western boundary of the park is also the Alberta/British Columbia border and a time-zone change. Set your watch back one hour when you cross into B.C.

The other route into the park is along the famous Icefields Parkway (Highway 93), connecting the town of Jasper with Lake Louise in Banff National Park. Be sure to check road conditions (☎ **403-762-1450**) before you venture onto the Icefields Parkway in winter. The remote, 230-km (143-mile) road crosses a number of avalanche paths, and may be closed for days at a time.

The town of Jasper, a main stop for VIA Rail, is located near the center of the park, not far from the junction of the Athabasca and Miette rivers. From here, it's about an hour to the park's east boundary and about half an hour to the park gate on the west.

East of the town, off Highway 16, the Maligne Road winds through the Maligne Valley and leads to popular hiking trails. Also off Highway 16 is the Miette Hot Springs Road, which is closed in winter. South of the town, off the Icefields Parkway, Highway 93A loops down to Athabasca Falls. In winter, the southern portion of Highway 93A is closed to traffic, but open for cross-country skiing.

Arriving in the Park

The mountain town of Jasper (fewer than 5,000 permanent residents) in the Athabasca Valley is the primary service center for the park. You'll find most shops, hotels, and restaurants along Connaught Drive, the main thoroughfare through town, and on Patricia Street, one block back of Connaught.

Jasper Townsite

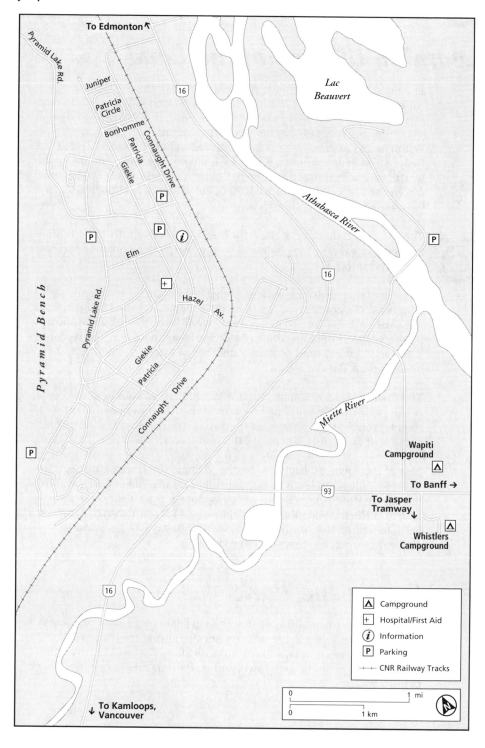

Finding information

When you arrive in the town, head for the rambling log and stone house at 500 Connaught Drive. This building, which dates to the early 1900s, initially housed the park's first superintendent. Today it's a National Historic Site and the **Jasper National Park Information Centre** (☎ 780-852-6176). The center opens daily at 9 a.m. and closes at 7 p.m. in summer, 6 p.m. in September, and 5 p.m. from October 1 through mid-June. **Parks Canada** staff here will help you plan a hike and provide the latest information on trail conditions, trail closures, avalanche warnings, and weather reports. If you need help finding a hotel, **Jasper Tourism** (☎ 780-852-3858) also has an office here (summer only). You can buy maps, hiking guides, and other books at the **Friends of Jasper** shop (☎ 780-852-4767) just inside the front door of the information center. This nonprofit group also puts on various educational programs, such as historical walking tours of the town. Call for information, or just check the posters in the information center.

The green area around the information center, by the way, is called **Athabasca Park.** Step out and take in the mountain views. The snow-capped peak to your right is Mount Edith Cavell, which is the tallest mountain near the town. That's the Maligne Range straight ahead, and the Colin Range to your left.

If you're traveling to Jasper along the Icefields Parkway in summer, there's also a **Parks Canada** information desk (☎ 780-852-6288) in the **Icefield Centre,** about 100km (60 miles) south of Jasper. It's not open in the off-season.

Paying fees

You'll need a **National Parks Pass** to travel in Jasper and other Canadian national parks. Your options are a day pass or an annual pass. A **day pass** costs C$7 (US$4.90) for adults; C$6 (US$4.20) seniors; C$3.50 (US$2.45) youth aged 6 to 16; and C$14 (US$10) for groups of between 2 and 7 people traveling in the same vehicle. If you'll be staying in the park for more than a few days, or if you also plan to visit Banff, Waterton, Kootenay or Yoho national parks, your best bet is the **annual pass,** which costs C$45 (US$32) for adults; C$38 (US$27) seniors; C$22 (US$15) youth aged 6 to 16; and C$89 (US$63) for groups of between 2 and 7 people in the same vehicle. This pass, good for one year from the date you purchase it, gets you into 27 national parks in Canada. Passes are for sale at park gates and information centers.

You will, by the way, need a parks pass to travel the Icefields Parkway between Lake Louise and Jasper. (In summer, there's a pass check just north of Lake Louise.)

Camping fees to stay in the frontcountry, or road-accessible, campgrounds in Jasper range from C$13 to C$26 (US$9 to US$18) a night. If you're planning an overnight hike, see "Backcountry adventures" later in this chapter. **Fishing licenses** cost C$7 (US$4.90) per day or C$20 (US$14) for an annual license.

Getting around

The small town of Jasper is easy to explore on foot. Most of the restaurants recommended later in this chapter are on or near Connaught Drive, as are the information center, the train station, and some of the hotels. You'll find more dining spots, shops, and services one block back of Connaught Drive on Patricia Street.

To rent a bicycle, visit **Freewheel Cycle** at 681 Patricia Street (☎ **780-852-3898**) or **On-Line Sport & Tackle** at 600 Patricia Street (☎ **780-852-3630**).

For travel through the park, your own (or a rented) vehicle will give you the most flexibility, but numerous tour companies also offer bus and train trips to the most popular destinations. **Hertz** (☎ **800-263-0600,** 780-852-3888) and **National** (☎ **780-852-1117**) car rental agencies are both located in the train station at 607 Connaught Drive. **Sundog Tours** at 414 Connaught Drive (☎ **888-786-3641,** 780-852-4056; Internet: www.sundogtours.com) offers trips from Jasper to Banff, the Columbia Icefield, Mount Edith Cavell, and other spots in the park. The same company runs a shuttle service between the Jasper Tramway and many hotels in town. **Brewster** (☎ **780-852-3332;** Internet: www.Brewster.ca), based in Banff, also offers a host of tours through the park along with bus service to Lake Louise, Banff, and Calgary.

Enjoying the Park

While Jasper isn't nearly as crowded as its neighbor to the south, it still attracts up to 2 million visitors a year. Most people arrive in July and August. You can dodge some of the crowds by visiting popular sites before 10 a.m. or in late afternoon.

Icefields Parkway

The 230-km (143-mile) drive along Highway 93 between Lake Louise and Jasper is a Canadian Rockies classic. You may want to earmark a day for this trip. If you're coming to Jasper from Banff, you travel the Parkway en route.

A highlight of the journey is the Columbia Icefield — basically, 325 sq. km (130 sq. miles) of solid ice. It's one of the biggest accumulations of ice and snow south of the Arctic Circle and visible even from the International Space Station. From the Icefields Parkway you can see a number of glaciers, including the **Athabasca Glacier,** which is the most accessible in the world.

The Icefields Parkway parallels the Continental Divide: Melting water feeds rivers that flow to the Pacific, Arctic, and Atlantic oceans. The highway also crosses two mountain passes — Sunwapta Pass at 2,035 meters (6,674 feet) and Bow Summit at 2,069 meters (6,786 feet).

Although it's open year-round, the parkway is best explored between June and September when driving conditions are more predictable and you can schedule a stop at the **Columbia Icefield Centre,** about 100km (62 miles) south of Jasper near the border of Banff and Jasper parks. Have your jacket handy — there's always a chilly wind up here. The center's open from May 1 to mid-October and has interpretive displays, a Parks Canada information desk, a restaurant, gift shop, and a 32-room hotel.

For a close-up look at the 6-km (over 3.5-miles) long **Athabasca Glacier,** take a tour on a specially designed **SnoCoach.** Tours take about 1.5 hours and cost C$29.95 (US$21) for adults, C$15 (US$11) for children aged 6 to 15. There's no charge for children under 6 sharing a seat with an adult. Buy a ticket at the Icefield Centre or by calling ☎ **877-423-7433.** For more information, e-mail icefield@brewster.ca or visit Internet: brewster.ca.

SnoCoach tours, which run April through September from 9 a.m. to 5 p.m. and in October from 10 a.m. to 4 p.m., are hugely popular. Avoid the crowds by arriving early in the morning or after 3 p.m.

You can also explore the Athabasca Glacier on foot, with a guide. A three-hour **Ice Walk** excursion costs C$45/US$32 (adult), or for C$50 (US$35) you can embark on a more ambitious five-hour hike. Buy tickets through the Jasper Adventure Centre, 604 Connaught Drive, Jasper, ☎ **800-565-7547,** or at the Columbia Icefield Centre at the front desk of the hotel (at the south end of the main floor). If you're buying tickets from the hotel, you'll need cash or traveler's checks. Space is limited on these hikes, so you should book a day or two in advance. If a hike isn't full, though, you can buy a ticket from a guide.

Also along the Icefields Parkway, you can visit **Athabasca Falls,** about 32km (20 miles) south of Jasper and **Sunwapta Falls,** 55km (33 miles) south of Jasper. Both sites have picnic areas and can be visited year-round. Don't forget your camera.

Maligne Lake

This lake in the beautiful Maligne Valley is the largest natural lake in the Canadian Rockies (22km/14 miles long). It's popular with fishermen (as is Medicine Lake, which you pass on the way to Maligne). You can also canoe, kayak, and hike. Boat tours on Maligne Lake, which include a visit to Spirit Island, run every hour in summer and take about 90 minutes. Tickets cost C$35 (US$25) for adults, C$17.50 (US$12) for children aged 6 to 12. For information contact **Maligne Tours, ☎ 866-625-4463.** Maligne Tours has offices in the town of Jasper at 627 Patricia Street, ☎ **780-852-3370,** and in the Jasper Park Lodge at the concierge desk, ☎ **780-852-3301.**

Bring a warm jacket. Raingear may come in handy, too.

Maligne Lake is 48km (30 miles) from Jasper Townsite. Take Highway 16 east for 5km (3 miles), turn right across the Moberly Bridge, and follow the paved road up the Maligne Valley. The road is open all year, but plan on delays in winter.

Miette Hot Springs

You will find hot springs in other parts of the Canadian Rockies (in Banff and Kootenay national parks), but these are the hottest — 54° Celsius/130° Fahrenheit. The water in the bathing pools is kept at about 40° Celsius/103° Fahrenheit. While you soak up the heat, you can also soak up the view of Ashlar Ridge. Swimsuits, towels, and lockers are available for rent. As well as two hot mineral pools and a colder pool, the Miette site has a gift shop, cafes, and hiking trails. On the road to Miette, which winds through the Fiddle Valley, watch for bighorn sheep, elk, moose, and deer.

This attraction is closed in winter, usually from mid-October to early May.

The hot springs are 61km (38 miles) northeast of Jasper Townsite. Take Highway 16 to Miette Hot Springs Road. Admission is C$6.25 (US$4.38) for adults, C$5.25 (US$3.68) for seniors and children. Open from May to mid-June, 10:30 a.m. to 9:00 p.m.; mid-June to September 1, 8:30 a.m. to 10:30 p.m.; and September 2 to mid-October, 10:30 a.m. to 9:00 p.m.

Mount Edith Cavell

This peak, named for a British nurse and World War I heroine, is the highest near the town of Jasper, at 3,363 meters (11,030 feet). Drive up to Cavell Lake, where you can venture out on a number of trails. Follow the Path of the Glacier, a short interpretive walk, or take a day hike to a wild-flower-filled meadow (the flowers are spectacular in July). The narrow, winding 14.5-km (9-mile) Cavell Road gets crowded, especially around midday. It's rough in places, with tight corners. (Don't bring the RV.)

Follow Highway 93A south of Jasper Townsite to the Cavell Road. It's about half an hour's drive. The road is usually open from about mid-June to October.

The Whistlers

On a clear day, the seven-minute trip to the top of Whistlers Mountain on the Jasper Tramway is truly memorable. This tramway is the highest in Canada (2,250 meters/7,500 feet above sea level). You'll have splendid views of five mountain ranges, including Mount Robson. From the tramway's upper terminal, you can climb a 1.5-km (1-mile) trail to the summit. Watch (and listen) for "the whisters," marmots that make a whistling sound.

If you'd rather hike, the Whistlers Trail starts in the tramway parking lot. It's a 7-km (4.3-mile) climb with a 1,200-meter (3,936-feet) elevation gain; allow about three hours for the trip up, two hours to return. In July, you have wildflowers to admire.

In spring and fall, the upper part of the Whistlers Trail is covered in snow and prone to avalanches. Be sure to check trail conditions at the Information Centre before you head out.

Take Highway 93 south of Jasper Townsite to Whistlers Road. Open from mid-April through September. Tickets cost C$20 (US$14) for adults, C$10 (US$7) for children aged 5 to 14, and free for children under 5.

Taking a Hike

Avid hikers have been known to liken a gorgeous day on a Canadian Rocky Mountain trail to a near-spiritual experience. These treks will help you understand why. They're all doable in about four to six hours. The folks at the Information Centre on Connaught Drive have the latest advice on trail conditions and wildlife activity. Check in with them before you hit the trails.

Cavell Meadows
Mount Edith Cavell

Gorgeous wildflowers and views of the Angel Glacier are the highlights of this popular day hike, which begins on the same trail as Path of the Glacier, a short, well-traveled trek past Cavell Pond and along Cavell Creek. Just past the paved section of the trail, you'll see the sign for the Cavell Meadows hike.

Distance: 8km (5 miles) round-trip. Level: Moderate. Access: End of Cavell Road. Drive 7km (4 miles) south of Jasper on Hwy. 93 to the junction of Hwy. 93A, turn right, and then travel 5.4km (3 miles) to Cavell Road

Don't go close to the Angel Glacier. Enormous blocks of ice sometimes fall down.

Opal Hills
Maligne Lake

This trail delivers a splendid view of Maligne Lake, although you work for it. You'll climb 460 meters (1,508 feet) over 3km (1.2 miles). After you cross the meadow near the trailhead, it's straight up through the forest for 1.5km (0.9 miles). When you come to a branch in the trail, follow the left branch above treeline. The trail loops back to the junction.

Distance: 8.2km (5 miles) round-trip. Level: Strenuous. Access: Maligne Lake parking lot (go to the farthest lot). Maligne Lake is 48km (30 miles) from Jasper Townsite. Take Hwy. 16 east to Maligne Road.

The hot springs area is a good choice if you're hiking early in the season, as trails here are generally clear of snow by late May.

Sulphur Skyline
Miette Hot Springs

This hike is a steep grind across an open mountainside to Shuey Pass, where the trail splits. Take the trail to your right and follow the switchbacks. The final stretch to the summit at 2,050 meters (6,724 feet) is a steep climb, but you're rewarded with views of the Fiddle River Valley and nearby peaks, including Utopia Mountain and Ashlar Ridge.

Distance: 9.6km (6 miles) round-trip. Level: Strenuous. Access: Drive 42km (26 miles) east of Jasper Townsite on Hwy. 16, then follow the Miette Road for 17km (11 miles). Park in front of the Miette Hot Springs.

Wilcox Pass
Columbia Icefield area

If you can manage only one hike in Jasper National Park, Wilcox Pass is a great choice. You'll be above the treeline in no time, wandering across meadows of wildflowers. The area's also a popular hangout for bighorn sheep. (The best time to hike here is after late July, when snow has melted from the pass.) You gain 330 meters (1,082 feet) and the resulting views of Snow Dome, Mount Athabasca, and Athabasca Glacier are unforgettable. If you're up for a longer day on the trail, you can trek on down to Tangle Falls, but you'll need a ride back to your car.

Distance: 8km (4 miles) round-trip, 11.2km (7 miles) to Tangle Falls. Level: Moderate. Access: Parking area to the left of the Wilcox Creek Campground road, 3.1km (2 miles) south of the Icefield Centre.

Tamer treks

For a shorter stroll, head up to the Fairmont Jasper Park Lodge and follow the 3.5-km (2-mile) trail around Lac Beauvert. Or explore the Mary Shaffer Loop at Maligne Lake — an easy and scenic 3.2-km (2-mile) walk on a paved trail.

Backcountry adventures

The most popular backpacking trip in Jasper is the **Skyline Trail,** a 45-km (28-mile) trek, largely above treeline, between Maligne Lake and Maligne Canyon. It takes at least two days. For other trip ideas, visit Internet: www.parkscanada.gc.ca (see "Backpacking").

For the Skyline hike and other top trails in the backcountry, you'll want to reserve campsites in advance. Call ☎ **780-852-6177** up to three months before your trip. A nonrefundable reservation fee of C$10 is charged.

You'll also need a **Wilderness Pass** (C$8/US$6 a night) to stay in the backcountry overnight. If you're planning serious time in the backcountry, invest in an annual pass (C$56/US$40). It's good for one year from the date you purchase it, and you can also use it in Banff, Yoho, Kootenay, or Waterton Lakes national parks. Pick up your pass at the Information Centre within 24 hours of your backcountry trip to get the latest reports on trail conditions and bear activity. If you have an annual pass, you should still check in with the Information Centre before your trip.

Staying Active

Hiking is just the beginning. Jasper National Park offers any number of opportunities to savor rugged peaks, alpine meadows, and glacial lakes. Here are just a few of your options.

Fishing

Anglers can try their luck at Maligne Lake, which is stocked with rainbow and brook trout. Other hot spots include Medicine Lake for rainbow trout, Talbot Lake for northern pike, and Maligne River for whitefish. The fishing season runs from June through October. You'll need a **Parks Canada permit** to fish in Jasper National Park. Permits cost C$7 (US$5) per day, C$20 (US$14) for an annual pass, and are available from the Information Centre on Connaught Drive, the boathouse at Maligne Lake, and most tackle shops. To hire a local guide, call **Currie's Guiding** (☎ 780-852-5650).

Golfing

For travelers who golf, the award-winning 18-hole course at **Jasper Park Lodge** (☎ 780-852-6090), designed by renowned golf architect Stanley Thomson, is a Canadian Rockies highlight. In this spectacularly scenic setting, the challenge is focusing on your game. In high season, green fees will set you back C$175 (US$123), including cart, C$130 (US$91) if you're a Canadian resident or a guest at the Jasper Park Lodge.

Mountain Biking

Mountain bikes are allowed on certain trails in the park. The brochure **Summer Trails,** available at the Information Centre, shows two-wheel compatible routes. To rent a bike, visit **Freewheel Cycle** (☎ 780- 852-3898) at 681 Patricia Street or **On-Line Sport & Tackle** (☎ 780-852-3630) at 600 Patricia Street.

Rafting

Tour operators in Jasper run trips for both novice rafters and those with a taste for roaring whitewater action. The Athabasca River, which originates in the Columbia Icefield and flows through Jasper, is a class I (novice) river, suitable for family trips. More experienced rafters could head for the Sunwapta River (Sunwapta is a Stoney word for turbulent river) or Kakwa River. To book a trip, visit **Maligne Rafting Adventures** at 627 Patricia Street (☎ **780-852-3370**). The cost for a two-hour trip starts at C$44 (US$31), including transportation to the river and all your gear. Another company to try: **Jasper Raft Tours** (☎ **888-553-5628**, 780-852-2665).

Skiing and snowboarding

Marmot Basin (☎ **780-852-3816**), a 25-minute drive south of Jasper Townsite, has 75 runs, about evenly divided among beginner, intermediate, and expert trails. A lift ticket costs C$54 (US$38). For cross-country skiers, Maligne Lake has a couple of easy trails along with more challenging terrain. Other options near town are the Whistlers Campground loop and the 26-km (16-mile) trail network at the Fairmont Jasper Park Lodge.

Where to Stay in Jasper National Park

If you're dreaming of a cabin in the wilderness, you can fulfill your fantasy in Jasper, whether it's a rustic log cottage you're looking for or a posh mountain chalet. Various styles of cabins are located along the Icefields Parkway, within about 5km (3 miles) of Jasper Townsite. In the town itself, you'll find a strip of conventional motels, some within a short stroll of shops and restaurants. Many local families also rent rooms to visitors.

I should point out that the prices listed here are high season (June through September) rack rates. You'll pay considerably less in the quieter months of October through April, especially in winter (November, December, and January), when some real deals can be had.

In and around Jasper Townsite

Alpine Village
$$$ **South of Townsite**

Many log cabins are described as charming. These ones really are. Alpine Village feels like a true wilderness retreat, yet it's only a kilometer or so from town. The cabins and spacious riverfront grounds are immaculately maintained. A small, one-room cabin goes for C$175 (US$123) per night in high season. Two-bedroom units (C$270/US$189 per night in high season) feature spiffy European applicances and lofts. All cabins have wood-burning fieldstone fireplaces. This setting, with the Athabasca River rushing by, is hard to top. There's no restaurant, so if you don't plan to cook, try nearby Tekarra Lodge or check out one of the restaurants in town.

Box 610, Jasper, AB TOE 1E0, 2.5km (1.6 miles) from Jasper Townsite (drive 2km [1.2 miles] south on Hwy. 93, then east on Hwy. 93A). ☎ 780-852-3285. Fax: 780-852-1955. E-mail: reservations@alpinevillagejasper.com. *Internet:* www.alpinevillagejasper.com. *Rack rates: Sleeping cabin $155 (US$109) double, 1-room cabin C$175 (US$123) double, Lodge suite C$210 (US$147) double, 2-bedroom cabin C$270 (US$189) double. MC, V. Open late Apr to mid-Oct.*

Bear Hill Lodge

$$–$$$ **Jasper Townsite**

This 33-cabin, super-friendly complex is a superb choice in Jasper. The quiet, treed setting feels removed from the town, but it's actually only two blocks from Connaught Drive. Cabin styles range from a small standard bungalow with two beds, a full bath, and eating area to roomy chalets that sleep eight. Everything's very tidy and nicely maintained. The complex also has a handful of rooms in the lodge. They're small but comfortable, with pine paneling and gleaming pedestal sinks. For C$8 (US$6) (C$4/US$3.20 for children) you can have breakfast in the main lodge. Breakfast goodies are from a great local bakery called the Bear's Paw.

100 Bonhomme St. ☎ 780-852-3209. Fax: 780-852-3099. E-mail: info@BearHill Lodge.com. *Internet:* www.bearhilllodge.com. *Rack rates: Standard bungalow C$145 (US$102) double, Queen kitchenette C$165 (US$116) double, Deluxe chalet suite C$350 (US$245) double. AE, MC, V. Open May 1 to mid-Oct.*

Becker's Chalets

$$$–$$$$ **South of Townsite**

These log cabins are along the Athabasca River (on the Icefields Parkway), a fine spot if you don't mind being a few kilometers from the townsite. Various cabin styles are available. Most have fireplaces and some have lofts. There's also a reputable restaurant in the complex. If you're hiking in Jasper, Becker's Chalets would make an excellent home base. Elk seem to enjoy this spot too. Whole herds of them regularly amble through the grounds at dusk.

P.O. Box 579, Jasper, AB TOE 1E0. 5km (3.1 miles) south of Jasper Townsite on Hwy. 93. ☎ 780-852-3779. Fax 780-852-7202. E-mail: info@beckerschalets.com. *Internet:* www.beckerschalets.com. *Rack rates: C$130–C$160 (US$91–US$112) double. AE, MC, V. Open late Apr to early Oct.*

Fairmont Jasper Park Lodge

$$$$ **East of Townsite**

This is as far as you can get from roughing it in the Rockies. In the early 1900s, accommodation here consisted of a handful of tents on the shores of Lac Beauvert. Today, a semi-secluded, year-round resort offers luxury suites in an upscale lodge and more than 50 chalets. Some have mountain views, others face the lake or the golf course. Besides spectacular scenery, you get an 18-hole golf course, restaurants, lounges, shops, a health club, and spa. Go canoeing on the lake or head out on a trail ride. You'll be pampered here. But you'll pay for it.

P.O. Box 40, Jasper, AB T0E 1E0. Hwy. 16, 4km (2.5 miles) east of Jasper Townsite. ☎ *800-441-1414, 780-852-3301. Fax: 780-852-5107. E-mail:* jasperparklodge@ fairmont.com. *Internet:* www.fairmont.com. *Rack rates: C$549–C$759 (US$384–US$531), double. AE, DISC, MC, V.*

Mount Robson Inn
$$$ Jasper Townsite

If you're planning to stay in one of the motels along Connaught Drive, this is your best bet. It's fairly generic (two levels, drive up to your door), but nicely kept, and you're just a stroll from shops and restaurants. Rooms are bright and all have fridges and coffeemakers. The suites with upstairs bedrooms are ideal for families.

902 Connaught Dr. ☎ *800-587-3327, 780-852-3327. Fax: 780-852-5004. E-mail:* info@mountrobsoninn.com. *Internet:* www.mountrobsoninn.com. *Rack rates: C$205 (US$144) double. AE, MC, V.*

Tekarra Lodge
$$$ South of Townsite

These cabins are slightly more rustic than those in the nearby Alpine Village complex, but also in top shape. And they're as close as you can get to town. All have wood-burning fireplaces. The smallest units feature kitchenettes with stove-top burners and small fridges, while larger units (room for six) have full kitchens. None have telephones or televisions — not that you'd want any distractions in this setting. Bed-and-breakfast accommodation is available in the main lodge. The small, wood-paneled rooms (just the basics) are bright and spotless. The restaurant here has an excellent reputation.

P.O. Box 669, Jasper, AB T0E 1E0. 1.5km (just under 1 mile) south of Jasper on Hwy. 93A. ☎ *888-404-4540, 780-852-3058. Fax: 780-852-4636. E-mail:* reservations@tekarralodge.com. *Internet:* www.tekarralodge.com. *Rack rates: Lodge room (includes breakfast) C$154 (US$108), 2-person cabin C$164–$C$184 (US$115– US$129), 4-person cabin C$214 (US$150). AE, MC, V. Open late Apr to mid-Oct.*

Runner-up lodgings

Jasper International Hostel

$ **Southwest of Jasper Townsite**

If you're searching for budget accommodation, C$23 (US$22) will buy you a bed in this chalet-style hostel (C$18/US$13 for members of Hostelling International). It's on the road to the Whistlers Tramway and near hiking trails. 7km (4.3 miles) southwest of Jasper Townsite.

Take Skytram Road. ☎ *877-852-0781, 780-852-3215. Internet: www.hihostels.ca.*

Marmot Lodge

$$$ **Jasper Townsite**

This older-style lodge is actually a complex of three two-story buildings. Popular with bus tours, it offers a range of room configurations, including some with kitchenettes.

86 Connaught Dr. ☎ *888-852-7737, 780-852-4471. Internet:* www.mpljasper.com

Lodging with the locals

If you like the idea of staying with a local family, you have plenty of options in the town of Jasper. You'll see houses everywhere advertising rooms. They range from spare bedrooms to apartments with fully equipped kitchens and cost anywhere from C$50 (US$35) to more than C$100 (US$70) a night. The **Jasper Home Accommodation Association** brochure (pick one up at the Information Centre on Connaught Drive) lists more than 100 homes that offer lodging. They're inspected by Parks Canada. Most don't provide breakfast. For B&B accommodation in Jasper, check the accommodations guide published by **Travel Alberta** (www.travelalberta.com) or the **Alberta Bed & Breakfast Association** (www.bbalberta.com) directory.

Campgrounds

The ten frontcountry (road-accessible) campgrounds in Jasper National Park vary from primitive tenting spots to fully serviced sites for RVs and cost C$12 to C$26 (US$8 to US$18) a night. They don't take reservations — it's first-come, first-served — so in the busy months of July and August, plan to arrive by early afternoon.

Lineups are longest at **Whistlers** and **Wapiti,** two campgrounds just south of the town of Jasper. These are the only camping areas in the park that offer serviced sites, and you may find them full by 11 a.m.

If you're planning to camp in the backcountry, see "Enjoying the Park" earlier in this chapter.

Where to Eat in Jasper National Park

Unlike Banff, where you come across popular chains on every corner, Jasper's dining scene is a little more uniquely Jasper. (The arrival of McDonald's in 2000 was met with a chorus of "Don't let it McHappen!") You can get a good meal in this town, and you probably won't have to wait in line.

Andy's Bistro
$$–$$$ **BISTRO**

Everybody raves about Andy's culinary skills, and this classy little bistro is the perfect spot for a special dinner. I can't say what Andy will be serving, but the menu's always tempting: roast lamb topped with mushrooms and served on polenta, or grilled pork tenderloin paired with chanterelles and roasted garlic. The mood is intimate, with candles and white tablecloths, but altogether low-key. It's next to impossible to get a table here without a reservation.

606 Patricia St. ☎ *780-852-4559. Reservations required. Main courses C$15–C$30 (US$11–US$21). MC, V. Mon–Sat 5–11 p.m.*

Caledonia Grill
$$–$$$ **INTERNATIONAL**

You won't mistake this big eatery across from the train station for anything but a hotel dining room (it's part of Whistlers Inn), but the menu goes beyond standard hotel fare. Should you be craving elk meatballs, for instance, you'll find them here. Caledonia also offers New Zealand lamb, red Thai curry prawns, vegetable samosas, and a black bean stir-fry. Everyone's very friendly and the service is efficient.

600 Connaught Dr. (in Whistlers Inn). ☎ *780-852-4070. Reservations not required. Main courses: C$16–C$23 (US$11–US$16). AE, MC, V. Daily 7:30 a.m.–2:30 p.m., 5–10 p.m.*

Coco's Café

$ **BAKERY**

If you like scrambled tofu for breakfast, head for Coco's. If you've never tried scrambled tofu, here's your chance. This wee vegetarian- and vegan-friendly spot (they'll vegetarianize virtually anything on the menu) serves an astonishing variety of breakfast and lunch dishes, from Belgian waffles to falafel and burritos. Great smoothies: Try mango juice with banana and strawberry. Coco's will prepare anything on the menu to go, which is just as well, since there's scarcely any place to sit.

608 Patricia St. ☎ *780-852-4550. Most items under C$10 (US$7). V only. Daily 7 a.m.–9 p.m. Closes 6 p.m. in winter.*

Fiddle River

$$$–$$$$ **SEAFOOD**

If you feel like dining on fish tonight, wander along Connaught Drive and see what's fresh at Fiddle River. Daily specials are posted on a blackboard at street level. The restaurant's upstairs. Look for inventive twists on everything from salmon and scallops to swordfish and snapper. While the focus is on fish, the chef also gets adventurous with beef and game. Do check out the dessert menu. You can't find chili-pepper ice cream just anywhere.

620 Connaught Dr. ☎ *780-852-3032. Reservations recommended. Main courses C$20–C$40 (US$14–US$28). AE, MC, V. Daily 5–10 p.m.*

Soft Rock Café

$ **BAKERY**

A cinnamon bun from this bakery will feed a family of five! Besides substantial baked goods, the Soft Rock serves breakfast all day, including eggs in a skillet with vegetables and cheese for C$8.95 (US$6). At lunch, try the Soft Rock's version of croque monsieur, a grilled ham and cheese sandwich with tomato and asparagus, served with a side of salad, roast potatoes, or fries (C$8.95/US$6). Order at the till and find a table inside or take a seat outdoors in the sun. While you're there, check your e-mail at the back of the cafe.

632 Connaught Dr. ☎ *780-852-5850. Most items under C$10 (US$7). MC, V. Daily 7:30 a.m.–9:00 p.m.*

Tekarra Restaurant

$$$–$$$$ **REGIONAL**

The Tekarra Lodge is a just a short drive from the town of Jasper (1km/just over half a mile) south on Highway 93A and the resort's upscale rustic restaurant is well worth a visit. The kitchen turns out buffalo and beef meatloaf and banana-crusted chicken with mango chutney. Rack of lamb is served in a macadamia nut crust. The signature dessert is a warm chocolate cake. When the weather's fine, you can dine on an outdoor deck.

1km south of Jasper on Hwy. 93A. ☎ *780-852-4624. Reservations recommended. Main courses: C$20–C$30 (US$14–US$28). AE, MC, V. May–Oct, daily 8–11 a.m., 5:30–10:00 pm.*

Fast Facts: Jasper

Area Code

☎ 708.

ATMs

Canadian Imperial Bank of Commerce, 416 Connaught Dr.; Toronto Dominion Bank, 606 Patricia St.

Emergencies

Dial **911.**

Fees

You need a National Parks Pass to visit Jasper. Daily passes (adults C$7/US$4.90; groups C$14/US$10) and annual passes (adults C$45/US$32; groups C$89/US$63) are available at park gates and information centers.

Fishing Licenses

Licenses are sold at information centers and fishing supply stores: C$7/US$4.20 per day or C$20/US$14 for an annual pass.

Hospitals

Seaton General Hospital, 518 Robson St., Jasper ☎ 708-852-3344.

Information

Jasper National Park Information Centre, 500 Connaught Dr. ☎ 780-852-6176.

Pharmacies

Cavell Drugs, 602 Patricia St.
☎ 780-852-4441.

Post Office

502 Patricia St. ☎ 780-852-3041.

Road Conditions and Weather

For road conditions, dial ☎ 403-762-1450. For weather information, call
☎ 780-852-3185.

Taxes

Alberta is the only province in Canada with no provincial sales tax. The 7% national Goods & Services Tax (GST), however, applies to most goods and services, although visitors can apply for a rebate on some purchases. You also pay a 5% hotel tax.

Time Zone

Mountain Standard.

Web Site

www.parkscanada.gc.ca

Part IV
Southwestern Alberta Rockies

The 5th Wave   By Rich Tennant

In this part...

*L*ace up your hiking boots. This part focuses on destinations in Alberta (*aside from* Banff and Jasper) that are worthy of your attention. The town of Canmore and its neighbor, Kananaskis Country, both favorites with Calgarians (and practically in their backyard), are superb spots to experience the Rockies, whether you intend to hike, ski, and mountain bike, or just gear up in Gore-Tex and look rugged. Waterton Lakes National Park, in the southern corner of the province, near the U.S. border, involves a bit of a detour from the main region covered in this book, but is well worth the time and effort. This part explains how to get to Waterton Lakes and tells you how much time to allow for the trip. I also give you the rundown on the park, including the best places to stay and where to eat (including where to go for pizza!). And I mention a couple of spots you may want to visit on your way to Waterton and beyond its borders.

Chapter 15

Canmore

- -

In This Chapter

▶ Getting to Canmore and finding your way around

▶ Locating the best beds and meals

▶ Touring the town

▶ Finding adventure

- -

Situated on the eastern edge of the Rocky Mountains, five minutes from Banff National Park and with Kananaskis Country in its very backyard, Canmore is a favorite home base for mountain climbers and outdoor enthusiasts. Thanks partly to development restrictions in nearby Banff, it's also one of the fastest growing communities in Canada. The small town's population is expected to more than double over the next decade, as is the number of folks who own vacation homes here.

Founded in 1883, Canmore, for the better part of a century, was a major coal-mining center. After the mines closed, the focus shifted to tourism, particularly after the 1988 Winter Olympics when the development of a Nordic center here helped put the town on the map. Canmore is far less touristy than Banff, but the hiking, climbing, skiing, and golfing on its doorstep are every bit as good.

Getting There

Canmore is a quick trip from Calgary, whether you're behind the wheel or riding the bus. If you're heading into Banff, you can take a detour into Canmore en route.

Driving in

From Calgary, drive 100km (60 miles) west on the Trans-Canada Highway (Highway 1). If you're traveling from Banff National Park, Canmore is just five minutes' drive east of the park gates on Highway 1.

Busing in

Greyhound (☎ 800-661-8747) offers regular bus service from Calgary to Canmore. The trip takes 1 hour, 15 minutes. In Canmore, the bus station is at 801–8th Street. Various shuttle services from the Calgary airport also stop in Canmore, including **Airport Shuttle Express,** ☎ 403-509-4799.

Orienting Yourself and Getting Around Canmore

Bow Valley Trail (Highway 1A) runs through Canmore, parallel to the Trans-Canada Highway and just east of the railway tracks. Most hotels are located here, as is the Information Centre (at the north end of the highway).

Follow Railway Avenue and Main Street across Policeman's Creek to the town center, where you find shops, restaurants, a post office, a museum, the Canmore Hotel, and a handful of other historic buildings. Avenues run north–south, and streets east–west. Park in one of the lots along 7th Street or 9th Street and check out the town center on foot. A network of trails runs along the Bow River and through neighborhoods, connecting with a boardwalk along Policeman's Creek.

Drive south on 8th Avenue across the Bow River to Rundle Drive, to reach Spray Lakes Road, the Canmore Nordic Centre, and the Smith-Dorrien Highway into Kananaskis Country.

The main route into Kananaskis Country, Highway 40, is about 30km (19 miles) east of Canmore.

A big **Visitor Information Centre** at 2801 Bow Valley Trail ☎ 403-678-1295 is open May 17 to September 2 from 8 a.m. to 8 p.m., and the rest of the year, from 9 a.m. to 6 p.m. Here you can pick up maps and brochures on Canmore, Kananaskis Country, and other Alberta destinations and get help finding a hotel.

Where to Stay in Canmore

Most Canmore hotels are along or near Bow Valley Trail (Highway 1A), east of the town center. To find B&Bs, pick up the **Canmore–Bow Valley Bed & Breakfast Association** brochure from the Visitor Information Centre. You can call the association to check on vacancies ☎ 403-609-7224.

Alberta

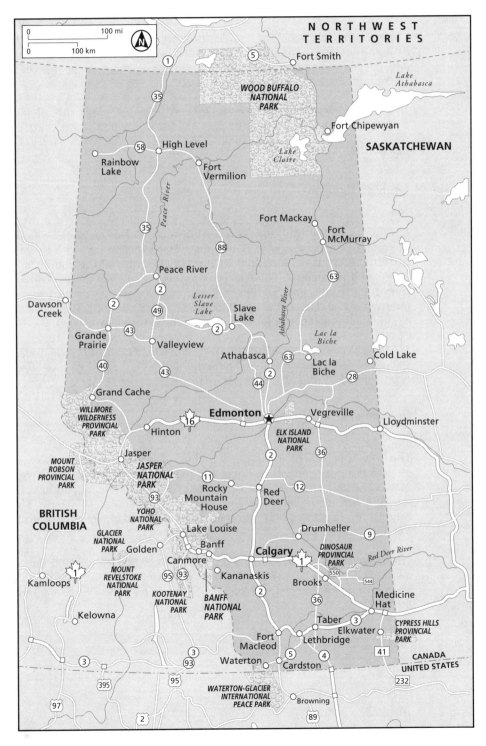

Canadian Rockies Chalets
$–$$$

These chalets are ideal for families or groups, especially if you plan to do some cooking — kitchens include full stoves and dishwashers. Hikers and skiers can find plenty of space to stash gear, and you can marvel at the mountains from your balcony.

1206 Bow Valley Trail. ☎ **800-386-7248***, 403-678-3799. Fax: 403-678-3413. E-mail:* info@canadianrockieschalets.com. *Internet:* www.canadian rockieschalets.com. *Rack rates: C$99–C$179 (US$70–US$125) double. AE, MC, V.*

Chateau Canmore
$$$

After a day on the trail, sink into the hot tub, soak in the pool, sweat in the sauna, or treat yourself to a massage. This big complex — it's the one with the red roof — along Bow Valley Trail delivers all the comforts of home, and then some. The spacious rooms feature gas fireplaces with river-rock fronts. For families, loft suites are equipped with fridges, microwaves, and two TVs. Kids like the separate check-in. To guarantee a good night's sleep, ask for a room away from the railway track.

1720 Bow Valley Trail. ☎ **800-261-8551***, 403-678-6699. Fax: 403-678-6954. E-mail:* info@chateaucanmore.com. *Internet:* www.chateaucanmore.com. *Rack rates: From C$179 (US$125) double. AE, DISC, MC, V.*

Georgetown Inn
$$

The only drawback of staying here is that the array of outdoor activities on your doorstep notwithstanding, it's so very tempting to linger in your room. The 25 guest rooms in this romantic Tudor-style inn, all unique, are adorned with antiques and boast lovely mountain views. The original inn (built in 1993) was renovated in 1997. Largest rooms are in the new section.

1101 Bow Valley Trail. ☎ **800-657-5955***, 403-678-3439. Fax: 403-678-6909. E-mail:* georgetowninn@cb.monarch.net. *Internet:* www.georgetowninn. ab.ca. *Rack rates: C$129–C$149 (US$90–US$104) double. Rates include breakfast. MC, V.*

Green Gables Inn

$$$

This long, narrow, motel-style accommodation is part of the Best Western chain. Opt for a second-floor room and savor the view from your balcony. A plus of lodging here: You can dine in one of Canmore's favorite restaurants, Chez François, without leaving your hotel.

1602–2nd Ave. (Bow Valley Trail). ☎ *800-661-2133, 403-678-5488. Fax: 403-678-2670. E-mail:* g_gables@telusplanet.net. *Internet:* www.pocaterrainn. com/greengables/index.html. *Rack rates: C$159–C$199 (US$111–US$139) double. AE, DISC, MC, V.*

Lady Macdonald Country Inn

$$$

This posh B&B-style inn offers 12 fresh and inviting rooms and a sunny breakfast area with gleaming oak floors that opens onto a patio. For C$180 (US$126) (C$130/US$91 if you visit between October 1 and May 31) you can nod off in a four-poster, wrought-iron bed and then awake to a view of the Rundle Range and Ha-Ling Peak.

1201 Bow Valley Trail. ☎ *800-567-3919, 403-678-3665. Fax: 403-678-9714. E-mail:* info@ladymacdonald.com. *Internet:* www.ladymacdonald.com. *Rack rates: C$155–C$255 (US$109–US$179) double. Rates include breakfast. AE, MC, V.*

Runner-up lodging

Canmore Suites

$–$$

Standard rooms don't include extras such as irons, hairdryers, and coffeemakers. Then again, neither do you pay for them. Two-bedroom suites feature basic kitchens.

10 Lincoln Park. ☎ *877-609-9099, 403-609-3999. Internet:* www.canmoresuites.net.

Drake Inn

$–$$

This hotel in the heart of downtown is older, but clean and spacious. Rooms overlooking Policeman's Creek are largest.

1km (0.6 mile) off Hwy. 1A. ☎ *800-461-8730, 403-678-5131. Internet:* www. drakeinn.com.

Restwell cabins

$$

The little cabins in the Restwell Trailer Park aren't the latest in decor, but hey, you're just a stroll from downtown.

#1A 502–3rd Ave. ☎ *403-678-5111. Internet:* www.restwelltrailerpark.com

Campsites

Head for the centrally located **Restwell Trailer Park,** #1A 502–3rd Avenue. It's along Policeman's Creek near the town center (call ☎ **403-678-5111** or visit Internet: www.restwelltrailerpark.com). Full-service sites cost C\$33 to C\$39 (US\$23 to US\$27) and unserviced tent sites C\$26 (US\$18).

Where to Eat in Canmore

To track down a coffee shop, pub, or dinner spot, wander around the 8th Avenue (Main Street) area. Latte lovers will have little trouble sourcing their favorite brew in this town. Canmore folks seem to love their coffee houses. In the Main Street/7th Avenue area, look for **Beaners,** the **Coffee Mine,** and **Rocky Mountain Bagel Company.**

Looking for trail snacks? You'll find the best selection of nuts, seeds, candies, trail mixes, and granolas at **Nutter's Bulk and Natural Foods** in the shopping complex at Railway and Main streets. Everything's sold from bulk bins. Buy as much or as little as you need.

Chez François

$$–$$$$ FRENCH

Chef Jean-François Gouin creates French classics in this reputable eatery in the Green Gables Inn. Start with beef and sherry broth, then sample shrimp in curry sauce, veal in wild mushrooms, or a delectable seafood stew. While you dine, enjoy the view.

1604 Bow Valley Trail (in the Green Gables Inn). ☎ *403-68-6111. Reservations recommended. Main course: C\$18–C\$30 (US\$13–US\$21). AE, DC, MC, V. Daily 6:30 a.m.–2:00 p.m., 5–11 p.m.*

Crazyweed Kitchen
$$ **REGIONAL**

This marvelous little spot serves very creative food, from lamb to duck and salmon to sablefish. The menu changes frequently, but everything's always fresh and imaginative. Look for highly original pizzas. Crazyweed has only a few tables and a handful of stools, but you can get food to go. It's usually closed one day a week, but not necessarily the *same* day. Call ahead to be sure it's open.

626–8th St. (Main St.). ☎ *403-609-2530. Reservations not accepted. Main course: C$18 (US$13). MC, V. Six days a week, 11:30 a.m.–3:30 p.m. and 5–11 p.m.*

The Grizzly Paw
$$ **PUB**

Outdoorsy types quench their thirst with Drooling Moose Pilsner and Beavertail Raspberry Ale on this micro-brewery's hugely popular patio. Umbrellas shelter you from the midday sun; heat lamps warm the night air. The kitchen, naturally enough, concentrates on food that goes with beer: munchy starters (dry garlic ribs, nachos, garlic prawns), hearty sandwiches, wraps, and fish and chips.

622–8th St. (Main St.). ☎ *403-678-9983. Main courses: C$10–C$14 (US$7–US$10). AE, MC, V. Daily 11 a.m.–2 a.m.*

Rocky Mountain Bagel Company
$ **COFFEE HOUSE**

Pop in for a quick breakfast and check your e-mail, or grab a coffee and breakfast-bagel to go. Coffee lovers have plenty of blends to choose from. Later in the day, have a salad, soup, or bagel sandwich.

830–8th St. (Main St.). ☎ *403-678-9978. Most items under C$10 (US$7). MC, V. Daily 6:30 a.m.–11:00 p.m.*

Sherwood House
$$ **CANADIAN**

You can't miss the big log cabin on the corner of Main Street and 8th Avenue. It's open at 8 a.m. for breakfast and picnic tables on the outdoor patio fill up at lunch. In the evening, move inside to dine on venison, caribou, ostrich, or lamb vindaloo. (The chef prepares a few things for vegetarians, too.) A pizzeria in the basement is open from 5 p.m. to midnight.

838–8th St. (Main St.). ☎ *403-678-5211. Main courses: C$15–C$20 (US$11–US$14). AE, DC, MC, V. Daily 8 a.m. to closing.*

Zona's

$$ **INTERNATIONAL**

This Canmore favorite, a block back from Main Street, dishes up wild mushroom ravioli, Mexican three-bean pie, and a house special, Moroccan molasses lamb curry with jasmine rice. Main courses are served with soup or avocado Caesar salad. Everything's very creatively presented. After 10 p.m., order from the tapas menu. You may find crab cakes with citrus soy dipping sauce or brie with roast garlic in filo. Zona's cheery patio is decked out in lanterns and flower boxes.

710–9th St. ☎ *403-609-2000. Reservations recommended. Main courses: C$15–C$20 (US$11–US$14). AE, MC, V. Daily, lunch: 11:30 a.m.–3:00 p.m.; dinner: 5–10p.m.; tapas: 10–12 p.m.*

Exploring Canmore

Canmore's main attraction is mountain adventure. But before you lace up your hiking boots, do take a stroll around town. Among the mountain gear stores and coffee shops, you find a number of historic buildings, including one of Alberta's oldest rooming houses (the Canmore Hotel).

From coal town to boom town

Unlike Banff, which had its beginnings in the luxury tourist trade, Canmore started out as a rough-and-tumble mining town. The discovery of coal here in the 1880s, together with the arrival of the Canadian Pacific Railway, lured workers to the small community, which ultimately became one of the most important mining centers in southern Alberta. Over the years, Canmore enjoyed booms and suffered busts, then took a downturn in the 1960s when the railway, which bought most of the town's coal, switched to diesel on the trains. After a few more years of ups and downs, the mines closed in 1979.

Tourism and condominium and resort construction are the driving forces in Canmore today. The town got an economic boost in the 1980s with the announcement that it would host Nordic events such as cross-country skiing and biathlon for the 1988 Winter Olympics. The Canadian government's decision to curb development in neighboring Banff National Park hasn't hurt, either. Canmore's location beside Banff and on the edge of Kananaskis Country makes it a popular base for outdoor enthusiasts and a trendy vacation-home spot.

Attractions

Canmore Museum

Pictures and artifacts on display here showcase Canmore's mining history from 1886 to 1979. You also learn about the geology of the Bow Valley. For more insight into Canmore's past, sign up for a heritage walking tour along Main Street. Tours run on from late June to late August, Thursdays at 3 p.m., and take about two hours. At press time, the Canmore Museum was planning a move to new digs across the street.

907–7th Ave. ☎ 403-678-2462. Admission by donation. Wed–Sun 1– 8 p.m. Closed Mon & Tues. Heritage tours: C$15 (US$11) adults, C$10 (US$7) seniors & students, C$8 (US$6) children under 12.

Travelers interested in Canmore's mining past can tour the town's original **North West Mounted Police barracks,** at Main Street and 5th Avenue, ☎ **403-678-1955.** There's no charge, although donations are welcome. June through August, you can visit the barracks from Wednesday to Sunday, 10 a.m. to 6 p.m. Winter hours vary. Call the Canmore Museum at ☎ **403-678-2462.**

Canmore Nordic Centre Provincial Park

Mountain bike enthusiasts, hikers, and in winter, cross-country skiers, have 72km (45 miles) of trails to explore at this facility, built for the 1988 Winter Olympics. You find showers, lockers, and a cafeteria in the Day Lodge. Ask for a trail map, showing easy, intermediate, and difficult routes. The 6-km/4-mile (one-way) trail from the Nordic Centre to the Banff National Park boundary is an easy cycle or stroll. Other trails have steep downhill sections, so cyclists should take care on the corners. A 2.5-km (1.5-mile) loop is set aside for roller skiing. An interpretive trail leads to the banks of the Bow River and the site of an early 1900s mining community called Georgetown.

Folk & blues in the Rockies

If you happen to visit Canmore in early August, catch Alberta's longest-running folk festival. See Internet: www.canmorefolkfestival.com for dates. On the Heritage Day (first Monday in August) long weekend, the **Canmore Folk Music Festival** takes over Centennial Park, near the town center. Tickets cost C$20 (US$14) a day or C$53 (US$37) for the three-day event. Order them through the Web site or from Ticketmaster outlets, ☎ **403-777-0000,** 780-451-8000. Tickets are also sold at the gate.

Trail Sports in the Nordic Centre Day Lodge (☎ **403-678-6764**) rents mountain bikes and cross-country ski gear. You pay C$40 (US$28) a day for a full-suspension mountain bike, C$15 to C$35 (US$11 to US$25) a day for cross-country ski gear. Hourly rates are also available.

4 km (2.5 miles) from the town center on Spray Lakes Rd. ☎ 403-678-2400. Winter trail fees C$5 (US$3.50) adult, C$4 (US$2.80) seniors and youth, C$3 (US$2.10) children 6–11. No charge to hike or bike the trails in summer.

Most of the trails around the Nordic Centre are one-way, so be sure to keep to the right.

Ways to relish the great outdoors

Rent just about any kind of outdoor equipment (bikes, canoes, skis, skates) at **Gear Up,** 1302 Bow Valley Trail (across from the hospital), ☎ **403-678-1636.** Bikes go for about C$35 (US$25) a day. **Rebound,** at 902 Main Street, ☎ **403-678-3668,** also rents bikes. Daily rates start at C$25 (US$18). Both shops also offer hourly rates.

Golfing

You have three courses within a few kilometers of town: the **Canmore Golf and Curling Club,** 2000–8th Avenue, ☎ **403-678-4785, SilverTip**, 1000 SilverTip Trail, ☎ **403-678-1600,** and **Stewart Creek,** in the Three Sisters Village, 4km (2.5 miles) from Canmore, ☎ **877-993-4653.**

Hiking

Families looking for an easy trek can explore the trails in town: the **Riverside Loop** follows the Bow River; you can also stroll along **Policeman's Creek.** For something more challenging, visit the **Canmore Nordic Centre.** You can meander all the way to Banff. Also in the Nordic Centre area, the **Grassi Lakes** trail is a good bet. The trail climbs through a forest above town to two emerald lakes and a panoramic view of Canmore. Near the Lac des Arcs exit from the Trans-Canada Highway, **Heart Creek** is an easy trek with interpretive signs. More experienced hikers may want to tackle **Ha Ling** peak or climb Mount **Lady MacDonald.** For hikes in nearby Kananaskis Country, see Chapter 16.

Mountain biking

Trail riding options are nearly endless in this town. Both beginners and experts find trails to their liking at the **Canmore Nordic Centre,** designed for cross-country ski and biathlon events for the 1988 Winter Olympics. Visit **Trail Sports (☎ 403-678-6764)** in the Day Lodge to rent a bike or sign up for lessons. The **Shark Mountain** biking trail system (drive 39km/24 miles past the Nordic Centre on the Smith-Dorrien/Spray Trail Highway) has scenic, easy to moderate trails. Two-wheelers can also venture out on many Kananaskis Country hiking trails.

A trail to write home about

For experienced hikers with energy to burn, **Centennial Trail** to the summit of Mount Allan is a magnificent hike in this area. Besides offering a real workout and some of the best views in the Rockies, you get bragging rights for climbing the highest marked trail in the Canadian Rockies (2,800 meters/9,200 feet). Give yourself 10 to 12 hours and bring plenty of water. Expect steep scrambles on some sections. On the south side of the summit, you pass through a row of 25-meter (82-foot) rock pinnacles, known as the rock garden. If you do the entire 19-km (12-mile) trip, from Canmore (Dead Man's Flats) to Ribbon Creek in Kananaskis Country, you need transportation back to your car. The trail is closed in the spring (until June 21).

Skiing

For downhill skiers, Banff's **Mount Norquay** (☎ 403-762-4421; Internet: www.banffnorquay.com), 23km (19 miles) from Canmore, is the closest hill — and the only resort in the area where you can go night skiing. **Fortress Mountain** (☎ 403-591-7108; Internet: www.skifortress.com) in the Kananaskis Valley, 83km (51 miles) from Canmore, is a challenging hill that's popular with snowboarders. **Nakiska** (☎ 403-591-7777; Internet: www.skinakiska.com), site of downhill events during the 1988 Olympics, boasts a broad range of terrain and is a good choice for families. Nakiska is also in the Kananaskis Valley, about 56km (35 miles) from Canmore. Cross-country enthusiasts can head for the **Canmore Nordic Centre,** where trails are mostly intermediate to advanced, or the **Mount Shark** trail system south of Canmore.

Shopping

Shops selling mountaineering and outdoor gear, and local art and crafts are concentrated in the town center, on and near Main Street (8th Street) and along Bow Valley Trail and Railway Avenue. **Valhalla Pure Outfitters,** 726 Main Street (☎ 403-678-5610), has hiking, climbing, and camping gear, along with clothing by Patagonia, Sierra Designs, and others. For kids' clothing, visit **Glacier's Edge,** 729–10th Street (☎ 403-678-4779). For works by local artists, check out the **Kinsella Art Studio,** 1302 Bow Valley Trail (☎ 403-678-4331) or **The Corner Gallery,** 705 Main Street (☎ 403-678-6090). In the town center area, you also find a handful of unique specialty stores, including **Rocky Mountain Soap Company,** #103 820 Main Street (☎ 403-678-9873), and the **Lavender Harvest Farms** shop at 737 7th Avenue (☎ 888-800-1921) .

Nightlife

For live music, the spots to head for are **The Drake,** 909 Railway Avenue (☎ **403-678-5131**), and the **Canmore Hotel,** 738 Main Street (☎ **403-678-5181**). Canmore's only nightclub, **Hooligans,** is at 103 Bow Valley Trail (☎ **403-609-2662**). Pick up a copy of the **Rocky Mountain Outlook** for the latest news on who's playing where. For a quiet brew, stop by the **Grizzly Paw,** 622–8th St. (☎ **403-678-9983**) or the **Rose & Crown,** 749 Railway Avenue (☎ **403-678-5168**). At the **Oh Canada Eh?!** dinner theater, 125 Kananaskis Way (☎ **800-773-0004**), you can be entertained by actors singing Canadian songs about Canadian themes (think Mounties and lumberjacks) and serving Canadian food (such as Atlantic haddock, roast Manitoba chicken, and PEI potatoes).

Fast Facts: Canmore

Area Code

Canmore's area code is **403**. You don't need to dial it if you're calling local numbers.

American Express

An American Express Travel Service office is located at #103 722–8th St. (Brewster Travel Service), ☎ **403-678-2662**. For card member services, including lost or stolen cards, call ☎ **800-668-2639**.

Emergencies

Dial **911**.

Hospitals

1100 Hospital Place (off Mountain Avenue). ☎ **403-678-5536**.

Internet Access and Cybercafes

The **Cyber Web,** 717–10th St., ☎ **403-609-2678,** is open daily from 9 a.m. to midnight. **Rocky Mountain Bagel Company,** 830–8th St., ☎ **403-678-9983,** also has computer terminals.

Maps

Drop by the **Visitor Information Centre,** 2801 Bow Valley Trail (☎ **403-678-1295**). Most Canmore outdoor gear shops also carry maps and guidebooks.

Newspapers

Local papers are the *Canmore Leader* and *Rocky Mountain Outlook*. The *Calgary Herald*, and two national papers, the *National Post* and *Globe and Mail,* are also widely available.

Police

Canmore RCMP. ☎ **403-678-5516**.

Weather

Environment Canada ☎ **403-762-2088**.

Chapter 16

Kananaskis Country

● ●

In This Chapter

▶ Arriving in K-Country

▶ Winding your way through wonderful wilderness

▶ Securing a campsite

● ●

Kana . . . *what?* Captain John Palliser, who led a British expedition through this area in the mid-1800s, named a river and two mountain passes in honor of a Native man named Kananaskis (kan-ann-*ass*-kis) who got an axe blow on the head and lived to tell the tale, thus achieving celebrity status.

Kananaskis Country, however, isn't famous at all. True, the region did host international athletes during the 1988 Winter Olympics. And in 2002, world leaders met here for the G8 Summit. But most years, the main visitors to "K-Country" are Albertans, happily toting hiking gear, mountain bikes, skis, fishing rods, and golf clubs to their own backyard playground.

Just east of Banff National Park on the eastern slopes of the Rocky Mountains, Kananaskis Country takes in a handful of parks, protected areas, and provincial forest lands, which together span 4,200 sq. km (1,640 sq. miles). Don't head here for shopping or nightlife: Kananaskis is largely undeveloped. You do find great campsites, a couple of hotels, and some guest ranches, but the region is mostly remote, pristine, and wild. Bighorn sheep are often glimpsed here, as are moose, elk, and bears. People who frequent the area love the outdoors.

You can have a lot of fun in this part of Alberta, and unlike Canada's national parks, where visitors must buy permits, Kananaskis Country offers its wonders to you *gratis.*

Kananaskis Country

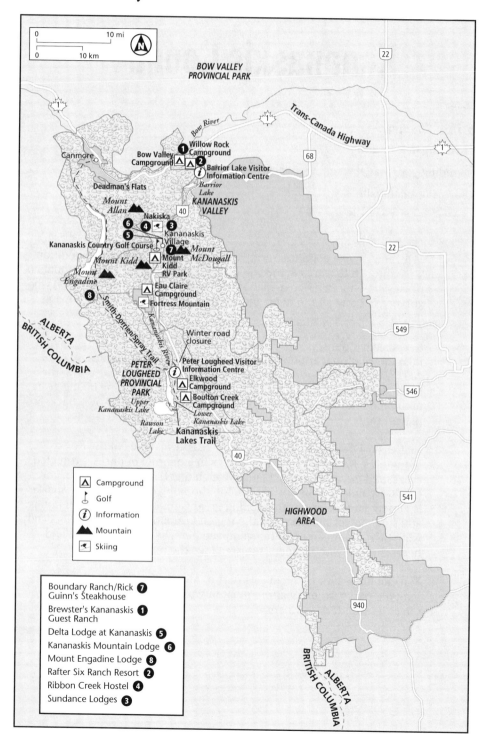

0 — 10 mi
0 — 10 km

BOW VALLEY PROVINCIAL PARK

Bow River

Trans-Canada Highway

22

1

1

68

1

Canmore

Willow Rock Campground ❶

Bow Valley Campground ❷

Barrier Lake Visitor Information Centre ⓘ

Deadman's Flats

Barrier Lake

KANANASKIS VALLEY

Mount Allan

Nakiska

40

❻ ❹ ❸

❺ Kananaskis Village

Kananaskis Country Golf Course

❼ Mount McDougall

Mount Kidd

Mount Kidd RV Park

Mount Engadine ❽

Eau Claire Campground

Fortress Mountain

22

ALBERTA
BRITISH COLUMBIA

Smith-Dorrien/Spray Trail

Kananaskis River

Winter road closure

PETER LOUGHEED PROVINCIAL PARK

Peter Lougheed Visitor Information Centre ⓘ

Elkwood Campground

Boulton Creek Campground

Upper Kananaskis Lake

Rawson Lake

Lower Kananaskis Lake

Kananaskis Lakes Trail

40

549

546

541

HIGHWOOD AREA

940

BRITISH COLUMBIA
ALBERTA

Legend:
- ⬛ Campground
- ⛳ Golf
- ⓘ Information
- ▲ Mountain
- 🎿 Skiing

Boundary Ranch/Rick Guinn's Steakhouse ❼
Brewster's Kananaskis Guest Ranch ❶
Delta Lodge at Kananaskis ❺
Kananaskis Mountain Lodge ❻
Mount Engadine Lodge ❽
Rafter Six Ranch Resort ❷
Ribbon Creek Hostel ❹
Sundance Lodges ❸

Must-See Attractions

The top draws in Kananaskis Country depend entirely on what you like to do. *Do* is the operative word here. The park contains remarkable hiking, biking, and cross-country ski trails, along with two ski hills and a couple of great golf courses. You can fish, canoe, or kayak. Conventional tourist attractions (places that charge admission) are nonexistent.

Getting There and Getting Around Kananaskis Country

Getting to Kananaskis Country is a picnic (providing you have wheels of one sort or another). From Calgary, drive 90km (56 miles) west on the Trans-Canada Highway (Highway 1) and head south on Highway 40, the main route through Kananaskis Country.

In summer (mid-June through December 1), you can continue south on Highway 40 over the Highwood Pass, the highest drivable pass in Canada, and loop back to Calgary through the heart of Alberta's ranching country.

There's no public transportation in Kananaskis Country, so you need your car (or bike) to get around.

Planning Ahead

To receive information before your trip, call **Travel Alberta** (☎ **800-252-3782**, 780-427-4321) or visit Internet: www.travel alberta.com. The official Kananaskis Country Web site, Internet: www.cd.gov.ab.ca/parks/kananaskis, is your best source of up-to-date news on trail conditions, avalanche reports, and park happenings and events.

Kananaskis Country offers a superb selection of campgrounds, including some that take reservations. Refer to the sections on Bow Valley Provincial Park, Kananaskis Valley, and Peter Lougheed Provincial Park for details. Hotels in the park are limited to two cushy spots in Kananaskis Village. There's also a backcountry lodge that you can drive to. You find a broader range of hotels and motels nearby, in Canmore (see Chapter 15).

You can take in award-winning interpretive musicals on summer evenings at the amphitheaters in the Bow Valley, Elkwood, Boulton Creek, and Mount Kidd campgrounds. Check with visitor centers for show times. Admission is free, although donations to the Friends of Kananaskis are appreciated.

To camp in one of the park's backcountry sites, you need a permit. They cost C$3 (US$2.10) and are available at the Barrier Lake or Peter Lougheed Provincial Park visitor centers, or by calling ☎ **403-678-3136.**

Visitor centers provide information on hiking trails and sell trail brochures (C$1.25) with maps and suggested routes. If you intend to do serious hiking, you probably want a topographic map (the Gem Trek series is widely available) and a guidebook, such as the two-volume *Kananaskis Trail Guide* by Gillean Daffern (Rocky Mountain Books). Order brochures, maps, and trail guides online from Friends of Kananaskis at Internet: www.kananaskis.org.

Figuring Out the Lay of the Land

Kananaskis Country encompasses some 4,200 sq. km (1,622 sq. miles) of mountains and foothills in southwestern Alberta, about a 45-minute drive from Calgary. About half of the region is designated provincial parkland. In other areas, you see commercial activities such as logging, cattle grazing, and oil and gas development. Highway 40, a paved highway and the main artery through the region, runs south from the Trans-Canada Highway along the Kananaskis River and past the Kananaskis Lakes before crossing the Highwood Pass.

Park facilities, which include two main visitor information centers, a couple of hotels, two ski hills, and a golf course, are concentrated in the Kananaskis Valley and Peter Lougheed Provincial Park areas, just west of Highway 40, as are many hiking and ski trails. South of Peter Lougheed Provincial Park, the highway closes in winter (December 1 to June 14) to protect a calving area for elk and because of avalanche hazards.

The other main route into Kananaskis Country is the Smith–Dorrien/ Spray Trail, a gravel road running from Canmore, on the northwest edge of Kananaskis Country, to Upper Kananaskis Lake. It links up with Highway 40.

The southern and eastern reaches of the park are accessible from several communities in Alberta, including Bragg Creek, Longview, and Turner Valley.

Arriving in the Park

You don't pass through an official park gate when you enter Kananaskis Country and you don't need a park pass.

Finding information

Visit the **Barrier Lake Visitor Information Center** (☎ 403-673-3985), on Highway 40, about 8km (5 miles) south of the Trans-Canada Highway, or the **Peter Lougheed Visitor Information Centre** (☎ 403-591-6322) farther south in Peter Lougheed Provincial Park. Both centers offer help planning hikes, ski trips, and other park adventures. You can also buy trail maps and guidebooks. Both information centers are open in summer daily from 9 a.m. to 5 p.m. In winter (after Thanksgiving), they're open most days, from about 9:30 a.m. to 4:00 p.m. Call ahead to check.

You can call visitor centers in Kananaskis Country toll-free from anywhere in Alberta. Dial ☎ **310-0000,** followed by the local number, including the area code.

Paying fees

Visiting Kananaskis Country is free, unless you plan to camp in the backcountry, in which case you require a backcountry permit. These cost C$3 (US$2.10) per person per night. Call ☎ **403-678-3136** to order by phone, or pick up your permit in person at the Barrier Lake or Peter Lougheed Provincial Park visitor center. You also pay a nonrefundable reservation fee of C$6 (US$4.20) per trip.

Bow Valley Provincial Park

This small park on the northern fringe of Kananaskis Country at the confluence of the Bow and Kananaskis rivers is a super spot to fish for trout and admire lovely mountain panoramas. It's also a convenient base for exploring Kananaskis Country or visiting nearby Banff National Park. This park is situated where the prairie meets the mountains. You find many short trails and no big uphill climbs, so it's a good spot for kids. In June and July, the wildflowers here are stunning, while winter is the best time to spot a herd of elk that lives in the park. You often see white-tailed deer, too.

Getting there

Bow Valley Provincial Park is about 80km (50 miles) west of Calgary on the Trans-Canada Highway.

Finding information

The **Bow Valley Park Administrative Office** (☎ 403-673-3663), north of the Trans-Canada Highway near Highway 1X, provides information on hiking trails and interpretive programs. The office is open Monday to Friday, from 8:00 a.m. to noon and 1:00 to 4:30 p.m. A larger visitor center is at **Barrier Lake** (☎ 403-673-3985), just south of the Trans-Canada Highway on Highway 40.

Where to stay

Just outside the park borders, two guest ranches offer accommodation in cabins and chalets along with trail rides, pack trips, wagon rides, and other western adventures. At the **Rafter Six Ranch Resort** (☎ 888-267-2624, 403-673-3622; Internet: www.raftersix.com), lodge rooms, log cabins, and chalets with kitchenettes range from C$149 to C$209 (US$104 to US$146) double. **Brewster's Kananaskis Guest Ranch** (☎ 800-691-5085, 403-673-3737; Internet: www.brewsteradventures.com) offers chalets and cabins for about C$188 (US$131) double, including breakfast and dinner.

Bow Valley Park Campgrounds (☎ 403-673-2163) operates two campsites within the park and several others throughout the Bow Valley Corridor. In the park, **Bow Valley Campground,** 75km (46.5 miles) west of Calgary, is the largest site; of its 169 spots, 39 have power and water. Reservations are accepted, beginning April 1, and fees range from C$17 (US$12) for an unserviced site to C$23 (US$16) for a spot with power and water. At **Willow Rock,** just northeast of the intersection of the Trans-Canada and Highway 1X, you find another 124 sites, including 34 with power only. Reservations are not taken. Rates are C$17 to C$20 (US$12 to US$14).

Exploring the park

The hikes in Bow Valley Provincial Park include a number of short (1- or 2-km, one-way) walks and interpretive trails, ideal for kids. Some hikes link up with trails in other parts of Kananaskis Country. Follow the **Flowing Water Interpretive Trail,** a 2.2-km (1.4-mile) loop that starts in the Willow Rock Campground. Another short loop, from **Middle Lake,** winds through forest and meadows. Other trails meander along the banks of the Bow and Kananaskis rivers. You also find a 4.4-km (2.7-mile) paved trail for explorers on bikes or in-line skates. A trail map is available from the park administrative office.

Kananaskis Valley

This region is the most developed part of Kananaskis Country. Along with hundreds of kilometers of hiking trails, it contains the main park visitor facilities, including hotels and restaurants, ski hills, and a golf course.

Getting there

From the Trans-Canada Highway, head south along Highway 40.

Finding information

Stop in at the **Barrier Lake Visitor Information Centre** (☎ **403-673-3985**).

Where to stay

In **Kananaskis Village**, about 25km (15.5 miles) south of the Trans-Canada, you find two hotels, several restaurants, tennis courts, a convenience store, and a sports rental shop.

Delta Lodge at Kananaskis
$$–$$$$ Kananaskis Village

This upscale Delta hotel is the largest resort in the village, with 250 rooms in a main lodge and, in a separate building, another 70 "signature club" rooms that include breakfast, evening hors d'oeuvres, and top views. In the lodge, standard rooms are spacious, with windows that open and lots of extras, including high-speed Internet. Some rooms have balconies. Upgrade to a loft room and you enjoy an extra sleeping area, TV, and bath on the second floor. You also find a spa, fitness center, and pool. Kids get a separate check-in and special menus in the lodge restaurants.

From the Trans-Canada Hwy., drive 25km (18 miles) south on Hwy. 40. ☎ *866-432-4322, 403-591-7711. Fax: 403-591-7770. Internet:* www.deltalodgeat kananaskis.ca. *Rack rates: C$129–C$319 (US$90–US$223) double. AE, DISC, MC, V.*

Kananaskis Mountain Lodge

$$$$ **Kananaskis Village**

The smaller of two hotels located in Kananaskis Village, this lodge offers 90 rooms in a variety of styles, including family suites and loft rooms. A restaurant, pub, spa, and fitness center are on-site, and tennis courts are nearby.

From the Trans-Canada Hwy., drive 25km (18 miles) south on Hwy. 40. ☎ *888-591-7501, 403-591-7600. Fax: 403-591-7633. E-mail:* info@kananaskis mountainlodge.com. *Internet:* www.kananaskismountainlodge.com. *Rack rates: C$210–C$270 (US$147–US$189) double. AE, DISC, MC, V.*

Ribbon Creek Hostel

$ **Nakiska Ski Hill**

Hostelling International accommodates travelers in two dorms (14 beds each) and five family rooms. Guests have use of a kitchen, outdoor barbecue, and coin laundry. In summer, check into horseback riding and whitewater rafting packages.

On Hwy. 40, turn right at the Nakiska Ski Hill access road, cross the Kananaskis River, and turn left. ☎ *866-762-4122, 403-283-6503. Internet:* www.hihostels.ca. *Rack rates: Dorm rooms: C$23 (US$16), C$19 (US$13) for members of Hostelling International. Family rooms: C$56 (US$40), C$50 (US$35) for members of Hostelling International. MC, V.*

Just south of Kananaskis Village, the **Mount Kidd RV Park** (☎ **403-591-7700**) has more than 200 campsites, including 74 full-service RV hookups. It's open year-round, and a camper's center offers conveniences such as lockers, showers, whirlpools, and saunas. The site also features children's play areas, tennis courts, and walking paths. If you intend to stay at least four nights, you can book a spot for summer (June 25 to September 6) as early as March 1. No minimum stay applies to reservations made after March 16. Fees range from C$22 (US$15) a night for a site without hookups to C$35 (US$24) a night for a full-service site.

The **Eau Claire Campground** (☎ **403-591-7226**) offers 51 tent sites, some near the banks of the Kananaskis River, and great views, to the north, of Mount Kidd. This site, open mid-May to mid-September, does not take reservations. The fee is C$17 (US$12).

Less conventional accommodation is available at **Sundance Lodges** (☎ **403-591-7122**), 22km (14 miles) south of the Trans-Canada Highway on Highway 40, where you can stay in a tepee or trapper's tent. This spot, which is open from mid-May to the end of September, borders the Kananaskis River, and some of the campsites are a short stroll from the river's banks. The tepees, which have wooden floors, kerosene heaters, and real beds (you can rent sheets and blankets if you don't have your own), cost C$46 to C$60 (US$32 to US$42) a night, depending on the size. Unserviced campsites go for C$18.70 (US$13). Reservations are accepted (beginning March 1) and a good idea.

Where to eat

In addition to dining rooms and restaurants in the Kananaskis Village hotels, you find this casual eatery at Boundary Ranch, just off Highway 40.

Rick Guinn's Steakhouse
$–$$ STEAK AND BURGERS

Barbecued burgers highlight a ranch-style menu that features, along with the classics, buffalo burgers and barbecued pork sausage topped with sauerkraut. For a quick meal, order a side dish, such as buttered corn on the cob or baked beans with cheese. Apple, bumbleberry, and strawberry-rhubarb pie are featured on the dessert menu, as are a mouth-watering selection of cookies. Guinn's is a big, bright place with lots of windows and a few picnic tables outside.

At Boundary Ranch, 26km (16 miles) south of the Trans-Canada Hwy. on Hwy. 40. ☎ *403-591-7171. Reservations required for dinner. Main courses: C$8–C$15 (US$6–US$11). Daily 11 a.m.–4 p.m. and 4:00–8:30 p.m.*

Exploring the park

Stop at the **Barrier Lake Visitor Centre** for help planning a hike and to get the latest news on trail conditions and wildlife activity. To rent mountain bikes, snowshoes, and other outdoor gear, visit **Peregrine Sports** (☎ **403-591-7453**) in Kananaskis Village.

Hiking

The hundreds of kilometers of trails through the Kananaskis Valley include short, scenic strolls, day hikes, and demanding backcountry trips. At the **Eau Claire Campground,** you can follow a gentle trail along the Kananaskis River. Pick up a brochure at the trailhead. Other family-friendly treks include the **Mount Kidd Interpretive Trail** in the Mount Kidd RV Park and the **Rim Trail,** an easy walk to awesome mountain viewpoints that begins near the hotels in Kananaskis Village. Favorite day hikes in the Kananaskis Valley area include **Lillian Lake,** a challenging 6.5-km (4-mile) climb past waterfalls and canyons to a backcountry campsite at Lillian Lake. From here, it's a 1.5-km (1-mile) hike to Upper Galatea Lake. **Ribbon Creek** is another popular trek that offers the option of a backcountry visit. The campsite is at Ribbon Falls, an 8-km (5-mile) ascent through a stunning valley surrounded by impressive ridges. From here, it's another 2km (1.2 miles) to Ribbon Lake. This section of the trail involves climbing a steep cliff, and chains are fastened into the cliff face.

Golfing

At **Kananaskis Country Golf Course** (☎ **403-591-7272**), 26km (16 miles) south of the Trans-Canada Highway, two courses offer 36 holes of spectacular scenery. Mount Lorette and Mount Kidd tower over the lush fairways, which sit at 1,524 meters (5,000 feet) above sea level. Green fees are C$70 (US$49).

Horseback riding

Boundary Ranch, 26km (16 miles) south of the Trans-Canada Highway on Highway 40, runs trail rides of between one and three hours along with overnight pack trips. Call ☎ **877-591-7177.**

Mountain Biking

Two-wheelers are welcome on numerous backcountry trails, including many that kick off from Kananaskis Village or the Ribbon Creek parking area. Maps are available at the visitor information centers. If you don't have a bike, rent one from **Peregrine Sports** in Kananaskis Village (☎ **403-591-7453**).

Skiing

Nikiska, downhill site for the 1988 Winter Olympics, features 28 runs and a vertical drop of 735 meters (2,412 feet). Farther south, **Fortress Mountain** offers six lifts, a snowboard half-pipe, and a 330-meter (1,082-foot) vertical rise. For snow conditions and ticket information, call ☎ **403-244-6665.** For cross-country skiers, the **Ribbon Creek** area just north of Kananaskis Village has 60km (37 miles) of groomed trails.

Peter Lougheed Provincial Park

This 500-sq.-km (195-sq.-mile) region, one of Alberta's largest provincial parks, features superb hiking, biking, and cross-country skiing along with a great selection of campgrounds. Peter Lougheed Provincial Park was named for a former Alberta premier who in the 1970s proposed setting aside land in Kananaskis Country for Albertans to enjoy.

Getting there

From the Trans-Canada Highway, drive 24km (15 miles) south on Highway 40.

Finding information

The **Peter Lougheed Visitor Information Centre** (☎ **403-591-6322**) is your first stop for news on trail conditions and park activities. In the interpretive area, you can learn about grizzlies, cougars, mountain sheep, and other park wildlife. The sunny lounge in this visitor center has a massive stone fireplace along one wall and is a favorite lunch spot for cross-country skiers. (Bring your lunch, there's no cafeteria.) Revive your overworked muscles in the coin-operated Shiatsu massage chair.

Where to stay

Mount Engadine Lodge

$$ North of Peter Lougheed Provincial Park

Unlike many backcountry lodges in the Canadian Rockies, this rustic getaway, just north of Peter Lougheed Provincial Park, is accessible by car. Lodge rooms go for about C$125 (US$88) a person in summer, very reasonable when you consider that rates include three meals. Baths and showers are shared. Two cabins are also available. The lodge is friendly, laid-back, and near great hiking, skiing, and wildlife watching.

On the Smith–Dorrien/Spray Lakes Rd., about 40km (25 miles) south of Canmore. ☎ *403-678-4080. E-mail:* info@mountengadine.com. *Internet:* www.mountengadine.com. *Rack rates: Lodge rooms C$125 (US$88) per person (double), Cabins from C$140 (US$98) per person. Rates include meals. MC, V.*

Kananaskis Camping (☎ 403-591-7226) operates six campgrounds in the park with a wide variety of trailer and walk-in tent sites. Most are first-come, first-served, but reservations are accepted at the **Boulton Creek** campground, which has a combination of pull-through, back-in, and tenting sites in private, treed areas along with a convenience store and casual eatery. Both Boulton Creek and the **Elkwood** campground, which is the largest in the park, have amphitheaters where you can catch interpretive theater programs on summer evenings. To reserve a spot at Boulton Creek or for information on other campsites in Peter Lougheed Provincial Park, call ☎ 403-591-7226 or visit Internet: www.kananaskis camping.com. On the Web site, you can check campsite vacancies and find reports on trail conditions. Rates are C$17 (US$12) per night.

Exploring the park

To really appreciate this park, summer or winter, you'll want to get out of your car and venture into the wilderness, on foot, by bike, or on skis.

Hiking

The park contains hundreds of kilometers of trails, including routes that link up with trails in Banff National Park, and Elk Lake Provincial Park in British Columbia. If you plan a backcountry trip, remember to get a permit. The Kananaskis Lakes Trail, which cuts off from Highway 40, takes you to the **Upper and Lower Kananaskis Lakes** and the starting points for numerous excellent day hikes. **Rawson Lake** is a 4-km

(2.5-mile) ascent through the forest to a lovely alpine lake ringed by mountain peaks. The trail up **Mount Indefatigable** is a tough grind, especially the first stretch, but totally worth it for stellar views of the Upper and Lower Kananaskis valleys. You gain 460 meters (1,500 feet) over about 2km (1.2 miles).

Mountain biking

Two-wheelers can explore 80km (50 miles) of trails. The 12-km (7.5-mile) paved trail that starts from the Visitor Information Centre is a family-friendly route. The Smith–Dorrien trail system, along old logging roads, is steeper and more challenging. Access is from Chester Lake or the Sawmill picnic area on the Smith–Dorrien/Spray Trail Road.

Skiing

The Kananaskis Lakes area is a favorite destination in winter, with more than 85km (53 miles) of groomed trails, most of which are suitable for novice and intermediate skiers. When you're ready for a lunch break, the park Visitor Information Centre has a lounge with a fireplace. Or, warm up at **Pocaterra Hut,** at the junction of Kananaskis Lakes Trail and the Smith–Dorrien/Spray Trail Road.

Fast Facts: Kananaskis Country

Area Code

☎ 403.

ATMs

Kananaskis Village, Mount Kidd RV Park.

Emergencies

Dial **911**.

Fees

No fee is charged to visit the park. Permits for backcountry camping cost C$3 (US$2.10) a night.

Fishing Licenses

For nonresidents of Alberta, a five-day permit costs C$20 (US$14) while an annual license is C$36 (US$25).

Hospitals

1100 Hospital Place (off Mountain Avenue), in Canmore. ☎ **403-678-5536.**

Information

Barrier Lake Visitor Information Centre (☎ **403-673-3985**).

Peter Lougheed Visitor Information Centre (☎ **403-591-6322**).

Post Office

Kananaskis Village.

Road Conditions and Weather

AMA Road Reports: ☎ **403-246-5853.** Call Environment Canada's 24-hour line ☎ **403-299-7878** for current conditions and storm warnings around the province.

Chapter 17

Waterton Lakes National Park

· ·

In This Chapter

▶ Exploring where mountain meets prairie

▶ Planning your stay in Waterton

▶ Hiking from lake to lake

▶ Finding the best beds and meals

· ·

*Y*ou're just as apt to encounter a mule deer or a bighorn sheep as a tourist in this park. Most visitors to the Canadian Rockies travel the Trans-Canada Highway through Banff National Park, perhaps with side trips to Jasper or stops at provincial parks along the way. Waterton isn't really on the road to anywhere, at least not anywhere in Canada. An out-of-the-way setting in the southwest corner of Alberta on the northern fringe of Montana's Glacier National Park (not to be confused with Glacier National Park in British Columbia) is precisely what makes Waterton special.

Even in the peak travel months of July and August, Waterton Townsite, the only commercial center in the park, isn't all that busy. (There aren't a lot of hotels, though, so you do need to book ahead.) In winter, the town looks deserted. As a matter of fact, it is: Fewer than 100 people live here year-round and all but a few hotels (and one restaurant) close before the snow flies. This all adds up to a tranquil, meditative kind of place that's a mecca for wilderness lovers.

Aside from its location off the traveled track, Waterton is unique among Canadian Rocky Mountain parks because of its diversity. Four ecological regions converge here: foothills parkland, montane, alpine, and subalpine. (Waterton is known as the place where mountain meets prairie.) In a mere 525 sq. km (202 sq. miles), this park shelters an amazing 250 species of birds and 60 species of mammals (moose, elk, deer, mountain goats, bears, wolves, and cougars, to name a few). And Waterton boasts more species of plants than Banff and Jasper parks combined.

Waterton Lakes National Park

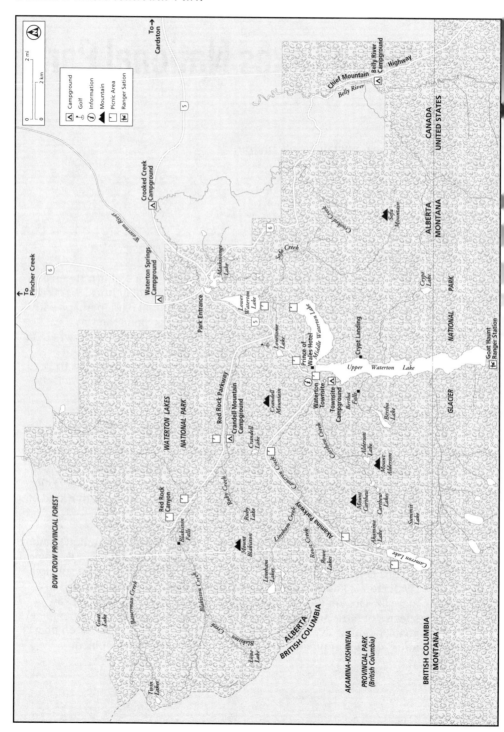

Much more wilderness lies on Waterton's southern border in Glacier National Park. (The two parks form the Waterton–Glacier International Peace Park.) In Glacier, the premier excursion (summer only) is Going-to-the-Sun Road, an 82-km (52-mile) journey across the park, east to west, known for some of the most incredible mountain scenery in the world.

One downside of Waterton (unless you're a sailboarder or power generator) is the park's notorious windy weather. Guard your RV awnings.

The mule deer you see throughout Waterton Townsite (the guys with the big ears) appear tame and approachable, but keep your distance. Like any wild animal, they're unpredictable, especially in the spring, when females are protecting their young. Watch small children carefully, keep your dog on a leash, and give the deer a wide berth.

Must-See Attractions

Waterton is open year-round, but it's largely a summer destination. Most people visit in July and August, when the weather is warmest and driest. In these busy months, you'll want to have a hotel booked before you arrive. Spring is generally rainy, particularly in April and June, but the wildflowers are exquisite. The hiking season officially starts in early June (although some trails at high elevation are still snow covered) and runs to October. Nature lovers also find lots to marvel at in September and early October, when bear, elk, and deer feed on lower mountain slopes, migrating birds touch down in the park, and autumn colors are at their showiest. The top attractions in this park are animals, birds, fish, flowers, canyons, peaks, and viewpoints. Here's where to find them:

- **Cameron Lake:** Follow the 16-km (10-mile) Akamina Parkway through the Cameron Valley to this lovely lake, which you can stroll around or explore by boat.

- **Chief Mountain Highway:** Admire the Waterton Valley as you travel this scenic route to Glacier National Park. In Glacier, the steep, winding Going-to-the-Sun Road will leave you breathless.

- **Crypt Lake Hike:** A boat shuttle to the trailhead and an exhilarating climb to an alpine lake make this among the most raved-about hikes in the Canadian Rockies.

- **Red Rock Canyon:** As you drive the scenic Red Rock Parkway, you appreciate Waterton's reputation as the place where prairie meets mountain.

- **Upper Waterton Lake Boat Cruise:** A two-hour tour of this lake, the deepest in the Canadian Rockies (nearly 150 meters/500 feet), showcases rugged mountain scenery and includes a stopover in Montana.

Getting There

Waterton isn't a quick trip from anywhere — which is more or less the point.

Flying in

The closest major Canadian airport is in Calgary, 270km (168 miles) north of Waterton. **Air Canada** (☎888-247-2262; Internet: www.aircanada.ca) operates nonstop flights to Calgary from many Canadian and U.S. cities. **WestJet** (☎ 888-937-8538; Internet: www.westjet.ca) flies direct from many places in western Canada.

In the U.S., the closest airports are at Great Falls and Kalispell, Montana.

Driving in

From Calgary, head south on Highway 2 to Fort Macleod, then drive west on Highway 3 to Pincher Creek and follow Highway 6 south to the Waterton Lakes National Park gate. (At Pincher Creek, you can't miss the row of power-generating windmills silhouetted against the mountains. This part of southern Alberta is famously windy.)

You can reach Waterton in about three hours from Calgary, but you may want to budget extra time to stop at **Head-Smashed-In Buffalo Jump** while you're in the Fort Macleod area. This interpretive center demonstrates an ancient Plains Indian buffalo hunting technique and is one of the oldest, largest, and best preserved of such sites in the world. Drive 18km (11 miles) north and west of Fort Macleod. (☎ 403-553-2731).

From Lethbridge in southern Alberta, Waterton is a little more than an hour away. Drive south to Cardston on Highway 2, then west into Waterton on Highway 5.

Travelers arriving from British Columbia go through the Crowsnest Pass on Highway 3, and then head for Pincher Creek.

From Glacier National Park in Montana, you can take the Chief Mountain International Highway to the Chief Mountain border crossing, which is open only from about mid-May to September. Your other option (year-round) is to head for Cardston, then take Highway 5 to Waterton. From St. Mary in Glacier Park, Waterton is about a one-hour drive. You cross the international border at the Piegan/Carway crossing, which is open year-round.

Planning Ahead

A Visitor Information Centre is open from early May to the end of September. Call ☎ 403-859-5133. In winter, call Park Headquarters at ☎ 403-859-2224; Internet: www.parkscanada.gc.ca.

For help booking accommodation, write or call the Waterton Lakes Chamber of Commerce and Visitors Association, Box 55, Waterton Park, AB T0K 2M0. ☎ 403-859-2224; Internet: www.watertonchamber.com.

Frontcountry (road-accessible) camping in the park is first-come, first-served. You can, however, reserve backcountry campsites. From April 1 to May 8, call the Warden's Office, ☎ 403-859-5140. After May 8, call ☎ 403-859-5133.

When you pack for a visit to Waterton, *windproof* and *rainproof* are the words to remember — any time of year. Next to the Crowsnest Pass, Waterton is the windiest place in Alberta. It also gets the most precipitation. Hikers can expect to encounter sun, wind, rain, and snow on backcountry trails — and all on the same day. Summers here are relatively cool, although the thermometer occasionally does hit 35° Celsius (94° Fahrenheit). Winters are fairly mild, thanks to chinooks, warm dry winds that sweep across southern Alberta and send temperatures soaring.

Figuring Out the Lay of the Land

Waterton sits in Alberta's southwest corner, bordered by the province of British Columbia to the west, the Bow-Crow Forest in Alberta to the north and east, and Glacier National Park, Montana, to the south.

Routes to Waterton park gates are Highway 6 through Pincher Creek, Alberta; Highway 5 through Cardston, Alberta; and in summer, the Chief Mountain Highway (Highway 17) through Glacier Park in the U.S.

On the Entrance Road (Highway 5), from the park gate into Waterton Townsite, you pass the chain of lakes for which this park was named (by Lieutenant Blakiston of the Palliser Expedition, in honor of British naturalist Charles Waterton). The largest, Upper Waterton Lake, drops into the U.S. and is the deepest lake in the Canadian Rockies. The Entrance Road also skirts by the turnoffs to Red Rock Parkway, the Prince of Wales Hotel, and Akamina Parkway before heading into the townsite, which crouches against Upper Waterton Lake.

Arriving in the Park

Waterton Townsite, where you find souvenir shops and restaurants, is essentially one main street (Waterton Avenue) near the shores of Upper Waterton Lake. Hotels are clustered along the lakeshore and near Windflower Avenue, one street back. For a quick tour of the town on foot, stroll the pathway that loops along the waterfront, past the campground, and out to Cameron Falls.

A currency exchange is located in **Tamarack Village Square** on Mountain Road, near the marina. If you need gear, Tamarack Village also sells hiking shirts, boots, packs, and guidebooks.

Finding information

The **Visitor Information Centre** (☎ 403-859-5133) is just minutes past the Waterton park gate on the road to the Waterton Townsite. It's open from early May to the end of September. Pick up a free map of Waterton's hiking trails and check in with park staff for the latest news on trail conditions and wildlife activity.

In the townsite, visit the **Heritage Centre** at 117 Waterton Avenue to find books on the park's history, wildlife, and trails. Run by the local natural history association, it's open from mid-May to September 30, daily from 10 a.m. to 6 p.m.

Paying fees

To visit Waterton, you buy either a daily pass (C$5/US$3.50 adults, C$4/US$3 seniors, C$2.50/US$2 youth, C$12.50/US$9 groups), or an annual pass (C$30/US$21 adults, C$22/US$15 seniors, C$15/US$11 youth, C$63/US$44 groups). If you're traveling to other national parks in the Rockies or elsewhere in Canada, an annual National Parks Pass (C$45/US$32 adults, C$38/US$27 seniors, C$22/US$15 youth, C$89/US$62 groups) gets you into 27 national parks in the country. It's good for one year from the date you purchase it.

Camping fees at the Townsite Campground, which has both tenting and full-service sites, are C$18 to C$24 (US$13 to US$17) a night. If you're planning an overnight hike, see "Backcountry adventures" later in this chapter. Fishing licenses cost C$7 (US$4.90) per day, C$20 (US$14) for an annual pass.

Getting around

Although you can start hiking on some trails right in town, most hikes begin along the Red Rock Parkway, Akamina Parkway, or at Cameron Lake, so you'll need to drive, cycle, or catch one of Waterton's Hiker Shuttles.

To rent a mountain bike, road bike, or scooter, visit **Pat's** at 224 Mountain View Road (☎ **403-859-2266**). Bikes cost C$30 to C$40 (US$21 to US$28) a day, scooters are C$65 (US$46). You can also rent by the hour.

For information on shuttle services to Cameron Lake and trails in the Goat Haunt area in Glacier Park, check in with **Waterton Outdoor Adventures** in Tamarack Village Square or call ☎ **403-859-2378.** For the shuttle boat to the **Crypt Lake** trailhead, call ☎ **403-859-2362.**

Enjoying the Park

Cameron Lake

The scenic Akamina Parkway through the Cameron Valley to Cameron Lake passes the trailheads for several popular hikes, including the Lineham and Rowe Creek Trails, as well as the site of western Canada's first producing oil well. At Cameron Lake, have a picnic, go fishing, take a hike, or rent a boat. Canoes, pedal boats, rowboats, and kayaks go for C$20 (US$14) an hour. (They don't take credit cards.) Kids can peer into a telescope to search for bears in the meadows on the other side of the lake.

Don't fish from the shore along the open slopes at the south end of Cameron Lake. It's a favorite grizzly bear hangout. In fact, the lake area in general is popular with bears. You must carry out fish and fish guts in odor-proof bags.

The road to Cameron Lake (Akamina Parkway) is just south of the Visitor Information Centre. It's 16km (10 miles) to the lake.

Chief Mountain Highway

If Glacier National Park in Montana is on your agenda, you travel this highway to the international border crossing (open mid-May to the end of September). Or, just take a drive. You travel through wetlands that provide important wildlife habitat, and get great views of the Waterton Valley. You also pass the site of the massive Sofa Mountain forest fire, sparked by lightning, that burned 1,521 hectares (3,756 acres) in September 1998.

Chief Mountain Hwy. runs south from Waterton park gates. It's 22km (14 miles) to the border.

Going-to-the-Sun Road

The spectacular summer-only highway across Glacier National Park, called the Going-to-the-Sun Road, winds along two lakeshores close to the cliffs below the Continental Divide. A visitor center is located at Logan Pass. You will notice lots of spots to turn off and ogle the views. Unfortunately, you can't drive the steepest sections if your vehicle is longer than 6 meters (21 feet) or wider than 2.5 meters (8 feet). And if you plan to cycle the Going-to-the-Sun Road, check in with a visitor center before you set out. Some stretches of the highway are closed to bicycle traffic from 11 a.m. to 4 p.m.

Red Rock Canyon

Check out views of Waterton's highest peak, Mount Blakiston (2,920 meters/9,580 feet), as you wind through the Blakiston Valley along Red Rock Parkway. June is the best time to appreciate the wildflowers. The parkway is also a good area to observe the sudden transition between mountain and prairie for which Waterton is known. You can follow a short hiking trail (less than 1km/half a mile) around the narrow, red-rocked canyon.

The Red Rock Parkway starts along the Entrance Rd. (Hwy. 5), 4.2km (2.6 miles) from the park gate. You drive 15km (9 miles) to the canyon.

Upper Waterton Lake Cruise

Boat tours of Upper Waterton Lake, the deepest lake in the Canadian Rockies, showcase gorgeous mountain scenery and get you close to the shoreline, where you're apt to spot deer, moose, bighorn sheep, or bears. The tour takes about two hours, including a visit to Goat Haunt in Montana's Glacier National Park. If you're just visiting the shore area with this tour, you don't need to clear Customs in the U.S. You must do so, however, if you're hiking into this area or staying overnight. Check in with the Park Rangers at Goat Haunt.

Buy tickets at the Marina in Waterton Townsite, ☎ 403-859-2362. C$25 (US$18) adults, C$13 (US$9) youth, C$9 (US$6) children 4–12. Early May to early Oct. Boats depart in July and Aug at 10 a.m., 1 p.m., 4 p.m., and 7 p.m., less frequently in spring and fall.

You can buy a one-way boat ticket to Goat Haunt in Montana (C$15/US$11) and hike back to Waterton Townsite along a 13-km (8-mile) trail.

Taking a hike

Waterton's 200km (120 miles) of trails, mostly doable in a day, deliver you to alpine lakes, spectacular falls, and marvelous mountain peaks. Beyond the park, Waterton's hiking network links to trails in Glacier National Park, Montana, and Akamina–Kishinena Provincial Park in B.C. Before you venture out, check with the **Visitor Information Centre** (☎ **403-859-5133**) for an update on trail conditions and wildlife activity. For guided hikes, call **Canadian Wilderness Tours,** ☎ **403-859-2058,** or **Waterton Outdoor Adventures** ☎ **403-859-2378.**

Bear's Hump

While you're in the vicinity of the information center, get your hiking legs into gear with a quick climb up this steep trail. Your reward: a great view of Waterton Townsite. The whole trip takes only about an hour.

Distance: 2.8km (1.8 miles) round-trip. Level: Moderately difficult. Access: Visitor Information Centre.

Bertha Lake

In spring, you're smitten with blue violets, yellow columbines, and a smashing mix of other wildflowers. This trail is also a good place to spot beargrass, a tall plant with tuft-like flowers that's considered the unoffical emblem of the park. You climb through a pine forest to Lower and Upper Bertha Falls, then hike a steeper section up to Bertha Lake. Bertha Lake makes an excellent half-day (four-hour) hike.

Distance: 11km (7 miles) round-trip. Level: Easy to Moderate. Access: Townsite: Cameron Falls.

Do bears eat this?

Waterton is the only national park in Canada where you see **beargrass,** a tall, showy lily with white, tuft-like blossoms. Some years, whole slopes are covered. (Individual plants flower only once in about every seven years.) Bertha Falls is a good spot to look. Don't panic: Despite its name, beargrass isn't common food for bears. Deer and elk nibble the flowers, though, and mountain goats snack on the leaves.

Day pack checklist

Before you head out for the day, put on your sturdy boots, grab a wide-brimmed hat, and toss the following into a day pack:

✔ two pairs of socks

✔ rain jacket/windbreaker

✔ wind pants

✔ something to pull on if the temperature drops

✔ sunscreen and sunglasses

✔ insect repellent

✔ flashlight

✔ first aid kit and matches

✔ map, guidebook

✔ camera, film

✔ food and lots of water

Carthew/Alderson

The trail to Carthew Summit, past Carthew and Alderson lakes, boasts some of the most stellar views in Waterton and, not surprisingly, is among the most popular hikes. From the summit, you gaze into Glacier Park. The hike starts at Cameron Lake on the Akamina Parkway and ends in the townsite, so you need a ride to the trailhead. (Or catch the Hiker Shuttle service from town ☎ **403-859-2378.** In summer, it runs hourly beginning at 8 a.m.) Plan to be on the trail for six or seven hours.

Distance: 20km (12.4 miles) one way. Level: Moderate. Access: Cameron Lake.

Crypt Lake

On this exhilarating trail, you gain 700 meters (2,296 feet). In the process, you pass four stunning waterfalls, climb through a narrow tunnel, and cross a sheer rock face along a narrow edge. (Hikers hold on to a cable that's fastened into the rock. All the same, if you suffer from vertigo, this may not be the trail for you.) Enjoy your lunch along the shores of a stellar alpine lake. But don't expect solitude; Crypt Lake is one of the best-known hikes in the Canadian Rockies. Access to Crypt Landing, where the trail starts, is by boat, so groups of hikers depart together. In July and August, boats leave from the marina in Waterton Townsite at 9 and 10 a.m. daily and return to pick up hikers at 4:00 and 5:30 p.m. To check departure times in other months, call ☎ **403-859-2362.**

Distance: 17.2km (10.6 miles), round trip. Level: Moderately difficult. Access: Crypt Landing. Buy tickets for the boat shuttle at the marina in Waterton Townsite. C$13 (US$9) adults, C$6.50 (US$4.50) children under 12.

Following family-friendly trails

The **Lakeshore Trail at Cameron Lake** is a popular family jaunt. The 3.2-km (2-mile) route takes about an hour and treats hikers to impressive views of the valley and surrounding peaks. For a shorter stroll, drive along the Red Rock Parkway and wander around **Red Rock Canyon.** It's 1.4km (1 mile) — allow about 20 minutes.

Being bear aware

Bear attacks are not common. Having said that, Waterton is home to both black bears and grizzlies, and when you trek through their territory, you need to take some safety measures.

Bears don't want to meet up with hikers; they prefer digging for roots and munching on buffalo berries. So don't sneak up on them. Hike noisily: sing, yodel, clap your hands. Hike in a group. Some hikers wear bells on their shoes or packs, but *don't rely on these.* Be especially loud near streams and in windy weather. If a bear hears you coming, it will probably move out of the way. Hike only on designated trails and avoid hiking early in the morning or after dark. Be alert for diggings, and turned-over rocks and logs — evidence that a bear has been in the area, and that you should leave.

You're no doubt wondering what to do if, despite heeding this advice, you run into a bear on the trail. Bears (like people) are hard to predict, but here are some guidelines.

✔ Stay calm and speak quietly. (This isn't the time to make noise.)

✔ Detour around the bear, if you can, but don't run.

✔ Be sure to give the bear an escape route.

✔ Back away slowly, but stop if this agitates the bear.

✔ Keep your pack on for protection.

✔ If the bear attacks, use pepper spray, if you have it. It's been shown to be effective in some situations.

✔ If the bear makes contact, play dead. Lie on your stomach with legs apart and your hands crossed behind your neck. Stay in this position until you're sure the bear has left the area.

Backcountry adventures

You need a Wilderness Pass (C$8/US$6 a night) to overnight in one of the 12 backcountry campsites in Waterton. Pick it up at the Visitor Information Centre. An annual Wilderness Pass (C$56/US$40) is good for Banff, Jasper, Kootenay, Yoho, and Waterton parks.

You can reserve a campsite up to 90 days before your trip. Between April 1 and May 8, call the Warden's Office ☎ **403-859-5410.** After May 8, call the Visitor Information Centre ☎ **403-859-5133.** The reservation fee (C$12/US$8 per trip) is payable by MasterCard or Visa.

Staying active

Providing you remember to pack your hiking boots or walking shoes, you'll have the basic gear for getting to numerous scenic spots in Waterton Lakes National Park. Having said that, you can rent more specialized equipment, should you require, for instance, a boat, a fishing rod, or perhaps a horse. Following are some of the park's more popular pursuits.

Biking

Four backcountry trails are designated for mountain bikes, and a map is available from the Visitor Information Centre. Aside from the hiking trails, Cameron Lake and Red Rock Canyon are popular destinations for two-wheelers. Rent wheels at **Pat's,** 224 Mountain Road (☎ **403-859-2266**).

Birding

Waterton's diverse habitat appeals to over 250 species of birds. Maskinonge Lake, near the park entrance, is considered the top spot for bird watchers. The best time to visit is fall, when geese, ducks, and swans migrate through the park.

Canoeing and Kayaking

The best spot is Cameron Lake, where you can rent boats for C$20 (US$14) an hour. The south end of the lake is grizzly bear territory, so *stay in your boat.*

Power boats are prohibited in most park lakes, the exceptions being Upper and Middle Waterton lakes.

Fishing

Rainbow trout, brown trout, and mountain whitefish are just a few of the species found in the park. The angling season generally runs from the end of June to the end of September, except in the case of Akamina, Cameron, Crandell, and Upper and Middle Waterton lakes, which are open until the end of October. Fishing licenses cost C$7 (US$5) a day, C$20 (US$14) for an annual permit. At **Pat's,** 224 Mountain View Road (☎ 403-859-2266), you can buy permits and rent gear.

Horseback riding

To saddle up and explore the park on horseback, visit **Alpine Stables,** just outside Waterton Townsite (across from the golf course road). Call ☎ 403-859-2462. You pay about C$20 (US$14) for a one-hour trail ride, C$110 (US$77) for eight hours. The four-hour Lion's Head trip up the Vimy Mountain Trail is known for great scenery. Another good bet is the five-hour ride through pine and aspen forests to Crandell Lake.

Golfing

Green fees at the Waterton Lakes 18-hole golf course (☎ 403-859-2074) are C$33 (US$23). You pay C$27 (US$19) to rent a cart. Book a tee time by calling ☎ 403-859-2114.

If you're over 55, inquire about seniors' specials at the Waterton Lakes golf course. On certain mornings, two seniors can golf for the price of one.

Sailboarding

Waterton has a windy reputation and Upper Waterton Lake, near the Townsite Campground, is one of the best spots to catch the gusts (pros only). *Note:* You need a wet suit. It's cold.

Where to Stay in Waterton Lakes National Park

Several hotels in the park are open year-round, but most close around mid-October and re-open in spring.

Aspen Village Inn
$$–$$$ **Waterton Townsite**

If you want to stay in your own cottage, head to the cheery Aspen Village complex, which offers duplex cottages ranging from a simple one-room unit with fridge and microwave to two-bedroom styles with full kitchens. Dine outside on your picnic table. Motel-style rooms are also available here, in two separate buildings.

111 Windflower Ave. ☎ *888-859-8669, 403-859-2255. Fax: 403-859-2255. E-mail:* reservations@aspenvillageinn.com. *Internet:* www.aspenvillage inn.com. *Rack rates: C$132–C$167 (US$92–US$117) double. May 1–Oct 15. AE, DC, DISC, MC, V.*

Bayshore Inn

$$–$$$ **Waterton Townsite**

The Bayshore is a big, two-story, motel-style complex near the marina. Step out your door and onto the lakefront pathway. Standard double rooms (C$135/US$95) are spacious, with high ceilings. The best locations are on the second level, overlooking the lake. If you feel like splurging, C$225 (US$158) buys you an enormous corner room with three windows and a dreamy lake view.

111 Waterton Ave. ☎ **888-527-9555**, *403-859-2211. Fax: 403-859-2291. E-mail:* info@bayshoreinn.com. *Internet:* www.bayshoreinn.com. *Rack rates: C$135–C$225 (US$95–US$158) double. May 1–Oct 15. AE, DC, DISC, MC, V.*

Crandell Mountain Lodge

$$–$$$ **Waterton Townsite**

One of the few spots in Waterton open year-round, this lovely inn, in a restored 1930s lodge, is run by an outgoing couple from southern Alberta. Each room is unique and all are charmingly country. Some have fireplaces. Suites with kitchens are also available. The lodge doesn't have a dining room, but in summer, restaurants are a short stroll away. The Lamp Post Dining Room in the Kilmorey Lodge is just across the street and open year-round.

102 Mount View Rd. ☎ **866-859-2288**, *403-859-2288. Fax: 403-859-2288. E-mail:* crandell@telusplanet.net. *Internet:* www.crandellmountainlodge. com. *Rack rates: C$139–C$199 (US$97–US$139) double. DISC, MC, V.*

Kilmorey Lodge

$$–$$$ **Waterton Townsite**

This historic inn was one of the first buildings in town. A favorite with many regular visitors to Waterton, Kilmorey Lodge has the look and feel of a traditional country inn, but you get modern touches such as high-speed Internet and jetted tubs. It's open year-round. Rates include breakfast, and the restaurant here is considered the top spot to dine in the park.

At townsite entrance on Emerald Bay. ☎ **888-859-8669**, *403-859-2334. Fax: 403-859-2342. E-mail:* kilmorey@telusplanet.net. *Internet:* www.kilmorey lodge.com. *Rack rates: C$108–C$213 (US$76–US$149) double. AE, DISC, MC, V.*

Prince of Wales Hotel
$$$$ **Waterton Townsite**

When you pass through the park gates and head into town, you spot the distinctive gabled roof, high on a wind-battered bluff. The Prince of Wales was built in 1927, and it's still kind of rustic and wild (no TVs, no air-conditioning). The cheapest rooms (C$269/US$188), on the fifth level in the former staff-quarters area, are tiny. Take the elevator to the fourth floor and a narrow staircase to the next level. You can, of course, splurge on more space, but for the money, Waterton has nicer rooms. All the same, the Prince of Wales has a certain romance. Check it out with a visit to the restaurant or have a before-dinner drink in the casual lounge.

Box 33, Waterton Park (turn off the Park Entrance Rd., across from the Visitor Information Centre). ☎ *403-859-2231. Fax: 403-859-2630. E-mail:* pwhmgr@ glacierparkinc.com. *Internet:* www.princeofwaleswaterton.com. *Rack rates: C$269–C$339 (US$188–US$237) double. May 1–Sept. AE, MC, V.*

Waterton Glacier Suites
$$$–$$$$ **Waterton Townsite**

This spiffy hotel, new in 1998, is decked out in fieldstone with a sky-blue metal roof. It's open all year, and rooms boast full amenities, including whirlpools and fireplaces. Glacier Suites is run by the same folks who own the Bayshore Inn, so guests get a 10% discount at the Bayshore's Kootenai Brown Dining Room (see "Where to Eat in Waterton Lakes National Park" later in this chapter).

107 Windflower Ave. ☎ *866-621-3330, 403-859-2004. Fax: 403-859-2118. E-mail:* info@watertonsuites.com. *Internet:* www.watertonsuites.com. *Rack rates: C$169–C$269 (US$118–US$188) double. AE, MC, V.*

Waterton Lakes Lodge
$$$–$$$$ **Waterton Townsite**

The 80 rooms in this elegantly rustic resort complex are located in nine separate buildings, including a main lodge. Rooms on the upper floors of the lodge have high ceilings and some bathrooms feature skylights. In the other buildings, deluxe rooms include jetted tubs and gas fireplaces. All buildings offer lovely mountain views. A hostel, located in the complex and operated by Hostelling International, can accommodate 21 people and is open year-round. Call the hotel for reservations.

101 Clematis Avenue. ☎ *888-985-6343, 403-859-2150. E-mail:* reservations@ watertonlakeslodge.com. *Internet:* www.watertonlakeslodge.com. *Rack rates: C$215-C$315 (US$151-US$221) double. AE, DISC, MC, V.*

Runner-up lodging

Northland Lodge

$–$$ Waterton Townsite

Built in 1929 as a private residence for the developer of the Prince of Wales Hotel, this quiet rooming house (mid-May to mid-October) is just south of Cameron Falls. Most rooms have private baths.

☎ *403-859-2353. Internet:* www.northlandlodgecanada.com.

Campgrounds

None of the park's frontcountry (road-accessible) campsites take reservations: It's first-come, first served. In July and August, they often fill up by early afternoon. The **Waterton Townsite Campground** (☎ **403-859-2224**) is open from about mid-May to October and offers 95 full-service sites (power, water, sewer) along with 143 unserviced sites. Camping fees are C$18 to C$24 (US$13 to US$17). No open fires are allowed, only gas stoves or barbecues. The kitchen shelters have woodstoves. The Townsite Campground is beside Upper Waterton Lake. Prepare for windy weather.

Beyond the town, you can pitch your tent at **Crandell Mountain** (☎ **403-859-5133**) off the Red Rock Parkway for C$14 (US$10) a night, or the **Belly River** site (☎ **403-859-2224**) on the Chief Mountain Highway for C$12 (US$8) a night. These two campgrounds don't have showers.

You also find a number of camping spots outside Waterton Park boundaries. The 31-hectare (77-acre) **Waterton Springs Campground** (☎ **403-859-2247**), 3km (1.2 miles) north of the park, has 60 full-service sites (C$24/US$17 per night), 13 with electricity only (C$19/US$13 per night), and more than 75 tenting spots (C$17/US$12 per night). A convenience store and laundry facilities are located on-site. Reservations are accepted. You can usually get a spot here, but sites close to the washrooms fill up fast, especially on weekends. The **Crooked Creek Campground** (☎ **403-653-1100**), operated by Waterton's natural history association, also takes reservations. It's 5.6km (3.5 miles) east of the park on Highway 5. Full-service sites cost C$18 (US$13) per night, sites with electricity only C$15 (US$11) per night, and tenting spots C$11 (US$8) per night.

If you're planning an overnight hike, see "Backcountry adventures" earlier in this chapter.

Where to Eat in Waterton Lakes National Park

Except for the **Lamp Post Dining Room,** which is open year-round, Waterton restaurants close from about mid-October until mid-May. Even in summer, the town doesn't offer a surplus of eateries, although you find something for every budget. For a fast coffee and muffin to go, stop by **Waterton Bagel or Borderline Books & Café,** both on Windflower Avenue.

Kootenai Brown Dining Room
$$$ Waterton Townsite   CANADIAN

The chef concentrates on conventional steak and seafood numbers (filet mignon, trout almondine), but look for a few Indian specialties such as Tandoori chicken. The samosas on the appetizer list are terrific. If you're a tea lover, ask to see the separate tea menu. The wood-paneled dining room opens onto a lakefront patio. If you're heading for the hiking trails, the folks at the Bayshore will pack you a lunch to go for C$10.50 (US$7).

Bayshore Inn (on Main St.). ☎ *403-859-2211. Main courses: C$25 (US$18). AE, MC, V. Daily 7 a.m.–10 p.m.*

Little Italian Cafe
$$ Waterton Townsite   ITALIAN

You'll find hefty portions of reasonably priced pasta here. Choose your noodles (penne, jumbo shells, and fettuccine, to name a few) and select a sauce (about 20 choices). This bright and breezy cafe also does halibut, veal, and a couple of veggie specials. On the wine list, four reds and four whites are available by the glass or half-liter. Kids under 12 eat for C$4.95 (US$3.47), which includes a main course, a beverage, and an ice-cream sundae.

Waterton Ave. ☎ *403-859-0003. Main courses: C$15–C$20 (US$11–US$14), pastas: C$12–C$14 (US$8–US$9). MC, V.*

Lamp Post Dining Room
$$$$ Waterton Townsite   ITALIAN

Ask any Waterton resident to recommend a restaurant and they point you in the direction of the Kilmorey Lodge. If you plan to check out the Lamp Post, be sure to call ahead. This place has a big following. The menu varies, but you're apt to see a strong lineup of Alberta beef, creative fish and seafood dishes, and regional numbers such as Canadian maple pork and triple-berry elk chops. Look for an awesome selection of Canadian wines.

In the Kilmorey Lodge. ☎ *403-859-2334. Main courses: C$20–C$28 (US$14–US$20). AE, MC, V. Daily 7:30 a.m.–10:00 p.m.*

Pizza of Waterton

$$ **Waterton Townsite**   PIZZA

Wander along Mountain View Road to Fountain Avenue to sample the best pizza in town. Okay, they don't have a lot of competition. But the pizza *is* good. This quaint little spot (blink and you miss it) also does soups, wraps, and other quick meals, but pizza's the best bet. The wine list includes both Canadian and imported selections. Dine inside or out on the deck.

103 Fountain Ave. ☎ *403-859-2660. Medium pizza: C$15 (US$11). MC. Mon–Fri 5–10 p.m., Sat & Sun noon to 10 p.m.*

Royal Stewart Dining Room

$$$$ **Waterton Townsite**   CONTINENTAL

Dine on filet of salmon in a fine herb crust, New York steak, or rack of lamb while you admire the scenery. The formal dining room in the Prince of Wales hotel boasts the top lake view in town: a sweeping hilltop panorama. You pay for it, of course. Main courses here are about $10 higher than those at the Kilmorey Lodge, Waterton's other fine dining establishment.

In the Prince of Wales Hotel. ☎ *403-859-2231. Main courses: C$30–C$35 (US$21–US$25). AE, MV, V. Daily 6:30–9:30 a.m., 11:30 a.m.–2:00 p.m., 5:00–9:30 p.m.*

Zum's Eatery

$$ **Waterton Townsite**   STEAK AND BURGERS

Fried chicken gets top billing at this always bustling, family-friendly eatery. Zum's also serves steak, grilled sandwiches, and burgers. Sit on the street-front patio and watch the deer stroll by. Or, eat inside and ponder the decor: a curious mix of license plates, beer posters, and patio umbrella lampshades. Service is friendly and fast. If you're traveling with kids, Zum's is a safe bet — nobody will notice a little extra commotion. It's also a good breakfast spot.

116B Waterton Ave. (Main St.). ☎ *403-859-2388. Main courses: C$10–C$15 (US$7–US$11). 8 a.m.–9 p.m.*

Fast Facts: Waterton Lakes National Park

Area Code

☎ 403.

ATMs

Banking machines are located in the Rocky Mountain Food Mart on Windflower Avenue, Tamarack Village Square, and Pat's, 224 Mountain View Rd.

Emergencies

RCMP (May to October) ☎ 403-859-2244. Park Wardens ☎ 403-859-2224.

Fees

A day pass to Waterton costs C$5 (US$3.50) for adults, C$12.50 (US$9) for groups. An annual National Parks Pass, for all national parks in Canada, is C$45 (US$31) for adults, C$89 (US$62) for groups.

Fishing Licenses

Fishing licenses are sold at the Visitor Information Centre, Cameron Lake Boat Rentals, and at Pat's, 224 Mountain View Rd.: C$7 (US$5) per day or C$20 (US$14) for an annual pass.

Hospitals

The closest hospitals are in Cardston (☎ 403-653-4411) and Pincher Creek (☎ 403-627-3333).

Information

Call ☎ 403-859-5133 in summer, ☎ 403-859-2224 in winter.

Post Office

Located at the corner of Windflower and Fountain avenues.

Road Conditions and Weather

To check road conditions in southern Alberta, dial ☎ 403-246-5853. For weather, call ☎ 403-299-7878, 24 hours.

Taxes

Alberta is the only province in Canada with no provincial sales tax. The 7% national Goods & Services Tax (GST), however, applies to most goods and services, although visitors can apply for a rebate on some purchases. You also pay a 5% hotel tax.

Time Zone

Mountain Standard.

Web Site

www.parkscanada.gc.ca

Part V

Across the Great Divide: The British Columbia Rockies

The 5th Wave   By Rich Tennant

GWEN AND EDMUND ENTER...
GRAND TEAPOT NATIONAL PARK

©RICHTENNANT

In this part...

This part deals with the British Columbia Rockies, which differ from the Alberta Rockies not only because they're on the opposite side of the Continental Divide, but also because they're somewhat less well known — and less touristy — than Banff and Jasper. (British Columbia, on the whole, is also way more laid-back than Alberta — but that's a subject for another book.) You may be only vaguely aware of Kootenay National Park or Yoho National Park (which is as fun to visit as it is to pronounce). In this part, I fill you in on the highlights of travel through both parks. I tour you around the town of Golden, which is surrounded by mountains. This section also includes information on several provincial parks in British Columbia. A couple of them are fairly challenging to reach, but, in case you're game, I do brief you on arranging helicopter flights.

Chapter 18

Golden

● ●

In This Chapter

▶ Getting to Golden and finding your way around

▶ Locating the best beds and meals

▶ Touring the town

▶ Blasting down mountains and leaping off cliffs

● ●

*T*his mountain town is full of people who think it's perfectly normal to hurl themselves off a more than 1,500-meter (5,000-foot) ledge, plunge down a river known for its 2.5-meter (8-foot) waves, or scale a wall of sheer ice. In Golden, you see mountains everywhere you turn: the Rockies to the east, and the Purcells and the Selkirks to the west. Add two rivers — the Columbia and the aptly named Kicking Horse, which converge here — and you have a town preordained for adventure.

Guided adventure has a long tenure in Golden. In the early 1900s, the newly completed Canadian Pacific Railway brought professional mountain guides here from Switzerland to lead climbers up as-yet-unnamed peaks. Nonetheless, the town's economy came to rely more on the forest industry than the visitor trade. Golden never really made the tourist circuit, except as a spot to fuel up on trips from Vancouver to Banff.

The town still has a raw edge — it's more lumber town than tourist attraction. (You don't find a lot of restaurants where work boots are out of place.) But these days, powder hounds are catching word of a great ski resort on Kicking Horse mountain that opened here in the winter of 2000–01, and new, upscale mountain lodges are starting to lure hikers and wildlife enthusiasts with outdoor hot tubs and sumptuous meals.

The community is also home to an amazing number of outfitters. If you've always wanted to try extreme whitewater rafting, here's your chance. If the rapids don't get your adrenaline pumping, investigate mountain bike racing, rock climbing, or paragliding. Numerous calmer pursuits, such as bird-watching float trips through the Columbia River wetlands, are possible as well.

Golden

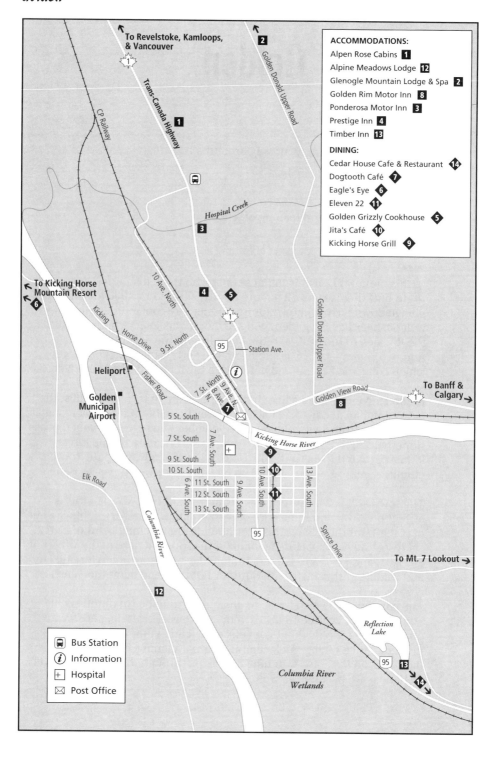

Getting There

Golden is surrounded by national parks: Yoho and Banff to the east, Glacier to the west, and Kootenay to the southeast. It's on the Trans-Canada Highway at the junction with Highway 95, which runs south through Radium Hot Springs to the Canada–U.S. border.

Driving in

From Calgary, follow the Trans-Canada Highway west through Banff and Yoho national parks. Allow about three hours. Golden is nine hours east of Vancouver. From the Canada–U.S. border at Kingsgate, drive about four hours (328km/205 miles) north on Highway 95.

Golden is in the mountain time zone, like Alberta, which is one hour later than most of British Columbia.

Busing in

Greyhound Canada (☎ **800-661-8747**) offers regular service between Golden and each of Calgary, Banff, and Vancouver. Greyhound also runs buses south to Cranbrook. The bus station in Golden (☎ 250-344-6172) is on the Trans-Canada Highway, next to Humpty's Restaurant at 1402 North Trans-Canada Highway. It's open Monday to Saturday from 8 a.m. to 7 p.m., and Sundays and holidays from 10 a.m. to 4 p.m.

Orienting Yourself and Getting Around Golden

Cruising the Trans-Canada Highway through Golden, you pass one motel after another, interspersed with service stations, family restaurants, and fast-food spots. It's easy to overnight here without investigating the downtown, but that's where you find the best meals.

Golden's modest downtown sits at the confluence of the Kicking Horse and Columbia rivers. From the Trans-Canada Highway, head south on Highway 95. You might want to stop by the **Visitor Information Centre** at 500–10th Avenue North (☎ **800-622-4653**, 250-344-7125).

Streets are in a numbered grid. To find an address, you need to know whether it's north or south of the Kicking Horse River. On the north side, along Main Street (10th Avenue North), you find a handful of cafes and restaurants, along with shops that sell and rent bikes and sports gear. A few more restaurants, grocery stores, and shops are found south of the bridge along Highway 95, which runs south to Radium Hot Springs.

To cross the Kicking Horse River on foot or by bike, follow 8th Avenue North to the covered pedestrian bridge. This masterpiece, completed in 2001, was built by volunteer timber framers from around the world, constructed on the riverbank and heaved into place by cranes.

Where to Stay in Golden

If you plan to visit during the height of summer (mid-July to mid-August), try to arrive before 3 p.m. — or better yet, reserve a hotel in advance.

Alpen Rose Cabins

$–$$

If you're looking for lodging on the main route through Golden and plan to fix some meals yourself, Alpen Rose is the spot to head for. These six log cabins, perched on a hill above the Trans-Canada Highway on the western edge of town, are fresh and airy with well-equipped kitchens. Each is lovingly furnished and immaculately maintained, with an impressive view from its deck.

448 Althoff Rd. ☎ ***250-344-5549.*** *Fax: 250-344-5375. E-mail:* infor@alpenrose cabins.com. *Internet:* www.alpenrosecabins.com. *Rack rates: C$75–C$125 (US$53–US$88) double. MC, V.*

To check your e-mail, drop by the Rumor Mill Café at 420B–9th Avenue North, where computer time costs 12¢ a minute. You can also use a fax and scanner. Elsewhere in town, you find computers at Jita's Café, 1007B–11th Avenue South, and 180 Rental Equipment, 423–9th Avenue North. The Golden Women's Resource Centre on 9th Avenue North has two terminals that women can use at no cost.

Alpine Meadows Lodge

$$

This great getaway, on a 60-hectare (150-acre) site just west of the Columbia River, appeals to wilderness lovers. The setting is semi-secluded (it's just off the road to the Kicking Horse ski resort) and you can hike, mountain bike, or cross-country ski from your doorstep. Ten rooms on two levels surround a common area with a big fireplace. Rooms have private baths and are tastefully and simply furnished. All have great views, and from the breakfast room on the main floor you gaze out at Mount 7, a hang-gliding hot spot. Alpine Meadows is more private than a B&B, but more personal than a hotel.

717 Elk Rd. ☎ ***888-700-4477,*** *250-344-5863. Fax: 250-344-5853. E-mail:* info@ alpinemeadowslodge.com. *Internet:* www.alpinemeadowslodge.com. *Rack rates: C$109–C$129 (US$76–US$90) double. Rates include breakfast. AE, MC, V.*

Glenogle Mountain Lodge & Spa
$–$$$

Situated in a private wooded setting about a 10-minute-drive from the Trans-Canada Highway, this sparkling new spot (builders were laboring over final touches at press time) is the epitome of a Rocky Mountain lodge: towering ceilings, huge windows, and tons of wood, slate, and tile. Have a seat by the massive stone fireplace if you're in the mood for conversation, or retreat to the balcony off your own spacious room to watch the sunset. Besides 14 rooms in the lodge, three cabins are available. All rates include breakfast. The owners definitely know their way around the kitchen; in their previous careers, they ran a popular Golden bakery.

913 Oster Rd. ☎ _**250-344-7638.** Fax: 250-344-7638. E-mail:_ info@glenogle lodge.com. _Internet:_ www.glenoglelodge.com. _Rack rates: C$150–C$375 (US$105–US$263) double. MC,V._

Golden Rim Motor Inn
$

Be sure to ask for a room with a view. This rambling motel, immortalized in a song by the Canadian band Tragically Hip, sits above the Kicking Horse River overlooking the town of Golden. It's on the Trans-Canada Highway, 1km (about 0.5 mile) east of the junction with Highway 95. Rooms don't include many extras, but they're bright, spacious, and reasonably priced. Bighorn sheep often hang around the green area in front of the hotel.

1416 Golden View Rd. ☎ _**877-311-2216,** 250-344-2216. Fax: 250-344-6673. E-mail:_ goldrim@rockies.net. _Internet:_ www.rockies.net/~goldrim/. _Rack rates: C$59–C$98 (US$41–US$69) double. AE, MC, V._

Prestige Inn
$$–$$$

These are among the priciest rooms along this stretch of the highway, but they're nicely appointed and contain coffeemakers, irons, and other extras you live without at most lower-cost motels along the strip. Kitchen suites are also available. A restaurant and small gift shop are on-site.

1049 Trans-Canada Hwy. ☎ _**877-737-8433,** 250-344-7990. Fax: 250-344-7902. E-mail:_ golden@prestigeinn.com. _Internet:_ www.prestigeinn.com. _Rack rates: C$140–C$210 (US$98–US$147) double. AE, DISC, MC, V._

Timber Inn

$–$$

About 20 minutes' drive south of Golden on Highway 95, five timber-frame chalets on a hill above the Columbia River offer splendid views of the river valley and Purcell Mountains. People drive for miles to visit the restaurant here, known for fresh, regional cuisine with a German twist. (Timber Inn is run by a family from Germany's Black Forest region.) Besides the spiffy chalets, new in 2000, six rooms are available in the main lodge. All have private baths. Neither the lodge rooms nor the chalets have kitchens, but breakfast and dinner packages are available.

3483 Hwy. 95 (in Parson). ☎ *877-348-2228, 250-348-2228. Fax: 250-348-2292. E-mail:* info@timberinn.com. *Internet:* www.timberinn.com. *Rack rates: C$75–C$150 (US$53–US$105) double. MC, V.*

Runner-up lodging

Ponderosa Motor Inn

$

This is a good choice in the "just the essentials" category, but avoid the "economy rooms" at the back, which have small windows and are rather dim.

1206 Trans-Canada Hwy. ☎ *800-881-4233, 250-344-2205. Internet::* www.ponderosamotel.bc.ca.

Are we roughing it yet?

Contemplate the day's agenda over breakfast, after you decide what to have: muesli, yogurt, fresh bread, croissants, cranberry French toast, waffles, eggs Benedict, roast potatoes. . . . Let's just say the food at **Purcell Lodge** (☎ **250-344-2639**; Internet: www.Purcell.com) is a step above what you normally associate with wilderness cooking. A big step. Yet wilderness is definitely what you find here, right on your doorstep. A stay at Purcell Lodge, situated at an elevation of 2,195 meters (7,200 feet) in a remote area along the eastern boundary of Glacier National Park near Golden, is probably as civilized as life gets in the backcountry. The setting is unimaginably gorgeous. Ski, snowboard, or snowshoe in winter. In summer, hike over mountain ridges and photograph meadows of wildflowers. Helicopters fly guests to the lodge a couple of times a week from the Golden airport. In summer, you also have the option of hiking in along a 14-km (9-mile) trail. Packages vary, depending on the season and on the number of people sharing a room. For a three-night stay in summer, including guided activities, accommodation, meals, and the helicopter transportation, you pay C$1,400 to C$1,500 (US$980 to US$1,050) per person.

Where to Eat

Cedar House Café & Restaurant
$$–$$$$ CANADIAN

A menu based on local, organic vegetables and free-range meats is only one reason to make a quick detour south of Golden to the Cedar House. Along with your serving of beef tenderloin in balsamic reduction with truffle oil or your plate of wild salmon with chili butter, you get to savor a view over the Columbia wetlands from a sunny deck. The owners grow some of their own produce and feature B.C. wines on the menu.

735 Hefti Rd. (5km/3 miles south of Golden on Hwy. 95). ☎ 250-344-4679. Reservations recommended. Main course: C$14–C$32 (US$9–US$22). MC, V. Daily 5:00–10:30 p.m.

Dogtooth Cafe
$ BAKERY/CAFE

Kick-start your morning with a foamy cafe latte or a loaded breakfast burrito (eggs, tomato, and cheese, with chips and salsa on the side). Later in the day, roasted vegetables, goat cheese, rosemary chicken, and other trendy fillings are sandwiched together and grilled (C$7/US$4.90). Add salad or soup for C$3/US$2.10. This order-at-the-counter eatery serves imaginative fast food and is a popular local hangout. Tables spill onto a patio. The Kicking Horse River rushes by.

506–8th Ave. N. ☎ 250-344-4547. Most items under C$10 (US$7). MC, V. Mon–Sat 6:30 a.m.–7:00 p.m. Sun 7 a.m.–5 p.m.

Eagle's Eye
$$–$$$$ CANADIAN

This is the ski cuisine of your dreams. When you can stop gasping at the 360-degree view from your table — Eagle Eye (at the Kicking Horse Mountain ski resort) is Canada's loftiest restaurant, at 2,350 meters (7,700 feet) — feast your eyes on the creations emerging from the kitchen. Choose buffalo steak or maybe scallop-and-prawn ravioli, and prepare for a memorable meal. Save room for dessert. Sweet potato cheesecake never tasted so good. Between 11:30 a.m. and 3:00 p.m., you can buy a "sky lunch" for C$24.99 (US$17), including the gondola trip.

Kicking Horse Mountain Resort. ☎ 250-439-5400. Reservations recommended. Main course: C$18–C$35 (US$7–US$11). Transportation to the restaurant, by gondola: C$17/US$12 (adult) Fri to Sat evenings C$13/US$9 (adult). Summer: Mon–Thurs, 11 a.m.–3 p.m., Fri–Sun 11:30 a.m.–9:00 p.m. Ski season: Sun–Thurs 11 a.m.–4 p.m., Fri–Sun 11 a.m.–9 p.m.

Eleven 22

$$–$$$ **INTERNATIONAL**

Eleven 22, which used to be called Sisters & Beans, is part of a B&B in a historic house on the south side of the Kicking Horse River. The comfortable restaurant is casual and relaxed with international appeal. Rice bowls and pad thai share the menu with hummus and buffalo rib-eye. And you can order in any language you like (okay, at least four).

1122–10th Ave. S. ☎ *250-344-2443. Main course: C$12–C$25 (US$8–US$18). MC, V. Daily 5 p.m.–closing.*

Golden Grizzly Cookhouse

$$ **FAMILY**

This upbeat, youthful eatery satisfies bear-size appetites with mountainous portions of burgers, pastas, and pizzas. The decor features tomato sauce and tomato juice cans (Heinz and Primo). When you sit down, a server breezes over, introduces himself (or herself) and jots his or her name on your tablecloth. For dessert, there's a chocolate, chocolate, chocolate cake. If you're still hungry, order a "kitchen sink," which is a combination of *all* the sweet food on the planet.

1002 N. Trans-Canada Hwy. ☎ *250-439-1833. Main course: C$8–C$15 (US$7–US$11). AE, DC, MC, V. Daily 11 a.m.–midnight.*

Jita's Cafe

$ **BAKERY/CAFE**

If you're in the neighborhood of Summit Cycle, the cafe next door serves the best chai in town. Other good bets here are chicken curry and chapati wraps. Jita's Indian dinner (a set menu), available on Fridays from 6:30 p.m., is very popular. This cafe is also a great choice for a quick breakfast. Choose a nice, fresh scone or order eggs and a bagel.

1007B–11th Ave. S. ☎ *250-344-3660. Most items under C$10 (US$7). MC, V. Daily 7 a.m.–6 p.m. Open Fri until 9:30 p.m.*

Kicking Horse Grill

$$–$$$$ **INTERNATIONAL**

The world is full of tantalizing flavors. And they all meld together at the Kicking Horse Grill. You may find paella from Spain, nasi goreng from Indonesia, or noodles from Singapore. Salads here are first-rate, and the chef will toss in shrimp or chicken to create a main course. As a matter of fact, Kicking Horse is extraordinarily flexible all around. Children's tastes and appetites are cheerfully accommodated (although the candlelit setting and pristine tables may make you wish you had left the kids at home).

1105–9th St. S. ☎ *250-344-2330. Main course: C$16–C$22 (US$11–US$32). AE, MC, V. Daily 4:30–11:00 p.m.*

Exploring Golden

Ringed by mountain ranges and surrounded by national and provincial parks, Golden makes a convenient base for wilderness adventure. There's also plenty to do in the Golden area, particularly if you have a taste for the extreme.

Rent gear for hiking, climbing, or skiing at **180 Equipment Rentals** (☎ **250-344-4699**), 423–9th Avenue North Ski packages (skis, boots, and poles) range from C$23 to C$41 (US$16 to US$29) a day. **Selkirk,** at 504–9th Avenue North (☎ **250-344-2966**), also rents a range of sports equipment, including mountain bikes.

Outdoor adventure and spine-tingling sports

Kicking Horse Mountain Resort

Kicking Horse is one of the top new ski resorts in North America, but more about that later. This place is a must-see, whether you're a powder hound or not. In summer (from late June until September 1), Kicking Horse is open for sight-seeing and mountain biking. An eight-person gondola, the Golden Eagle Express, hoists you 3,380 meters (11,266 feet) to the top in 12 minutes. From here, **hike** along lofty ridges, blast down one of 18 **mountain bike trails,** or treat yourself to a meal in the stunning **Eagle Eye restaurant,** encircled by one of the most spectacular panoramas in the Rockies. The mountain bike trails are open Friday, Saturday, and Sunday from noon to 8 p.m. You can rent bikes, helmets, and other gear at the resort.

The newest addition to Kicking Horse is a 9-hectare (22-acre) **grizzly bear refuge.** In summer, from the gondola, you can usually spot the first residents, a pair of orphaned grizzly cubs that were moved here in 2003 after their mother was illegally shot. The refuge is a conservation, research, and education center for grizzly bear preservation. To learn more about the cubs and plans for the refuge, sign up for an interpretive tour.

1500 Kicking Horse Trail (4km/9 miles off the Trans-Canada Hwy.; just follow the signs). ☎ *866-754-5425, 250-439-5400; Internet:* www.kickinghorseresort.com. *Gondola sightseeing tickets: C$17 (US$12) adult, C$10 (US$7) children 7–12, free for children 6 and under. For Grizzly Bear Interpretive Program, add C$5 (US$3.50). Mountain bike trail day pass, including gondola: C$30 (US$21).*

The best times for birding in the Columbia River wetlands are spring and fall, when thousands of migratory birds pass through the area.

Hiking

Head east to the Rockies or west to the Selkirks and Purcells. A favorite half-day trip near town, and a good choice for families, is **Gorman Lake,** an easy-to-manage 3-km (2-mile) trek to a subalpine lake in the Dogtooth Range of the Purcell Mountains. Watch for mountain goats on nearby rock faces. The trail starts about 23km (14 miles) from Golden, past the Golf and Country Club. Or, take a 60-km (37-mile) trip north of town to the Blaeberry Valley and climb the **Mummery Glacier** trail in the Rockies. This popular 3-km (2-mile) route leads you through a lovely old-growth cedar and hemlock forest and delivers views of waterfalls and the toe of the glacier. **Kootenay Wilds Backcountry Adventures** (☎ **866-303-9453,** 250-344-4966; Internet: www.kootenaywilds.com) runs weekly trips to both destinations.

In Golden, you can follow the **Rotary Trail** (the Visitor Information Centre has maps) along the Kicking Horse River, or for something more demanding, head for **Mount 7.**

A number of local companies hire out hiking guides. Aside from Kootenay Wilds, there's **Golden Mountain Adventures** (☎ **800-433-9533,** 250-344-4650; Internet: www.adventurerockies.com). For a half-day hike, expect to pay C$50 to C$125 (US$35 to US$88). Family rates are available. A good site to explore when you're planning a hike is Internet: www.goldenhikes.ca, developed by a local resident.

Water, water, everywhere

The Columbia River wetlands, which run south of Golden, extend for 180km (112 miles), making them the longest undeveloped wetlands in North America. The bogs, marshes, ponds, and cottonwood groves here support a fantastic variety of resident and migratory birds: more than 265 species. These wetlands provide homes for 300 pairs of great blue herons, along with bald eagles and osprey, not to mention critters such as moose, deer, beavers, otters, and bears.

Several companies in Golden run float trips on the wetlands, usually lasting about two or three hours. Expect to pay C$46 to C$50 (US$32 to US$35). Try **Kinbasket Adventures** (☎ **866-344-6012,** 250-344-6012; Internet: www.bcrockies adventures.com) or **Golden Mountain Adventures** (☎ **800-433-9533,** 250-344-4650; Internet: www.adventurerockies.com). Don't forget your binoculars.

Heli-skiing/hiking

The Purcell and Selkirk mountains west of Golden are renowned for deep, dry powder, located in very inaccessible terrain. Inaccessible unless you have a helicopter, that is. If your goal is to ski fresh tracks in open bowls or on glaciers, investigate one of the handful of heli-ski operators in Golden. **Great Canadian Helicopters** (☎ **866-424-4354,** 250-344-2326; Internet: www.canadianheli-skiing.com) charges C$3,200 to C$4,300 (US$2,240 to US$3,010), depending on the season, for a three-day package including meals and accommodation in its cushy Heather Mountain Lodge. Weekly packages are also available. **Canadian Mountain Holidays** (☎ **800-661-0252,** 403-762-7803; Internet: www.cmhski.com), based in Banff, Alberta, operates seven remote mountain lodges in the Selkirks, Purcells, and other mountain ranges in eastern British Columbia. The company offers packages for skiers, hikers, and mountaineers.

Mountain biking

If you've got a mind to explore the wilderness on two wheels, you're in the right town. Folks in Golden get *very* excited about mountain biking. For a good range of intermediate-level trails, explore the **Moonraker** system, a combination of single track and old roads that pass through forests, over creeks, and alongside lakes and ponds.

 Don't get so distracted by the scenery that you neglect to keep an eye out for exposed roots, slippery stretches, and, along Canyon Creek, cliff drop-offs. Also remember that bikes share these trails with hikers and horseback riders.

Access to the Moonraker trail system is off the road to Kicking Horse Mountain Resort. On Friday, Saturday, and Sunday, you can also bike down trails at the **Kicking Horse Mountain Resort.** (A day pass for the gondola costs C$30/US$21.) The fastest downhill trails (the steepest trails in B.C., as a matter of fact) are on **Mount 7,** which attracts daredevils of various persuasions — it's also a launching spot for hang gliders and paragliders. There's a maintained road to the top of the mountain. (You don't need a four-wheel drive.) If you intend to tackle Dead Dog, Skid Marks, or one of the other vertical drops off this hill, you definitely need to know what you're doing. Another option is to watch other bikers blast down the mountain: Catch the **Psychosis** race, held annually here in June. It's considered one of the toughest downhill bike races on the continent.

Don't try this at home

Golden's Mount 7 is a top spot for hang gliders and paragliders. The warm temperatures and steep mountains in this area produce thermals that attract pilots from around the world, and some record-breaking flights have taken off here. You too can soar with the eagles by booking a tandem flight with an instructor. (I confess I haven't personally checked this out.) Call Golden Mountain Adventures, ☎ **800-433-9533**, 250-344-4650. A 20-minute flight costs C$140 (US$98), including transportation to and from the launch site. You need about 1.5 hours for the whole trip. You must also be in good shape and be able to run.

Skiing

Golden's new **Kicking Horse Mountain Resort** (☎ **866-754-5425,** 250-439-5400; Internet: www.kickinghorsemountainresort.com) boasts fine, dry "champagne powder" snow and the highest vertical drop in the Canadian Rockies (1,260 meters/4,133 feet). Skiers and snowboarders can glide down 96 runs on 1,619 hectares (4,000 acres) of terrain, about half beginner and intermediate and half advanced to expert. An eight-person gondola whisks you to the top of the hill in 12 minutes. Wonderful food, a massive fireplace, and awesome views are available in the mountaintop restaurant, the Eagle's Eye. A day pass (adult) for the ski hill is C$53 (US$37), a half-day pass is C$39 (US$27).

You can catch a shuttle service to the Kicking Horse Resort from a number of hotels on the Trans-Canada Highway. The round trip costs C$5.50 (US$3.85). For schedule information, call **Mount 7 Taxi** ☎ **250-344-5237.**

Whitewater rafting

The Kicking Horse River is one of the top spots for rafting in Canada. The upper section of the river, through Yoho National Park, is the easiest, whereas the lower canyon section is the most intense with 4km (2.5 miles) of class IV (powerful) rapids. The rafting season runs from May until September. About a dozen local outfitters run trips on the Kicking Horse, ranging from family excursions to multi-day whitewater adventures. Expect to pay about C$55 (US$39) for a half-day trip. Day trips go for C$90 to $C95 (US$63 to US$67), including lunch. Check with **Alpine Rafting** (☎ **888-599-5299;** Internet: www.alpinerafting.com) or **Glacier Raft Company** (☎ **250-344-6521;** Internet: www.glacierraft.com).

Nightlife

The local dance club is **Packers Place** at 429–9th Avenue North
(☎ **250-344-5951**). It's open daily from noon until 2 a.m. and has a
patio facing the Kicking Horse River. If you're looking for a casual beer
and a quieter scene, head down the street to the **Mad Trapper Pub**
(☎ **250-344-6661**). The **Moberly Pub,** just west of town at 1398 Hartley
Road (☎ **250-344-6566**), is a local favorite.

Fast Facts: Golden

Area Code

Golden's area code is ☎ **250.** You don't need
to dial it if you're calling local numbers.

Emergencies

Dial **911.**

Hospitals

Golden District General Hospital, 835–9th
Ave. S., ☎ **250-344-5271.**

Internet Access and Cybercafes

Rumor Mill Café at 420B–9th Ave. N.
(☎ **250-344-5057**), **Jita's Café,** 1007B–11th
Ave. S. (☎ **250-344-3660**), and **180 Rental
Equipment,** 423–9th Ave. N.
(☎ **250-344-4699**).

Maps

Drop by the **Visitor Information Centre,**
500–10th Ave. N. (☎ **250-344-7125**).

Newspapers

The local paper is the **Golden Star.** National
papers, the *National Post* and *Globe and
Mail,* are also widely available.

Police

☎ **250-344-2221.**

Road reports

☎ **800-665-8001.**

Chapter 19

Yoho National Park

. . . .

In This Chapter

▶ Getting to know Yoho

▶ Planning your stay in the park

▶ Marveling at waterfalls and other wonders

▶ Finding the best beds and meals

. . . .

*B*ordered by Banff National Park to the east and Kootenay National Park to the south, this small parcel of wilderness on the western slopes of the Continental Divide contains more than two dozen mountain peaks that are over 3,000 meters (about 10,000 feet) high. Within the park's boundaries, 400km (250 miles) of trails deliver hikers to picture-perfect settings: Snow-capped mountains tower overhead, lakes glisten in the sun, waterfalls plunge over cliffs. Almost 2,500 meters (some 8,000 feet) above sea level, on a ridge above Emerald Lake, the Burgess Shale fossil beds hold the remains of more than 120 species of marine animals that lived 500 million years ago. And farther south, close to the Great Divide, the beauty of the Lake O'Hara region inspires almost spiritual respect and awe. Spend even a few hours traveling through this region and it's easy to see how it came to be called "Yoho," a Cree word that translates roughly as "Wow!"

Must-See Attractions

A trip through Yoho National Park is a memorable journey, even if you never venture far from the Trans-Canada Highway. Some of the park's most impressive settings are just north of the highway and accessible by car. Exceptions are Lake O'Hara, which is protected by a quota system (you either walk 13km/8 miles or reserve a seat on a bus) and the Burgess Shale fossil site, which you can visit only in the company of a guide.

> ✔ **Emerald Lake:** The stunning blue-green waters of the "jewel of the Rockies" can be admired from various vantage points along a 5-km (3-mile) lakeshore trail. If you book in to the Emerald Lake Lodge, you can swoon over this gorgeous scenery from your room.

 ✔ **Lake O'Hara:** This remote lake is so beautiful that some people make annual pilgrimages to hike, ski, or just be there. This chapter includes information on accommodation options. Day trips are also doable.

 ✔ **Takakkaw Falls:** *Takakkaw* is a Cree word meaning "magnificent," which is essentially what most people say when they catch sight of the water thundering over the cliffs at this powerful waterfall.

Getting There

From Banff National Park, head west on the Trans-Canada Highway, which crosses the Kicking Horse Pass. The tiny town of Field, a service center for the park, is only about 80km (50 miles) from Banff Townsite. If you're traveling from British Columbia, Field is 55km (34 miles) east of Golden on the Trans-Canada Highway.

Flying in

The closest international airport is in Calgary, about a 2.5-hour drive from Field. **Air Canada** (☎ **888-247-2262;** Internet: www.aircanada.ca) and **WestJet** (☎ **888-937-8538;** Internet: www.westjet.ca) operate nonstop flights from many Canadian cities. From the U.S., Air Canada flies direct to Calgary from Los Angeles, San Francisco, Las Vegas, Spokane, Phoenix, Houston, and Chicago. **Continental Airlines** (☎ **800-231-0856;** Internet: www.continental.com.), **Northwest Airlines** (☎ **800-447-4747;** Internet: www.nwa.com), and **United Airlines** (☎ **800-241-6522;** Internet: www.ual.com) also offer nonstop flights from various U.S. centers.

Driving in

Field is 210km (130 miles) west of Calgary on the Trans-Canada Highway, just past Lake Louise. If you're traveling from British Columbia, Field is less than 60km (37 miles) east of Golden.

Planning Ahead

For information about travel in the B.C. Rockies, write **Tourism Rockies, Box 10, 1905 Warren Avenue, Kimberley, B.C., V1A 2Y5,** or call ☎ **250-427-4838.** You can request brochures by calling ☎ **800-661-6603.** On the Web, visit Internet: www.bcrockies.com. You find information about Yoho and other Canadian national parks at Internet: www.parkscanada.gc.ca.

Mountain weather is unpredictable: It can snow anytime. Having said that, you can usually count on enjoyable summer weather from about mid-June through September. The park is open year-round, although storms and avalanches sometimes cause delays and road closures in winter. The Yoho Valley Road to Takakkaw Falls closes around the beginning of October and re-opens in June.

If a visit to Lake O'Hara is on your agenda, decide first whether or not you want to stay overnight. If not, you need only worry about bus transportation to the lake. Call ☎ **250-343-6433** to make a reservation on the bus, which runs from mid-June to mid-October. Reservations are accepted (and highly recommended) up to three months in advance. If you have your heart set on spending a few days exploring the hiking trails around Lake O'Hara, see "Enjoying the Park" and "Where to Stay" below for information on booking a campsite or room at Lake O'Hara Lodge.

Paleontology buffs may also want to arrange a hike to the Burgess Shale fossil site. Call the Yoho–Burgess Shale Foundation, ☎ **800-343-3006,** or visit Internet: `www.burgess-shale.bc.ca.`

Figuring Out the Lay of the Land

Yoho is the smallest of the four adjoining national parks that form part of the Canadian Rocky Mountain Parks world heritage site. It borders Banff National Park to the east, and Kootenay National Park to the south. It's just west of the Continental Divide and the Alberta–British Columbia border.

Yoho is on Mountain Standard Time, like Alberta: one hour ahead of most of British Columbia.

On the Trans-Canada Highway (Highway 1), which cuts through the heart of Yoho National Park, you pass the town of Field (27 km/17 miles west of Lake Louise). It has a hotel, a few B&Bs, and a couple of restaurants along with a large Visitor Centre. Not far from Field, secondary roads wind north of the Trans-Canada to Takakkaw Falls (summer only) and Emerald Lake.

Arriving in the Park

There's a booth at the western park gates where you can buy a pass, required if you intend to stop inside the park. Or, just stop in at the Visitor Centre in Field.

Finding information

The **Yoho National Park Visitor Centre** (☎ **250-343-6783**) in Field is open mid-September through late April from 9 a.m. to 4 p.m., May 1 to late June 9 a.m. to 5 p.m., and late June to September 1 (summer) 9 a.m. to 7 p.m. Park passes are sold here, along with backcountry camping permits. If you're planning a hike, you can pick up a map of trails in the park and check in with Parks Canada staff for trail information. A Friends of Yoho shop sells books, maps, and souvenirs.

Learn more about Yoho by taking in an interpretive program. Put on by Parks Canada staff and guest speakers, the free programs usually start around 8 p.m. and run about an hour. You can catch interpretive programs in the Kicking Horse Campground and the Field Community Centre. Check in with the Visitor Centre in Field for program details.

Paying fees

This national park, like others in the Canadian Rockies, requires you to buy a **National Parks Pass** if you intend to stop for a visit. A day pass costs C$7 (US$4.90) adults; C$6 (US$4.20) seniors; C$3.50 (US$2.45) youth aged 6 to 16; or C$14 (US$9) for groups of between two and seven people in the same vehicle. If you already have an annual park pass, of course, you don't need to pay a daily entry fee. The annual pass is your best bet if you're traveling in the park for longer than a week or if you plan to visit one of 27 other national parks in Canada within a year of the date on which you purchase the pass. The cost is C$45 (US$32) adults; C$38 (US$27) seniors; C$22 (US$14) youth; and C$89 (US$63) for a group pass.

If you plan to camp in the wilderness, you need a **Wilderness Pass,** which costs C8 (US$6) per night or C$56 (US$39) for an annual pass that you can also use in Banff, Jasper, and Kootenay national parks.

A fishing license costs C$7 (US$4.90) per day or C$20 (US$14) a year.

If a visit to Lake O'Hara is on your itinerary, you need to pay for a bus trip to the lake — C$15 (US$11) adult, C$7.50 (US$5) youth aged 6 to 16 — unless you opt to hike or ski in.

Getting around

You need a vehicle — or bicycle — to explore Yoho and travel to neighboring parks.

Yikes ... this is a big hill

The original Canadian Pacific Railway line through the Rockies featured the steepest grade of any railway in North America. Trains traveling west from Lake Louise to Field climbed the Kicking Horse Pass, then headed down a frighteningly steep stretch known as ""Big Hill." Accidents were common and several lives were lost. After more than two decades, a CPR engineer came up with a plan to construct two spiral-shaped tunnels that would lengthen this dangerous section of the railway but reduce the grade from 4.5% to just over 2%. The spiral tunnels were completed in 1909 and are still being used today. The track forms a figure-eight pattern. To watch trains wind their way through the tunnels, stop at the **spiral tunnel viewpoint** on the Trans-Canada Highway, 8km east of Field. You can also check out displays on the construction of the railway. A second viewpoint is located higher up on the Yoho Valley Road, north of the Kicking Horse Campground.

Enjoying the Park

Waterfalls, lakes, and magnificent peaks make Yoho an excellent choice for hikers and cross-country skiers. Whether you're an outdoor enthusiast or not, if you're traveling through this park on a sunny summer or fall day, don't miss the chance to detour into Emerald Lake or Takakkaw Falls. You'll want your camera. Yoho! (Wow! Remember?)

Exploring the top attractions

The sites in this section, easy trips from the town of Field, showcase Yoho's majestic scenery. You can drive to Emerald Lake year-round, but the road to Takakkaw Falls is only open in summer.

Emerald Lake

The remarkable jewel color of this lake comes from rock flour (particles of rock ground off the bed of a glacier) suspended in the water. The trail around the lakeshore (just over 5km/3 miles) makes a nice family jaunt. At the end of the lake, the trail connects with the Emerald Basin trail, a half-day hike to a natural amphitheatre of hanging glaciers and avalanche paths. Like other scenic wonders in the Rockies, Emerald Lake is busiest in July and August, particularly through the middle of the day. For the calmest experience, aim to visit first thing in the morning or late in the afternoon. In the picnic area, you find a display on the famous Burgess Shale fossil site, situated on a ridge high above Emerald Lake (at an elevation of 8,000 meters [over 26,000 feet], to be exact).

From Field, drive 11km (7 miles) east on the Trans-Canada Hwy.

Emerald Sports (☎ 250-343-6000) at Emerald Lake rents canoes and kayaks for about C$25 (US$18) an hour. In winter, cross-country ski packages go for C$8 (US$6) an hour or C$22 (US$15) per day. All major credit cards are accepted. Emerald Sports is open July and August, daily from 9 a.m. to 7 p.m., and in spring and fall, daily 10 a.m. to 5 p.m. Winter hours are Monday to Friday from 10 a.m. to 4 p.m. and weekends 10 a.m. to 5 p.m.

It's *how* old? Yoho's famous fossils

Once upon a time, approximately 500 million years ago, a multitude of unusual creatures lived in a warm, shallow ocean at the edge of the North American continent. (Everything lived in the water then; land animals hadn't evolved.) Some of these creatures were ancestors of animals we know today; many others were unlike anything you've ever heard of (five-eyed beings with elephant trunks, for example). Every once in a while, underwater mudflows washed over these ancient animals and killed them. Over time, their remains became fossils and eventually were buried under miles and miles of rock. Rather recently — beginning about 175 million years ago — geological processes that led to the formation of mountains unearthed the fossils and deposited them on a ridge high above Emerald Lake, between Mount Field and Mount Wapta.

Paleontologist Charles D. Walcott of the Smithsonian Institution, who discovered the fossils in 1909 and named the site **Burgess Shale** after nearby Mount Burgess, collected thousands of specimens here. The site was declared a UNESCO World Heritage Site in 1981.

The Burgess Shale fossils are significant not only because of their age but on account of how perfectly the ancient soft-bodied marine animals have been preserved and the light they've shed on the mysteries of human evolution. Yoho National Park's famous fossils are the subject of a best-selling book, *Wonderful Life*, by Stephen J. Gould, published in 1989.

The fossil sites are protected areas. You can't visit them on your own, but guided hikes are offered. Contact the Yoho–Burgess Shale Foundation, ☎ **800-343-3006**; Internet: www.burgess-shale.bc.ca. The hikes are fairly demanding, particularly the trip to Walcott Quarry, a 10-hour, 20-km (12-mile) round trip. You can learn more about the Burgess Shale fossils by visiting the Yoho National Park Visitor Centre in Field. There's also a display at Emerald Lake.

Lake O'Hara

Lake O'Hara is one of the most beautiful spots in the Canadian Rockies — "an explosion of the senses," as one Parks Canada employee describes it, "even if you just get off the bus and stand there." Hiking trails around the lake and surrounding valley are all the more inviting in that they aren't jam-packed with tourists. That's because you have to park your car 11km (7 miles) away near the Trans-Canada Highway. The road to Lake O'Hara is closed to regular traffic: From the parking lot, you either catch a bus, which makes round trips several times daily from about mid-June to early-October, or walk.

You can reserve a seat on the bus up to three months before your trip by calling ☎ **250-343-6433.** You pay by credit card when you make the reservation. There's a C$12 (US$8) reservation fee, which is nonrefundable. A handful of seats are also available on a first-come, first-served basis (the day before departure), as are a few one-night spots at the Lake O'Hara campground, but these must be reserved in person at the **Lake O'Hara office** in the **Yoho National Park Visitor Centre** in Field. And you probably won't be the only person in line. The Lake O'Hara office opens at 8 a.m. (sometimes by 7:45 a.m.), and determined backcountry enthusiasts have been known to camp outside the door.

If a visit to Lake O'Hara is high on your Canadian Rocky Mountain agenda, get on the phone early. Seats on the bus go fast, as do camping spots at the lake, which can also be reserved three months ahead (☎ **250-343-6433**). Late July and August are the best times to hike. Earlier in the season, some of the higher trails are still snowy and wet.

If you plan to score a spot on the bus to Lake O'Hara at the last minute but you don't luck out, don't give up. Hang around until the bus departs. Sometimes people with confirmed reservations don't show up. If you decide to walk, there's a bonus: You're guaranteed a free trip out on the bus.

Accommodation at Lake O'Hara includes a campground (30 sites), two huts operated by the Alpine Club of Canada (☎ **403-678-3200;** Internet: www.alpineclubofcanada.ca), and a backcountry lodge. See the "Where to Stay" section later in this chapter.

*The Lake O'Hara parking lot is 15km (9 miles) east of Field, just off the Trans-Canada Hwy. Bus fare is C$12 (US$8) adults, C$5 (US$3.50) youth 6 to 16. Camping at Lake O'Hara costs C$8 (US$6) per night (unless you have an annual Wilderness Pass, in which case you're covered). For reservations, call ☎ **250-343-6433**. You pay bus fare and camping fees when you reserve, along with a C$12 (US$8) reservation fee. AE, MC, V.*

Takakkaw Falls

In summer, motor up the spectacular Yoho Valley Road for about 13km (8 miles) to check out one of Canada's highest waterfalls. The water crashing 254 meters (833 feet) over the cliffs into the Yoho River Valley originates in the Daly Glacier, part of an icefield on the Continental Divide. From the Takakkaw Falls parking lot, you can follow an interpretive trail to the base of the falls. When you see and hear the water thundering over cliffs, you immediately appreciate how these falls came to be called "Takakkaw," which means "magnificent" in Cree. If you're inclined to savor this environment for a few days, pitch your tent at the walk-in Takakkaw Falls campground. It's about a ten-minute walk from the parking lot and features more than 30 sites and some awesome panoramas. A number of wonderful hikes also begin in this area, including the Iceline Trail, with views of the Daly and Emerald glaciers. In the surrounding backcountry, campsites are located at Twin Falls, Laughing Falls, and Yoho Lake. If you plan to stay overnight, remember to get a Wilderness Pass.

Don't head up the Yoho Valley Road with a trailer in tow — it's steep with tight corners.

If you visit after early October, you find the Yoho Valley Road closed to traffic until spring. If there's lots of snow and you cross-country ski, though, you're in luck. In winter the road is converted to a cross-country ski trail.

On the Trans-Canada Hwy., just east of Field, travel north on the Yoho Valley Road for 13km (8 miles).

Taking a hike

For hikers, Yoho is a treasure, with 400km (250 miles) of trails, most of which are far less frequented than those in neighboring Banff. At the park Visitor Centre in Field, pick up a copy of the *Yoho National Park Backcountry Guide*, which points you in the direction of six short walks, a handful of half-day hikes, and some day trips. Many spectacular treks kick off in the Takakkaw Falls area, including the Iceline Trail, which starts at the Whiskey Jack Hostel and runs along the edge of the Emerald Glacier and through the Yoho Valley. The hike can be stretched into a two- or three-day backcountry trek with marvelous views of waterfalls and glaciers. There's also fantastic hiking at Lake O'Hara.

Backcountry adventures

You need a Wilderness Pass to spend the night in one of Yoho's five backcountry campgrounds. They cost C$8 (US$6) per night or C$56 (US$39) for an annual pass that you can also use in Banff, Jasper, and

Kootenay national parks. Pick up a pass at the Visitor Centre in Field or at the visitor information centers in Banff or Lake Louise. The maximum stay in one campground is three days.

To reserve a backcountry campsite (up to three months in advance of your trip), call ☎ **250-343-6783.** You pay a C$12 (US$8) reservation fee.

Staying active

Besides hiking in Yoho National Park, you may want to travel the park trails mountain bike or cross-country skis. The closest golf courses and ski resorts are in Golden, 55km (34 miles) west of Field, and in Lake Louise, just across the Alberta border in Banff National Park.

Cross-country skiing

Yoho's spectacular peaks and valleys are breathtakingly gorgeous in winter, and gliding through the wilderness on skis is a wonderful way to experience this park. From the town of Field, you can head out along the **Kicking Horse River trail** and connect with a trail that leads to Emerald Lake. You can also ski on the road to **Takakkaw Falls**. The lower portion (7km/4 miles) is track set and passes some great viewpoints. Higher up, this trail is more challenging and crosses some avalanche paths. Other trips start at the **Lake O'Hara** parking lot, including the road to Lake O'Hara, a 23-km (14-mile) round trip. You also find various shorter trips on easier terrain, including several 4- and 5-km (2.5- and 3-mile) loops. The Visitor Centre in Field provides a list of trails, and staff will help you select a trip that matches your ability and energy level.

Before your ski trip, check in with staff at the park Visitor Centre (☎ **250-343-6783**) for the latest information on weather and avalanche hazards. You can also call ☎ 403-762-1460 to hear avalanche danger forecasts for Yoho, Kootenay, and Banff national parks. Stay in safe areas. If you intend to ski across avalanche paths, you should definitely carry an avalanche transceiver (and know how to use it), a probe, and a snow shovel.

Mountain biking

Two-wheelers can travel on eight former fire roads in Yoho, including a trail to Lake Louise and a 21-km (13-mile) route that parallels the Kicking Horse River. You share the trails with hikers and horses.

A golden trail for pedal-pushers

The Trans-Canada Highway through Yoho National Park is part of a popular Rocky Mountain cycling route called the **Golden Triangle,** which loops through Banff, Radium Hot Springs, and Golden. The 320-km (198-mile) trip tours through three national parks (Banff, Kootenay, and Yoho), crosses the Continental Divide twice, and features stunning mountain scenery, glaciers, waterfalls, and hot springs. Hundreds of members of an Alberta cycling group tackle this trip each year on the Victoria Day long weekend in May. To bike the Golden Triangle in three days, you need to be in top shape and willing to log roughly 100km (62 miles) a day. A more leisurely pace, of course, gives you more time for such pursuits as soaking in hot springs, rafting down rivers, or just taking in the grand views.

Where to Stay in Yoho

Standard motel rooms are scarce in this park. In the town of Field, which is the main service center for Yoho, you find a hotel along with some B&Bs and guesthouses. In the vicinity of Field are a few lovely mountain lodges and cabins, most of which you can drive to. The park also contains numerous scenic sites in which to pitch a tent.

Cathedral Mountain Lodge
$$$–$$$$

Whether you opt for one of the original log cabins, which date from the 1930s, or a more recent addition, this enchanting resort in a wooded setting along the Kicking Horse River just 6km (4 miles) west of Field is a treat. Twenty-one romantic log cabins feature wood-burning fireplaces and pine furnishings. Most have splashy baths with big soaker tubs. The original buildings, which are the most economical, have showers instead. A few cabins have lofts containing two twin beds — suitable for kids who don't mind scrambling up a ladder. Breakfast, which is included in your rate, is a buffet of fruit, yogurt, cereals, and baked goodies, served in the main lodge. Cathedral Mountain Lodge also houses a popular restaurant. If you'd like a table for dinner, you should reserve ahead.

Yoho Valley Rd. (23km/14 miles west of Lake Louise). ☎ 250-343-6442. Fax: 250-343-6424. E-mail: info@cathderalmountainlodge.com. *Internet:* www.cathedralmountainlodge.com. *Rack rates: C$195–C$350 (US$137– US$245) double. Rates include continental breakfast. June 1–Oct 1. AE, MC, V.*

Emerald Lake Lodge

$$$–$$$$

If your notion of a rustic wilderness escape includes in-room hairdryers, telephones, cable TV, and coffeemakers, you'll most likely love these gorgeous chalet-style rooms on the shores of Emerald Lake. Besides enjoying numerous conveniences, you can kick back beside your in-room fieldstone fireplace (wood is delivered daily). Most rooms also boast balconies. The restaurant here, which concentrates on upscale regional cuisine, is well worth a splurge. You can also dine in a more casual cafe, Cilantro on the Lake. Some excellent day hikes begin near Emerald Lake. Alternatively, you could spend a lazier afternoon paddling a canoe across blue-green water or exploring the 5-km (3-mile) trail that meanders along the lakeshore.

Take Emerald Lake Rd., 2km (1 mile) west of Field. ☎ *800-663-6336, 250-343-6321. Fax: 250-343-6724. E-mail:* emlodge@rockies.net. *Internet:* www.crmr.com. *Rack rates: C$140–C$450 (US$98–US$315) double. AE, MC, V.*

Kicking Horse Lodge

$–$$

Rooms in this hotel in the small town of Field are simply adorned but bright and fresh. Some have kitchen facilities. On the main level, you find a dining room with a few tables spilling onto an outdoor deck, which is a mellow spot to catch some sun while you lunch on salmon pie, an elk burger, or a smoked portobello focaccia. If you stay in Field, a couple of other dining spots are within walking distance, including the funky little Truffle Pigs Café (see "Where to Eat" below) across the street. After August, when the summer crowds thin, rates at the Kicking Horse drop considerably. Between mid-October and April 30, you can stay here for as low as C$56 (US$39) a night.

100 Centre St., Field. ☎ *800-659-4944, 250-343-6303. Fax: 250-343-6355. E-mail:* khorselodge@rockies.net. *Internet:* www.kickinghorselodge.net. *Rack rates: C$126–C$138 (US$88–US$97) double. MC, V.*

Lake O'Hara Lodge

$–$$

This historic backcountry lodge, in one of the most stunning settings in the Canadian Rockies, is accessed only by an 11-km (7-mile) road that's closed to regular traffic. In summer, bus transportation to and from Lake O'Hara is included in your rate. The most economical rooms, with shared baths, are in the main lodge. For an additional C$150 (US$105), you can stay in a lakeshore cabin with a private bath. Either way, you have 80km (50 miles) of incredible hiking trails on your doorstep. For skiers and snowshoe enthusiasts, the main lodge is also open in winter (mid-January to mid-April). It can handle 16 people. The bus to Lake O'Hara doesn't run in winter. Both summer and winter rates include all meals, and you can count on eating well.

Buses depart from the parking area off the Trans-Canada Hwy., 15km (9 miles) east of Field. ☎ ***250-343-6418*** *(in off-season, 403-678-4110). Internet:* www. lakeohara.com. *Rack rates: Summer (mid-June–mid-Sept) C$400–C$550 (US$280–US$385) double. Winter (mid-Jan–mid-April) C$230 (US$161) per person. All rates include breakfast, lunch, and dinner.*

West Louise Lodge
$$

This motel on the Trans-Canada Highway at the summit of Kicking Horse Pass between Field and Lake Louise offers moderately priced rooms, some of which have balconies with views of Wapta Lake. Family suites are available in a separate building. It's only a 10-minute drive west to the Lake Louise ski hill.

Across from Wapta Lake, Lake Louise. ☎ ***800-258-7669****, 250-343-6311. Fax: 250-343-6786. E-mail:* westlouiselodge@skilouise.com. *Rack rates: C$119 (US$83) double. Rates include breakfast. MC, V.*

Whiskey Jack Hostel
$

Just a stroll away from Takakkaw Falls, this hostel is ideally situated for hiking. Whiskey Jack has 27 beds in 3 dorms along with kitchen facilities, lockers, and storage room for gear. It's closed from October until mid-June.

Yoho Valley Rd. ☎ ***866-762-4122****, 403-670-7580. Fax: 403-283-6503. Internet:* hihostels.ca. *Rack rates: C$29 (US$20) per person. C$19 (US$13) for members of Hostelling International. MC, V.*

None of Yoho's frontcountry (road-accessible) campgrounds take reservations, so the best strategy is to get there early, especially in the peak seasons of July and August. The **Kicking Horse** and **Monarch** campsites are just east of Field along the Kicking Horse River. Kicking Horse has hot showers, flush toilets, a kitchen shelter, a playground, walking trails, and interpretive programs. It's usually full by early afternoon in high season. The Monarch Campsite, in a meadow just a stroll away, is more basic. You can also camp at Takakkaw Falls and enjoy close-up views of the falls. The tent site here is a short walk from the parking lot. A cart is available for moving your gear. The Kicking Horse and Takakkaw Falls campgrounds are open from the end of June through to the end of September. Monarch opens around mid-May and closes September 1.

Where to Eat in Yoho

The Cathedral Mountain, Emerald Lake, and Kicking Horse lodges all serve reputable food. For casual dining and goodies to go, head for this funky cafe in Field.

Truffle Pigs Café
$–$$ Field BAKERY/CAFE

This petite bistro, which doubles as a general store, turns out an astonishing variety of tasty meals. Dine on spinach salad with gorgonzola, an elk burger, or gourmet beef stew. Or, have a fresh-from-the-oven muffin, cookie, or brownie to go. The pies have a loyal following and the coffee's fresh and strong. In hiking season, Truffle Pigs is usually bustling. On sunny days, the outdoor tables fill fast.

318 Stephen Ave., Field. ☎ 250-343-6000. Bistro menu: C$11–C$14 (US$21–US$25). Bakery items: under C$10 (US$7). Summer: daily 8 a.m.–10 p.m. Winter: Mon–Thurs 9 a.m.–7 p.m., Fri & Sat 8 a.m.–9 p.m., Sun 8 a.m.–6 p.m.

Fast Facts: Yoho National Park

Area Code
☎ 250.

ATMs
In the Truffle Pigs Café on Stephen Avenue in Field.

Emergencies
Dial **911**.

Fees
A day pass to Yoho National Park costs C$7 (US$4.90) for adults, C$14 (US$9) for groups. An annual National Parks Pass, for all national parks in Canada, is C$45 (US$31) for adults, C$89 (US$63) for groups.

Fishing Licenses
Fishing licenses are sold at the Visitor Centre in Field. They cost C$7 (US$4.90) for a day pass or C$20 (US$14) for the year.

Hospitals
The closest hospitals are in Golden (☎ 250-344-5271) and in Banff Townsite (☎ 403-762-2222).

Information
Call ☎ 250-343-6783.

Post Office
Across from the Community Centre on Stephen Avenue in Field.

Road Conditions and Weather

For weather, call ☎ **403-299-7878**, 24 hours. For road conditions, check the Mountain Parks Road Report ☎ **403-762-1450**.

Taxes

British Columbia's provincial sales tax is 7.5%. The 7% national Goods & Services tax (GST) applies to most goods and services, although visitors can apply for a rebate on some purchases. Most hotels charge an 8% hotel room tax.

Time Zone

Mountain Standard.

Web Site

www.parkscanada.gc.ca

Chapter 20

Kootenay National Park

. . . .

In This Chapter

▶ Getting to know a region of cactus and ice

▶ Planning your stay

▶ Traveling the Parkway and soaking in the hot springs

▶ Finding the best beds and meals

. . . .

*T*he landscape in this long, skinny park is so diverse that you see glaciers and icy lakes in the northern corner, while prickly pear cactus and sagebrush inhabit the south. Kootenay National Park flanks Highway 93, between Vermilion Pass in Banff National Park, Alberta, and Radium Hot Springs in British Columbia. The park was created in 1920, through an agreement between the Canadian government, which paid for the highway, and the province of B.C., which provided an 8-km (5-mile) stretch of land on each side of the highway for a national park. That's why this park is so narrow. Highway 93, also called the Banff–Windermere Highway or the Kootenay Parkway, was the first motor road over the Rockies when it opened in 1922. Motoring through here today, you discover numerous viewpoints, picnic areas, and pathways that unveil this region's natural attractions. Some fascinating hikes also start from parking areas and camping spots right along the highway.

The most popular destination in Kootenay National Park is a hot springs pool near the southwest corner. On the whole, this park is far less visited than neighboring Banff, which makes it an ideal spot to seek some solitude. You won't find any towns or service centers in the park. If you're in need of a room or a meal, drive through Kootenay's southern gate to Radium Hot Springs, a Bavarian-flavored village whose residents include about 700 people and approximately 200 bighorn sheep.

Fall, winter, and spring are the best times to spot the bighorn sheep.

Must-See Attractions

If you don't plan to hike, half a day is sufficient to travel through the park, inspect its natural attractions, and reflect on the experience with a soothing soak in the hot springs.

✔ **Kootenay Parkway:** The 94-km (58-mile) scenic parkway takes you through the heart of the park. On the way, investigate natural attractions such as the **"paint pots,"** where mud has been pigmented by iron-rich springs. Native people used to collect clay here to produce paints for decorating their tepees. In the north, check out interpretive displays that illustrate how forests recover from fire.

✔ **Radium Hot Springs:** These hot pools, so named because tests have shown the water to be slightly radioactive, are considered therapeutic by many visitors. Unlike some mineral springs, the water here doesn't contain sulphur, so it's odor-free. A day spa is a relatively recent addition to the site.

Major wild fires that swept through southern British Columbia during the summer of 2003 burned about 12 percent of Kootenay National Park. (This park is very prone to lightening. In fact, the area around Vermilion pass is referred to as "lightening alley.") Most fire damage occurred in the northern part of the park, in the region between Vermilion Pass and the Kootenay Park Lodge. At press time, some trails in the park were blocked by fallen trees and were closed to the public. Some picnic areas were also closed, as was the marble Canyon Campsite. Before your visit to Kootenay National Park, get the latest information on park conditions by visiting Internet: www.parkscanada.gc.ca/kootenay or by calling a visitor information centre in Kootenay National Park (☎ **250-347-9505**) or in Lake Louise (☎ **403-522-3833**).

Getting There

A trip through Kootenay National Park is simple to work into your itinerary. Highway 93, which cuts through the heart of the park, links up with routes to Banff in the north and the Canada–U.S. border in the south. Another road links Kootenay's southern gate with Golden, on the Trans-Canada Highway.

Although the road through the park is open year-round, it closes once in a while during winter if driving conditions are dangerous. Call ☎ **403-762-1450** to check the highway situation before you head out. The law requires winter drivers to have snow tires or all-season radials. It's also a good idea to pack a few emergency supplies in your car: a shovel, a flashlight, warm clothing.

Flying in

The closest Canadian international airport is in Calgary, about a three-hour drive from the park. You could also fly to Vancouver, B.C. **Air Canada** (☎ **888-247-2262;** Internet: www.aircanada.ca) and **WestJet** (☎ **888-937-8538;** Internet: www.westjet.ca) operate nonstop flights to both cities from many Canadian destinations. From Calgary and Vancouver, Air Canada flies to Cranbrook, about 140km (98 miles) from, Kootenay National Park. If you're traveling from the U.S., you might book a flight to Spokane and then rent a car.

Driving in

From Calgary, head west on the Trans-Canada Highway through Banff National Park to Castle Mountain Junction and drive south on Highway 93 through Kootenay National Park. The village of Radium Hot Springs, at the park's southern gate, is 264km (165 miles) from Calgary. From Golden, Radium Hot Springs is about an hour's drive south on Highway 95.

Highway 95 is a smart choice if you're a birding enthusiast; the road parallels the Columbia Valley wetlands, a protected area that's home to great blue herons, bald eagles, and numerous other species.

From the U.S., head for the border crossing at either Kingsgate, Idaho, or Roosville, Montana. Both are open round the clock. Radium Hot Springs is 224km (140 miles) north of the border.

Planning Ahead

To receive information before your trip, write **Tourism Rockies,** Box 10, 1905 Warren Avenue, Kimberley, B.C., V1A 2Y5, or call ☎ **250-427-4838.** Call ☎ **800-661-6603** to request brochures. You also can find information about Kootenay National Park on the Parks Canada Web site at Internet: www.parkscanada.gc.ca.

The village of Radium Hot Springs offers hundreds of hotel rooms. All the same, in the peak seasons of July and August, reservations are advisable. Campgrounds within the national park are first-come, first-served. You can, however, reserve ahead at most privately run camping areas. See the section "Where to Stay in Kootenay" later in this chapter for suggestions.

Calling all birders

More than 260 species of birds, including magnificent golden eagles or great blue herons, have been spotted in the Upper Columbia Valley. You can learn more about them — and have fun in the process — if you time your visit to coincide with the **Wings Over the Rockies bird festival,** held in the valley each spring, usually in early May. Activities during the week-long naturalist event include float trips on the Columbia River and horseback trips in the grasslands. You can take in guided nature walks, a children's festival, live music, and a flock of presentations of interest to birders. For dates and event schedules, call ☎ **888-933-3311** or 250-342-3210, or visit Internet: www.adventurevalley.com/wings. Field trips usually cost about C$5 to $C10 (US$3.50 to US$7) per person. For other events and presentations, you can pay up to C$50 (US$35). Some are free.

If you intend to venture into the wilderness by hiking the Rockwall Trail or other routes that involve overnight stays in the backcountry, you can reserve a campsite up to three months before your trip. Between June and September, call the **Kootenay National Park Visitor Centre, ☎ 250-347-9505.** In winter, make your reservations through the **Lake Louise Visitor Centre, ☎ 403-522-3833.**

Figuring Out the Lay of the Land

Kootenay is the southernmost of the parks that make up the Canadian Rocky Mountain Parks United Nations World Heritage Site (Banff, Jasper, Kootenay, and Yoho national parks; and Hamber, Mount Robson, and Mount Assiniboine provincial parks). Kootenay National Park is a 1,406-sq.-km (543-sq.-mile) strip of wilderness, bordered to the north and east by Yoho, Banff, and Mount Assiniboine parks.

Highway 93, also called the Banff–Windermere Highway or the Kootenay Parkway, is the only road through the park. It runs north–south for nearly 100km (about 60 miles) through the Kootenay and Vermilion River valleys, ushering you past viewpoints and interpretive trails that showcase the park's beauty and history.

At the northern edge of the park, the summit of Vermilion Pass marks the Continental Divide. In the south, near the park's western gate, the highway descends into a stunning canyon and emerges in the village of Radium Hot Springs above the Columbia River Valley.

Arriving in the Park

It's easy to get your bearings in this park — there's only one road. The main gate is in the western corner of the park, just past the village of Radium Hot Springs. If you haven't already purchased a park pass, you can buy one here. Passes are also sold at the visitor center in Kootenay Park Lodge, 63km (39 miles) north of Radium, but only between April and early October.

If you stay in the village of Radium Hot Springs, you don't require a park pass if you're only visiting the hot springs.

Finding information

Head for **Kootenay National Park Visitor Centre** at 7556 Main Street E. in the village of Radium Hot Springs (corner of Main Street East and Redstreak Campground Road), ☎ **250-347-9505.** It's open in spring (mid-May to mid-June) daily from 9 a.m. to 5 p.m. and in summer (late June to Sept. 1) daily from 9 a.m. to 7 p.m. In the first half of September, the centre is open 9 a.m. to 5 p.m. From mid-September to mid-October, it's open Friday and Saturday from 9 a.m. to 4 p.m. Here you can pick up hiking maps, buy park passes, check trail conditions, and get help finding a campsite or hotel. A Friends of Kootenay shop sells books and souvenirs.

An information center is also located at **Kootenay Park Lodge,** 63km (39 miles) north of Radium Hot Springs at Vermilion Crossing. You can buy park passes, fishing licenses, and wilderness passes here, but the center is closed in winter. There's no telephone. Summer hours (mid-May to late September) are 10 a.m. to 7 p.m., and spring and fall hours are 11 a.m. to 6 p.m.

Paying fees

A day pass to visit the park costs C\$7 (US\$5) adults; C\$6 (US\$4) seniors; C\$3.50 (US\$2.45) youth aged 6 to 16; or C\$14 (US\$9) for groups of between two and seven people in the same vehicle. If you already have an annual park pass, of course, you don't need to pay a daily entry fee. The annual pass is your best bet if you're traveling in the park for longer than a week or if you plan to visit one of 27 other national parks in Canada within a year of the date on which you purchase the pass. The cost is C\$45 (US\$32) adults; C\$38 (US\$27) seniors; C\$22 (US\$14) youth; and C\$89 (US\$63) for a group pass.

If you plan to camp in the wilderness, you need a **Wilderness Pass,** which costs C\$8 (US\$6) per night or C\$56 (US\$39) for an annual pass that you can also use in Banff, Jasper, and Yoho national parks.

A fishing license costs C\$7 (US\$5) per day or C\$20 (US\$14) a year.

Getting around

Hop in the car or grab your bike. The highway through this park is an attraction in itself. You pass plenty of inviting spots where you can break to stretch your legs.

Enjoying the Park

Gas stations, hotels, and restaurants are found just outside the park's west gate in the village of Radium Hot Springs.

Exploring the top attractions

The 94-km (58-mile) drive along Highway 93 (the **Kootenay Parkway**), between the village of Radium Hot Springs and the British Columbia–Alberta border, is dotted with picnic sites, viewpoints (bring your camera), and short trails that display Kootenay National Park's most prominent features.

At the southern gateway to the park, as you snake through **Sinclair Canyon,** the sheer walls of the Redwall Fault tower overhead. The water that ends up in the nearby Radium Hot Springs pools originates here. Bighorn sheep are frequent visitors to the area. About 13km (8 miles) farther north, at the top of **Sinclair Pass,** take a stroll around **Olive Lake,** then motor along to the **Kootenay Valley Viewpoint,** where you may wish to have your photo taken. The mountains you admire here are part of the Mitchell and Vermilion ranges.

At **Vermilion Crossing,** 63km (39 miles) from Radium Hot Springs, you find **Kootenay Park Lodge,** which houses a visitor center in summer. It's miraculous that this historic lodge is still standing, considering that huge forest fires blazed through this area in both 2001 and 2003. Farther north, you can picnic at **Numa Falls** and stop by the **"paint pots."** A 1.5-km (1-mile) pathway leads to a site where iron-rich springs have tinted the earth. Displays explain the history of these ochre beds, which were used by Native people.

A few kilometers along, the **Marble Canyon Trail** climbs through a spectacular gorge, eroded by the waters of Tokumm Creek. It's just 7km (4 miles) to the summit of Vermilion Pass and the **Continental Divide.** From here, waters flow either east toward the Atlantic or west to the Pacific. This is also the border between Alberta and British Columbia. A massive forest fire tore through the Vermilion Pass area in 1968. Today, this region is bursting with wildflowers. It's also an important habitat for lynx. To see how the area is regenerating and to learn more about the recovery of forests after fire, follow the **Fireweed Trail,** a short interpretive walk through a young forest. It starts in the Continental Divide parking lot.

So . . . it isn't smelly?

Hot springs form when water seeps deep into the ground, heats up, and gets percolated back to the surface. When the water gets hot, it dissolves minerals in the surrounding rock. As the minerals break down, they release hydrogen sulphide gas, which is kind of smelly (like rotten eggs). You notice the sulphur smell if you visit the hot pools in Banff and Jasper, a result of minerals such as pyrite and gypsum that have dissolved in the springs. Thanks to the type of rock found in the area around the Radium Hot Springs, the water in these pools is odorless.

Radium Hot Springs Pools

The steaming water in the hot springs pools (the largest in Canada) is thought by some to ease the pain of arthritis and rheumatism. Whether or not it's healing for the body, a soak in Radium Hot Springs, under the steep, towering walls of Sinclair Canyon, is probably good for the soul. Relax in the 40° Celsuis (104° Fahrenheit) hot mineral pool, or dive into the swimming pool, where the water is kept at a cool 27° Celsuis (84° Fahrenheit). If you don't have a swimsuit with you, you can rent one, along with a towel and a locker for your gear. If you feel like being pampered, call the **Pleiades Spa** ☎ **250-347-2100** to schedule a massage or spa treatment. For a one-hour hot stone massage, you pay C$75 (US$52) an hour.

The hot springs pools are 3km (about 2 miles) east of the village of Radium Hot Springs. ☎ *250-347-9485. Admission: C$6.50 (US$4.55) adults, C$5.50 (US$3.85) seniors & children. Summer (early May to mid-Oct) daily 9 a.m.–11 p.m. Other months Sun–Thurs 12–9 p.m., Fri & Sat 12–10 p.m.*

Taking a hike

The 200km (125 miles) of trails in the park include scenic strolls with informative displays (see the Kootenay Parkway section, above), day hikes of various lengths, and backcountry excursions.

Day trips start from various parking lots along the Kootenay Parkway (Highway 93). In the Radium Hot Springs area, the **Redstreak Campground Trail** is a manageable 2.2-km (1.4-mile) hike through the forest to the nearby hot springs pools. From there, you can enjoy impressive views over the Columbia Valley if you follow the **Juniper Trail,** which runs along the edge of Sinclair Canyon and down along Sinclair Creek.

For a longer trek, a stellar choice is the 5.5-km/3.5-mile (one-way) **Stanley Glacier Trail,** near the northern edge of the park. The trail ascends into a lovely hanging valley and offers a view of the glacier. This moderately steep hike also leads you through a region that burned during a huge forest fire in 1968. You can see how the forest is reinventing itself.

Other hikes are listed in the Kootenay National Park Backcountry Guide, which you can pick up at the visitor center in Radium Hot Springs.

Backcountry adventures

The top backcountry trip in Kootenay National Park, and one of the finest in the Rockies, is the **Rockwall Trail,** a rugged 55-km (34-mile) journey beneath a sheer, towering limestone wall and across three alpine passes. The trail, in the northwest corner of the park, is usually hike-able by early to mid-July. It's an up-and-down trek (stamina comes in handy) highlighted by hanging glaciers, alpine lakes, and pretty meadows. Most people take three days to do the trip. If you start at the southern end of the trail, you depart from Highway 93, 70km (44 miles) north of Radium Hot Springs, and hike to a campground at **Floe Lake.** Four camping spots are located along the route, including **Helmet Falls** at the north end.

Campsite reservations can be made up to three months before your trip. Between June and September, call the Kootenay National Park Visitor Centre at ☎ **250-347-9505.** Prior to June, call the **Lake Louise Visitor Centre,** ☎ **403-522-3833.** You pay a C$12 (US$8) reservation fee. If you're overnighting in the backcountry, be sure you have a wilderness pass. These are available at information centers for C$8 (US$7) per night. An annual permit, also good for Banff, Jasper, and Yoho, costs C$56 (US$39).

Staying active

Besides touring through the national park, you may want to set aside some time for a round of golf or a river rafting trip in the Radium Hot Springs/Invermere area.

Cycling and mountain biking

With its majestic scenery and numerous picnic sites, the 94-km (58-mile) Kootenay Parkway makes a memorable bike excursion. The highway is part of a popular cycling trip through Kootenay, Yoho, and Banff national parks. For mountain bikers, a couple of former fire roads are open in the park.

Mountain biking is not allowed on hiking trails in Kootenay National Park.

Golfing

With a golf season that stretches from March to October, and 11 area courses, the Columbia Valley is a favorite spot to hit the links. Just west of the village of Radium Hot Springs on the banks of the Columbia River, the **Springs Course** is ranked among the best in the province. Green fees for 18 holes run around C$65 (US$46). Farther south above the Windermere Valley, the **Resort Course** features awesome views of both the Rockies and the Purcell Mountains. Green fees for 18 holes are C$40 (US$28). Both resorts are owned by Radium Resort (☎ **800-667-6444;** Internet: www.radiumresort.com).

Rafting

Several companies run raft trips on the Kootenay River and gentler float trips along the Columbia River. **Kootenay River Runners** (☎ **800-599-4399,** 250-347-9210; Internet: www.raftingtherockies.com) has offices in both Radium Hot Springs and Invermere. Its one-day, 48-km (30-mile) Kootenay River trip is a good family excursion, with gorgeous Rocky Mountain scenery and opportunities to see wildlife. The trip costs C$89 (US$62) for adults, C$69 (US$48) for kids aged 14 and under, including a morning snack and buffet lunch. A half-day trip is also available.

Where to Stay in Kootenay

Except for the Kootenay Park Lodge, located in the heart of the park, these hotels are just outside the park gate, mostly in the village of Radium Hot Springs. You'll note that some are closed in the winter. A few more hotels are found in Invermere, about 14km (9 miles) farther south. The Kootenay National Park Visitor Centre (☎ **250-347-9505**) has a list of area B&Bs.

Alpen Motel
$ Radium Hot Springs

Look for the flowers. Now look for the *most* flowers. All hotels on this stretch of highway sport rows of window boxes stuffed with purple petunias, white geraniums, and other cheery blossoms. Alpen Motel is more like a collection of flower boxes decorated by a hotel. Besides smelling the flowers, you can have a soak in the nearby hot springs; a pass is included in your rate. If you like to light up, however, you should look elsewhere. Ditto if you have Fido or Fluffy in tow.

5022 Hwy. 93, Radium Hot Springs. ☎ ***888-788-3891,*** *250-347-9823. Fax: 250-347-9823. E-mail:* info@alpenmotel.com. *Internet:* www.alpenmotel.com. *Rack rates: C$59–C$99 (US$41–69) double. AE, MC, V. Mar–Oct.*

Chalet Europe

$–$$ **Radium Hot Springs**

Look up, way up. It's the spot with the wooden balconies and white stucco arches. A stunning location high above Radium Hot Springs is only part of the appeal of this rambling lodge, which houses 16 one-bedroom suites along with a family suite. In addition to unbelievable views, the spiffy rooms feature fridges, microwaves, Internet access, and fireplaces. Some even have telescopes. Chalet Europe is run by an outgoing family and a dog named McKinley.

5063 Madsen Rd., Radium Hot Springs. ☎ *888-428-9998, 250-347-9305. E-mail:* info@chaleteurope.com. *Internet:* www.chaleteurope.com. *Rack rates: C$99–C$159 (US$69–US$111) double. Rates include continental breakfast. AE, MC, V.*

Crystal Springs Motel

$ **Radium Hot Springs**

If Highway 93 seems too busy for your taste, select a motel on one of the quieter side streets just west of the highway. Crystal Springs is a reliable and economical choice. A variety of room styles are available and even the most basic units are equipped with telephones, TVs, coffeemakers, and little fridges. The affable owners, who recently moved to Radium Hot Springs from Korea, keep everything tidy and trim.

Radium Blvd. (1 block west of the Esso Station), Radium Hot Springs. ☎ *800-347-9759, 250-347-9759. Fax: 250-347-9736. E-mail:* contact@crystal springsmotel.bc.ca. *Internet:* www.crystalspringsmotel.bc.ca. *Rack rates: C$68–C$75 (US$48–US$53) double. AE, MC, V.*

Gateway Motel

$ **Radium Hot Springs**

Of the many motels that line Highway 93 through Radium Hot Springs on the fringe of Kootenay National Park, the Gateway is a standout. Although simple and basic, it's bright, fresh, and positively sparkling. The main floor is newly renovated. If you enjoy hiking, you'll be in good company here. The outdoorsy owners are extremely knowledgeable about park trails and attractions.

Hwy. 93, Box 301. ☎ *800-838-4238, 250-347-9655. Fax: 250-347-9655. Rack rates: C$45–C$65 (US$32–US$46) double. MC, V. Apr–Nov.*

Kootenay Park Lodge

$ **Kootenay National Park**

Kootenay Park Lodge is situated right in the national park, about 60km (37 miles) from Radium Hot Springs. The Canadian Pacific Railway built it in 1923. Cabins were added in the 1930s. The historic site narrowly escaped the flames of two major forest fires in the area, in 2001 and 2003. The ten cabins are equipped with fridges and coffeemakers. Most also feature fireplaces, and one contains a complete kitchen. The lodge houses a dining room. There's a park information center here, where you can pick up park passes, wilderness passes, and fishing licenses.

Vermilion Crossing, Kootenay National Park. ☎ *403-762-9196 (off season: 403-283-7482). Fax: 403-283-7482. E-mail:* info@kootenayparklodge.com. *Internet:* www.kootenayparklodge.com. *Rack rates: C$89–C$125 (US$62–US$88) double. MC, V. Mid-May–mid-Oct.*

Mountain View Lodge

$ **Invermere**

These are the most reasonably priced motel rooms in Invermere, but they're well maintained and centrally located, a quick stroll from restaurants and shops. Kitchen suites are available.

747–12th St., Invermere. ☎ *250-342-6618. Fax: 250-342-6720. E-mail:* info@mtnviewlodge.ca. *Internet:* www.mtnviewlodge.ca. *Rack rates: C$65 (US$42) double. MC, V.*

Prestige Inn

$$$–$$$$ **Radium Hot Springs**

The newest and priciest hotel rooms in Radium Hot Springs are in the Prestige Inn. The location is convenient, at the intersection of highways 93 and 95, and after your day in the park you'll welcome the pool, hot tub, and day spa. Aromatherapy massages start at C$40 (US$28) for half an hour. The hotel restaurant is uninspiring, but you can find interesting alternatives without wandering far.

7493 Main St. W., Radium. ☎ *877-737-8443, 250-347-2300. Fax: 250-347-2345. E-mail:* radium@prestigeinn.com.ca. *Internet:* www.prestigeinn.com. *Rack rates: C$170–C$300 (US$119–US$210) double. AE, MC, V.*

Super 8 Motel

$–$$ **Invermere**

This standard highway motel, which opened in 2000, is the newest spot in Invermere. Its location on a main thoroughfare isn't exactly picturesque, but it's easy to find and efficient. Amenities include a family restaurant and a hot tub. Family suites are available.

8888 Arrow Rd., Hwy. 93/95, Invermere. ☎ *888-408-7388, 250-342-8888. Fax: 250-342-8889. E-mail:* invermeresuper8@excite.ca. *Rack rates: C$90–C$135 (US$73–US$95) double. AE, MC, V.*

Parks Canada runs three main campsites in Kootenay National Park. The best — and the largest, with 240 sites — is the **Redstreak Campground,** near the village of Radium Hot Springs (watch for the turnoff beside the Visitor Centre). Of the campgrounds within the park, Redstreak is the only one with full hookups and hot showers. You can also take in evening interpretive programs at the campsite amphitheater. Some interesting walks and hikes begin in the campground, and you can stroll to the hot springs in about half an hour. Nightly rates range from C$22 (US$15) for an unserviced site to C$30 (US$21) for a site with water, sewer, and electricity.

If you're camping within Kootenay National Park, remember that you require a park pass.

Other spots to pitch your tent include the **McLeod Meadows Campground,** about 16km (10 miles) farther north in a wooded area along the banks of the Kootenay River and the **Marble Canyon Campground,** closer to the park's northern entrance. None of these park campgrounds take reservations: it's first-come, first-served.If you're camping within Kootenay National Park, remember that you require a park pass.

The Marble Canyon Campground was closed at press time because of fire damage to the surrounding region. Be sure to call ahead.

You can, however, reserve a spot at one of the nearby commercial campgrounds. The **Canyon Camp RV Resort** is conveniently situated in the village of Radium Hot Springs, just outside the Kootenay National Park gates. It's an attractive site, with spots for both RVs and tents along with showers, washrooms, and a place to do your laundry. To reserve a spot, call ☎ **250-347-9564.** Tent sites go for C$21 (US$15) a night; fully serviced sites cost C$28 (US$20) per night. Reservations are also accepted at the **Mountain Shadows Resort,** 6km (4 miles) south of Radium Hot Springs. Mountain Shadows is a smaller site, with numerous amenities, including showers, a laundromat, a convenience store, and a playground. Call ☎ **250-347-9095.** Rates are C$23 to $C26 (US$16 to US$19).

Where to Eat in Kootenay

Head for the village of Radium Hot Springs, where you can always find something to please your palate, particularly if you're fond of schnitzel and spatzle. Invermere, about 14km (9 miles) south, contains a couple of special-occasion spots along with some pubs and cafes. Can't make a decision? Stop by the front desk of your motel or hotel. Many innkeepers are happy to show you menus from popular area restaurants.

Blue Dog Café

$ **Invermere   BAKERY/CAFE**

Order at the counter and grab a stool by the window or head for the sunny patio in the back. Creative sandwiches and wraps, served with soup, salad, or tortilla chips, go for C$7.95 (US$6). Try tuna, Thai, or marinated roast beef. An abbreviated version (C$4.95/US$3.46) is offered for kids, who can dine on a grilled cheese, peanut butter and jam sandwich, or cheese-only quesadilla accompanied by a small serving of chips or soup. The iced tea here (C$1.50/US$1) is refreshing and delicious. You can also enjoy a frothy cappuccino with your breakfast or a chilled beer at lunch.

1213–7th Ave. (Main St.), Invermere. ☎ *250-342-3814. Most items under C$10 (US$7). MC, V. Mon–Sat 10 a.m.–5 p.m. (in summer, open Thurs, Fri & Sat until 9 p.m.). Sun 11 a.m.–4 p.m.*

While you're waiting for your lunch at the **Blue Dog Café,** you can **check your e-mail.** Computer time costs C$2 (US$1.40) for 15 minutes, or C$3.50 (US$2.45) for half an hour. More terminals are located in the **Book Cellar** on 12th Street and 7th Avenue (downstairs). You pay 20¢ per minute.

Helna's Stube

$$–$$$ **Radium Hot Springs   AUSTRIAN**

Stube (a warm and cozy room) is an apt description of this polished little Austrian eatery on Main Street, where candlelit tables are adorned with miniature vases of fresh pansies. The menu includes warm appetizers, such as a trilogy of deep-fried cheeses paired with cranberry sauce. For dinner, try homemade pasta (spatzle) with ham, bacon, and mushrooms or the house special, Wiener schnitzel. For fish lovers, a delectable dish is filet of sole in potato crust, served in a delicate white sauce and accompanied by parsley potatoes.

7547 Main St. W. (1 block south of the liquor store), Radium Hot Springs. ☎ *250-347-0047. Main courses: C$13–C$24 (US$9–US$17). MC, V. Daily 5–10 p.m. (in winter, closed Tues & Wed).*

Parkside Café

$ **Radium Hot Springs BAKERY/CAFE**

The cafe at the Parkside Mini Golf is a pleasant spot to start your day. Between 8:00 and 11:30 a.m., you can breakfast on French toast, eggs Benedict, or oatmeal and bananas, among other menu items. Or down a power shake prepared with low-fat yogurt, juice, honey, protein powder, bran, and wheat germ. Parkside Café also offers light lunches and yummy desserts, including a famous warm apple strudel.

4873 St. Mary's St., Radium Hot Springs. ☎ *250-347-9592. All items under C$10 (US$7). Cash only. Daily 8 a.m.–6 p.m.*

Peppi's Italian Fuel

$–$$ **Invermere ITALIAN**

Peppi's likes to boast that some of its regular customers come all the way from Calgary, which is a three-hour drive. Who knows? All these customers have to come from *somewhere*. Peppi's is a hugely popular little eatery with a very extensive pizza menu. In addition to pepperoni, onions, and other ordinary pizza fixings, you find trendier toppings such as roasted garlic, bruschetta, banana peppers, and coconut. If nothing on the 20-pizza lineup appeals to you, create your own: The toppings and sauces (secret sauce, sweet BBQ, pesto, garlic, or tomato) are all mix-and-matchable.

1018–8th Ave., Invermere. ☎ *250-342-3421. Reservations not accepted in summer. Medium pizzas: C$12.95–C$17.95 (US$9–US$13). Pastas: C$7.95–C$11.95 (US$6–US$8). MC, V. Daily 4:30–11 p.m.*

Strand's Old House

$$–$$$$ **Invermere INTERNATIONAL**

This beautifully restored 1912 home is just a few blocks from Invermere's main street on a manicured lot with a gazebo and views of the Rockies. It's a lovely spot for an elegant, special dinner and the food garners rave reviews. The chef serves up West Coast salmon, pork fusilli, veal schnitzel, and various game dishes. Prime rib is featured on Sundays. If you don't object to dining between 5:00 and 6:15 p.m., you can take advantage of a three-course early-bird dinner for C$11.95 (US$8). Four dinner choices are available.

818–12th St., Invermere. ☎ *250-342-6344. Reservations recommended (call after 3 p.m.). Main courses: C$17–C$30 (US$12–US$21). MC, V. Daily from 5 p.m.*

If you're camping in the park, detour into Invermere to stock your picnic basket with mega-grain bread or a loaf of sunflower rye from the **Quality Bakery.** It's at the bottom of Main Street: 1305–7th Ave., ☎ **250-342-9913.** (There's a giant pretzel over the door.) Run by a Swiss baker and pastry chef, the shop also sells marvelous flax-seed crackers, tasty cookies, and fresh-from-the-oven scones. The doors open at 7:30 a.m. and the goodies go fast. A few tables are also available and light lunches are served. The menu is usually posted by the sidewalk.

Fast Facts: Kootenay National Park

Area Code
☎ 250.

ATMs
In the village of Radium Hot Springs: Mountainside Market on Main St. E. next to the Visitor Centre and in the Petro Canada service station, corner of Highway 93 and Highway 95.

Emergencies
Ambulance: ☎ **250-342-2055**; Fire: ☎ **250-347-6590**; Police: ☎ **250-342-9292**.

Fees
A day pass to Kootenay National Park costs C$7 (US$4.90) adults, C$14 (US$9) groups. An annual National Parks Pass, for all national parks in Canada, is C$45 (US$31) adults, C$89 (US$63) groups.

Fishing Licenses
A fishing license for the national park costs C$7 (US$4.90) a day, C$20 (US$14) for the year. Pick one up at the Visitor Centre, the Radium Hot Pools, or a campground kiosk.

Hospitals
Invermere & District Hospital, 850–10th Ave., Invermere. ☎ **250-342-9201**.

Information
Call ☎ **250-347-9505**.

Post Office
Radium Boulevard, Radium Hot Springs.

Road Conditions and Weather
Road conditions: ☎ **403-762-1450**. Weather: ☎ **403-762-2088**.

Taxes
British Columbia's provincial sales tax is 7.5%. The 7% national Goods & Services tax (GST) applies to most goods and services, although visitors can apply for a rebate on some purchases. Most hotels charge an 8% hotel room tax.

Time Zone
Mountain Standard.

Web Site
www.parkscanada.gc.ca

Chapter 21

British Columbia Provincial Parks

*E*ven though 8 to 10 million people visit the Canadian Rockies each year, places exist where you can dodge the crowds and more or less be at one with the wilderness. One sure way to retreat is to visit a region that nobody can get to by car. This chapter presents two parks that fit that description: **Hamber Provincial Park,** near Jasper, and **Mount Assiniboine Provincial Park,** farther south and beside Banff. If you're an experienced backpacker, it's possible to reach both of these spots on foot. Each park also contains a backcountry lodge that (for a price) will happily fly you in and feed you.

The other destination in this chapter, **Mount Robson Provincial Park,** also near Jasper, is a bit off the traveled track but accessible by car. In fact, it's on a major highway: The Yellowhead. This park protects the highest peak in the Canadian Rockies, Mount Robson, and features one of Canada's top backpacking adventures, the Berg Lake Trail.

Unlike their four neighbors (Banff, Jasper, Kootenay, and Yoho), which are Canadian national parks, these three wilderness regions are managed by the province of British Columbia. All seven parks, however, are part of the same World Heritage Site, comprising one of the largest protected areas in the world.

British Columbia Provincial Parks

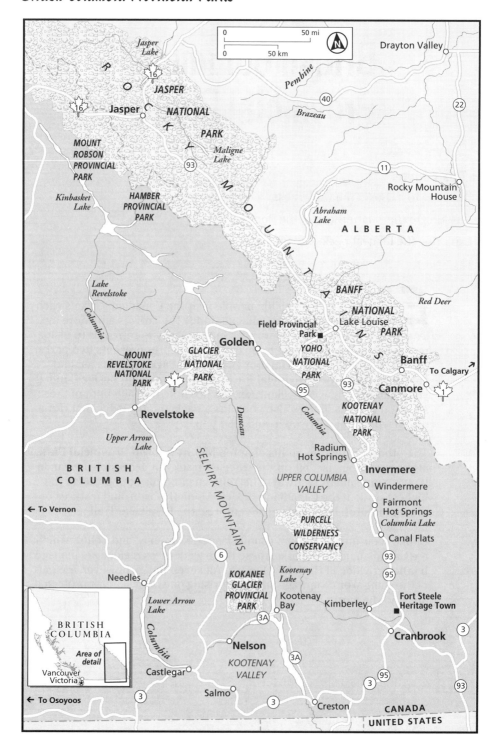

Hamber Provincial Park

You may have heard of Kootenay National Park, or Yoho, maybe even Mount Assiniboine . . . but *Hamber?* This small piece of northern Rockies wilderness (24,000 hectares/over 59,000 acres) on the Alberta–British Columbia border beside Jasper National Park, is the least developed and most remote of all the parks in this book. Hamber Provincial Park protects **Fortress Lake,** a beautiful 15-km (9-mile) long mountain lake that's chock-full of eastern brook trout. Here you find some of the best trout fishing in the Rockies, along with some of the most pristine wilderness scenery. Icefields surround the lake: the Chaba, Clemenceau, and Columbia icefields to the south and east, and the Hooker Icefield and Serenity Glacier at the west end. The park is also a prime habitat for black and grizzly bears. Not many people visit Hamber Provincial Park, because it's accessible only on foot (unless you fly) and the nearest road is more than 20km (12 miles) away.

Getting to Hamber Provincial Park isn't as simple as driving along the highway and wheeling through a park entrance. You either hike in and pitch your tent or fly in to a lodge.

Roughing it (backpacking)

The hiking trail to Hamber Provincial Park starts on Highway 93 (the Icefields Parkway) at Sunwapta Falls, about 55km (34 miles) south of the Jasper Townsite in Jasper National Park. Refer to Chapter 14 for information on visiting Jasper. (Although Hamber Park is located in the province of British Columbia, the closest highway is in Alberta.) You can leave your car in the Sunwapta Falls parking lot as long as you have a National Parks Pass.

The 24-km (15-mile) trail from Sunwapta Falls to Fortress Lake is well marked, but about 3km (2 miles) before you reach the lake, you have to cross the Chaba River, which can be treacherous if not impossible, particularly in July and August, when the river is fast and high.

Jasper National Park operates the campsites along the trail, and you require a Wilderness Pass. In Hamber Provincial Park, there's a primitive campground at the east end of Fortress Lake, with a bear-pole for storing your food. If you intend to fish, make sure you have a license.

Not roughing it

The other way to see the park is as a guest of **Fortress Lake Wilderness Retreat** (☎ **250-344-2639;** Fax: 250-344-5520; Internet: `www.fortresslake.com`). In that case, the park is a one-hour trip, by floatplane, and you depart from Golden, B.C., about a three-hour drive from Calgary (for information on visiting Golden, see Chapter 18). The retreat, located on the lakeshore, consists of a main lodge and five rustic cabins. In addition to fishing for eastern brook trout (the average catch weighs 1 kilogram/2.5 pounds and is 45 centimeters/18 inches long), you can canoe, kayak, and hike through the wilderness. This spot is run by the same folks who operate Purcell Lodge (see "Where to Stay" in Chapter 18). Expect three scrumptious meals a day. Rates are about C\$400 (US\$280) per person a day, and include round-trip transportation along with all your food.

Mount Assiniboine Provincial Park

This triangular-shaped, 39,000-hectare (96,000-acre) chunk of wilderness, bordered by Banff National Park to the east and Kootenay National Park to the west, is a Rocky Mountain wonderland of peaks, lakes, forests, and meadows. Grizzly bears, mountain goats, deer, and bighorn sheep reside here, along with about 100 species of birds. Daisies, Indian paintbrush, and scores of other wildflowers carpet the mountain slopes in summer. The whole park sits at an elevation of more than 1,500 meters (nearly 5,000 feet) above sea level and a few mountains tower above 3,100 meters (10,168 feet). The star attraction is **Mount Assiniboine,** a 3,618-meter (11,867-foot) distinctive, Matterhorn-like peak and the tallest mountain in the southern Rockies. Mount Assiniboine is visible from the Sunshine Village ski area in Banff National Park. The top views, of course, are reserved for those who visit the park. What you will not find in Mount Assiniboine Provincial Park are highways. To reach the park, you have three options: hike, ski, or fly by helicopter.

Getting there

Mount Assiniboine Provincial Park is 48km (30 miles) southwest of Banff and just west of the Alberta/B.C. border. It's accessible by hiking trail from Kananaskis Country or Banff National Park in Alberta and from Kootenay National Park in British Columbia.

The most popular trail into the park, **Assiniboine Pass,** starts in the Mount Shark day-use area in Kananaskis Country and takes you along Bryant Creek in Banff National Park. It's a 28-km (17-mile) trek. Give yourself at least six hours. The hike from the **Sunshine Village ski area in Banff** National Park is a more ambitious journey, covering 30km (19 miles). This distance assumes you catch a shuttle bus from the ski area parking lot to Sunshine Village. Otherwise, plan for a further 6km (4 miles) . . . all uphill. There's also a trail through **Kootenay National Park,** but it's a long haul. The 45-km (28-mile) hike starts at the junction of the Vermilion and Simpson Rivers near Highway 93, about 56km (35 miles) north of Radium Hot Springs.

If you want to ski to Mount Assiniboine park, take the Assiniboine Pass Trail. Call Mount Assiniboine Lodge (☎ **403-678-2883**) before you head out to check on trail conditions.

The easiest and fastest (8 minutes) way to reach Mount Assiniboine Provincial Park is by helicopter. Flights depart at 1 p.m. Mountain Standard Time on Sundays, Wednesdays, and Fridays from the Mount Shark Heliport in Kananaskis Country, Alberta, near Mount Engadine Lodge. The heliport is a one-hour drive from Canmore. If you're coming from Calgary, allow 2.5 to 3 hours. Mount Assiniboine Lodge handles flight arrangements. Call ☎ **403-678-2883.** The fare is C$100 (US$70) one-way, and you pay when you book, by MasterCard or Visa. If you're hiking or skiing to the park, you can lighten your load by sending your gear on the helicopter. You pay C$1.50 (US$1.05) per pound, each way.

Planning ahead

No supplies are available in the park, so you must be self-sufficient or have a reservation at the lodge.

The best months for hiking are July, August, and early September. Weather can be lovely in summer, with warm sunny days and temperatures up to 25° Celsius (80° Fahrenheit). But prepare, as well, for rain and cold. The thermometer may dip to –8° Celsius (20° Fahrenheit) at night. In winter, temperatures of –30° Celsuis (–20° Fahrenheit) aren't unheard of, but a chinook wind can warm things up considerably.

To reach the park by helicopter, you should reserve your flight about two weeks ahead. The helicopter operates from mid-June to early October in the hiking season and mid-February to mid-April for skiers.

If you're hiking in through Banff National Park and plan to camp in the park on the way, you need a Wilderness Pass and you should reserve a campsite. See "Backcountry adventures" in Chapter 12. To reserve accommodation in the **Naiset Huts** in Mount Assiniboine Provincial Park, call ☎ **403-678-2883.**

For information on travel in British Columbia, contact **Tourism Rockies,** Box 10, 1905 Warren Avenue, Kimberley, B.C., V1A 2Y5, or call ☎ **250-427-4838.** You may also want to visit the B.C. Parks Web site at Internet: www.bcparks.ca.

Paying fees

If you're staying in Banff National Park, you require a National Parks Pass, which costs C$7 (US$4.90) a day for adults, and C$14 (US$9) a day for a group. Annual passes go for C$45 (US$36) or C$89 (US$62) for groups. A Wilderness Pass, to camp in the backcountry in Banff, costs C$8 (US$6) a night or C$56 (US$39) for the year.

Camping fees at Mount Assiniboine are C$5 (US$3.50) a night. You can also get a bed in a wilderness hut for C$20 (US$14) a night.

Where to stay in Mount Assiniboine Provincial Park

Your options in the park, from comfortably rustic to roughing-it rustic, are a lodge room or private cabin, a bed in a backcountry hut, or your tent.

Mount Assiniboine Lodge
$

This is as cushy as it gets in the park. The historic Mount Assiniboine Lodge, situated at an elevation of 2,180 meters (7,200 feet), was built by the Canadian Pacific Railway in 1928. Now owned by B.C. Parks and privately run, the lodge offers rustic but comfy accommodation and tasty meals. The Norwegian-style main building features a communal dining room and six rooms (upstairs) with shared bath and shower. Nearby are six one-room cabins with cold running water and propane heat and light. Guests share outhouse and shower house facilities. Minimum stay is two nights. Rates include all meals, along with the services of hiking guides. For winter guests, the lodge provides climbing skins, avalanche transceivers, and snowshoes.

In Mount Assiniboine Provincial Park. ☎ *403-678-2883. Fax: 403-678-4877. E-mail:* info@assiniboinelodge.com. *Internet:* www.assiniboinelodge.com. *Rack rates: Summer: Lodge room C$190 (US$133) per person, cabin for two C$240 (US$168) per person. Winter: Lodge room C$170 (US$119) per person, cabin for two C$210 (US$147) per person. Rates include all meals. MC, V. Helicopter transportation for guests of the lodge is C$100 (US$70) each way.*

About a five-minute walk from the lodge, the **Naiset Huts,** built by the Alpine Club of Canada in 1925, offer basic accommodation for C$20 (US$14) per person a night. The four one-room huts (think trapper cabins) sleep about five to eight people each, so don't plan on privacy. You're pretty much on your own here. You need your own sleeping bag, gas stove, cooking equipment, soap, and toilet paper. Sweep the floor and close the door snugly before you leave. The C$20 (US$14) nightly rate includes a C$5 (US$2.80) reservation fee. In winter, reservations (☎ **403-678-2883**) are required to stay in these huts. In summer, you don't have to book ahead, but it's a good idea. If you come without a reservation, be ready to pitch your tent should the huts be full.

The main camping area, on the west side of **Lake Magog,** has 25 sites with gravel pads, two outhouses, and a water tap. You can also camp at Og Lake. Camping fees are C$5 (US$2.80) per night. Reservations are not accepted for the campsites, but you can count on finding a spot here. Open fires are not permitted in the campgrounds.

Hitting the trails

Once you arrive in the park, you can meander to nearby lakes and viewpoints or embark on more strenuous trips.

Hiking

Many trails start near Mount Assiniboine Lodge. If you're staying at the lodge, you have the option of joining a guided hike.

The hikes to nearby **Elizabeth Lake** and **Sunburst Lake** are lovely, or you might wander up to **Og Lake,** about 6km (4 miles) from the lodge. The climb to **Windy Ridge,** roughly the same distance, is more of a grind, but worth the effort, as is the trail to **Nub Peak,** with panoramic views of nearby peaks, valleys, and lakes.

The fairly strenuous hike to **Wonder Pass** and Banff National Park also promises memorable scenery, including picturesque views of **Marvel Lake.** Ultimately, this trail connects with the Assiniboine Pass/Bryant Creek trail to the Mount Shark day-use area in Kananaskis. The entire trip covers 28km (17 miles).

For information on trail conditions, check in at the visitor center in Banff National Park (☎ **403-762-1550**) or call Mount Assiniboine Lodge (☎ **403-678-2883**).

Skiing

This park is a magnificent spot for cross-country skiing and tele-marking. You may be treated to deep layers of fantastic powder as late in the year as April. The Assiniboine Pass Trail into the park from Kananaskis Country in Alberta is a favorite trip. If you're heading into this park in winter, you definitely want to be familiar with avalanche safety. Guests at Mount Assiniboine Lodge are provided with avalanche transceivers (for locating buried people in the event of an avalanche) and climbing skins for skis. Snowshoes are available, and you can rent tele-mark ski packages if you call ahead.

Mount Robson Provincial Park

Mountaineers from around the world come to this park to climb Mount Robson, and many visitors who aren't climbers come here just to gaze at the peak. At 3,954 meters (12,972 feet), Mount Robson is the highest mountain in the Canadian Rockies. Early trappers, hunters, and explorers were awestruck when they caught sight of it. The First Nations people called it "mountain of spiral" because of its layered appearance. Climbers first reached the summit of Mount Robson in 1913. The provincial park, created in the same year, is one of the oldest in British Columbia, spanning nearly 225,000 hectares (556,000 acres) of largely undeveloped wilderness. Keep your eyes peeled for deer, moose, elk, wolves, coyotes, and bears. This park also protects the headwaters of the Fraser River, which empties into the Pacific Ocean.

Getting there and getting around

If Jasper National Park is on your travel agenda, it's easy to include a side trip to Mount Robson. Highway 16, the Yellowhead Highway, which runs through Jasper, takes you right through the heart of the provincial park.

Flying in

The closest major airports are in Edmonton, Calgary, and Vancouver, British Columbia. Major car rental companies are well represented in all three airports. Air Canada (☎ 888-247-2262) operates nonstop flights to these cities from many parts of Canada and the U.S., while **WestJet** (☎ 888-937-8538) flies from many Canadian destinations. Air Canada also flies to Kamloops, B.C., which is about a four-hour drive from Mount Robson.

Driving in

See Chapter 14 for advice on travel to Jasper National Park. From Jasper Townsite, drive west on Highway 16 for about 95km (59 miles). If you're coming through B.C., Mount Robson is about 4 hours north of Kamloops on Highway 5, or 3.5 hours east of Prince George on Highway 16.

Planning ahead

Contact Mount Robson Park Headquarters, Box 579, Valemount, B.C., V0E 2Z0. Internet: www.bcparks.ca.

B.C.'s campsite reservation line is ☎ **800-689-9025.** Use this number to book a spot at the **Robson Meadows Campground** in the park and for backcountry campsites on the **Berg Lake Trail.** Call Monday to Friday between 7 a.m. and 7 p.m. (Pacific Time), weekends and holidays 9 a.m. to 5 p.m. You pay (by MasterCard or Visa) the campsite fee and a reservation fee when you book. Visit Internet: www.discovercamping.ca for more information.

If you use B.C.'s toll-free (☎ **800-689-9025**) or online (Internet: www.discovercamping.ca) campsite reservation system, make sure your travel plans are relatively firm. It costs an extra C$6.42 (US$4.49) to change your reservation. If you opt out altogether, you pay up to C$26 (US$18) (depending on how many nights you had booked) for cancellations with more than seven days' notice and up to C$46 (US$32) if you cancel less than seven days in advance.

For information on travel to Jasper National Park, see Chapter 14. For information on Valemount, B.C., which is about 40km (25 miles) west of the Mount Robson Provincial Park, check out Internet: www.valemount.org.

Arriving in the park

A gas station, convenience store, and cafeteria are located inside the park's western gate, beside the visitor center.

Finding information

The **Mount Robson Park Visitor Centre** is open from May to October. Call ☎ **250-566-4325.** Here, you can check trail conditions, pick up information on park activities and other B.C. destinations, and check out displays and exhibits. Meander along an interpretive trail through the open fields behind the center, where you can admire Mount Robson from various vantage points.

Paying fees

No admission fee is charged to visit Mount Robson Park. If you hike the Berg Lake Trail, you pay a backcountry camping fee of C$5 (US$3.50) per night. There's a C$6.42 (US$4.49) per night charge to reserve a campsite. See "Planning Ahead" above.

Anglers are required to buy a fishing license. In B.C. a daily license costs C$10 (US$7) for B.C. residents, C$20 (US$14) for nonresidents. Buy one at the Robson Shadows Campground, 5km (3 miles) west of the park on Highway 16. Eight-day and annual permits are also available.

Exploring the park

The big draw in Mount Robson Provincial park is, well, Mount Robson. You can admire the peak from the various vantage points, depending on what type of recreation you prefer. Here are some top choices.

Cycling and mountain biking

Two-wheelers are allowed on the first 7km (4 miles) of the Berg Lake Trail, up to the Kinney Lake campground. You can do the round trip (from the Mount Robson Park Visitor Centre) in less than two hours. You can also peddle along the Trans-Mountain Pipeline right-of-way, which follows the Fraser River.

Mountain bikes are only allowed on the first 7 kilometers (4 miles) of the Berg Lake trail.

Hiking

Aside from hiking the well-known **Berg Lake Trail** (see below), you can explore some memorable backcountry in the east end of the park. On the **Yellow Mountain Trail,** you see Mount Fitzwilliam, Waddington Peak, Yellowhead Pass, and two nearby lakes. It's a fairly steep climb, gaining 800 meters (2,625 feet) over 8.5km (5 miles). The trail starts about 53km (33 miles) east of the Mount Robson Park Visitor Centre, near Whitney Lake. Plan to be on the trail for three to five hours. The **Mount Fitzwilliam Trail,** a 14-km/9-mile (one-way) overnight trip, begins at Yellowhead Lake and ascends through timbered switchbacks to backcountry campsites and trailheads for several day hikes. Mount Fitzwilliam (2,911 meters/9,538 feet) is visible from Highway 16. Stop by the Visitor Centre to register for travel in the backcountry, pick up maps and check trail conditions.

Shorter strolls and easy walks, some with interpretive displays, start near the Robson River, Robson Meadows, and Lucerne campgrounds and behind the park visitor center.

The **Berg Lake Trail** in Mount Robson Provincial Park is one of the most popular backpacking trips in the Canadian Rockies. It begins beside the Robson River and climbs to Berg Lake on the north face of Mount Robson, showcasing scenery so compelling that many hikers return again and again.

The 21-km (13-mile) trail starts near the Visitor Centre and winds gently through a lush, coastal-like forest of cedar and hemlock to Kinney Lake. About 7km (4 miles) from the trailhead, you arrive at the Kinney Lake campsite, and a few kilometers farther along, the Whitehead campsite. From here, it's a tougher grind, as you switchback through the Valley of a Thousand Falls, gaining about 500 meters (1,640 feet) over the next 4km (2.5 miles). The final stretch of the trail, which offers marvelous views of the north face of Mount Robson, delivers you to the stunning, blue-green waters of Berg Lake, fed by the Berg, Mist, and Robson glaciers. The Berg Glacier is one of the few advancing glaciers in the Canadian Rockies. As you catch your breath near the lakeshore, you may see a massive ice chunk calve off the glacier.

The hiking season at Mount Robson runs from June to September. Wildflowers are spectacular through July and August, and you can take in rich fall colors later in the year.

If you have time to stay at Berg Lake for more than one night, you can venture off on shorter hikes that lead to nearby lakes, waterfalls, glaciers, and viewpoints.

Along the Berg Lake Trail, camping is allowed at seven designated sites. The largest campsite, at the lake, has 26 tent pads. To reserve a campsite, call ☎ **800-689-9025** up to three months before your trip. The camping fee is C$5 (US$3.50) per person a night. There's also a reservation fee of C$6.42 (US$4.49) a night to a maximum of C$19.26 (US$13.48). You pay when you make the reservation, by MasterCard or Visa. Some campsites are also available for hikers without reservations, on a first-come, first-served basis. Before you head into the backcountry, you must register with the Mount Robson Visitor Centre.

If you're determined to visit Berg Lake, but short on time or not enthusiastic about shouldering a heavy pack, local companies offer a variety of heli-hiking trips and guided tours. **Robson Heli-Magic** (☎ **250-566-4700;** Internet: www.robsonhelimagic.com) will transport you to Berg Lake for C$175 (US$123), and you can hike out on your own. If you're reasonably fit and have some hiking experience, you can probably handle this trip. Expect to be on the trail for six to eight hours. Robson Heli-Magic also offers sight-seeing tours of Mount Robson by helicopter. **Hike Inc** (☎ **866-445-3462,** 250-968-4457; Internet: www.hikeinc.ca) runs four-night guided hiking trips in July and August and five-night trips in the fall. They cost C$150 (US$105) per day.

So . . . salmon follow the stars?

If you visit Mount Robson Provincial Park in late August or September, you can see salmon returning home to their birthplace in the Fraser River.

Chinook salmon that begin life in the Fraser River eventually make their way to the Pacific Ocean, where they grow to full size over the course of three to four years. When the fish are mature, they head back home, covering nearly 30km (19 miles) a day, swimming against strong currents, through rapids, and up waterfalls. Scientists believe that the salmon may recognize star patterns that help guide them home.

By the time these fish reach their freshwater birthplace, 1,200km (745 miles) from the ocean, their silver-colored bodies have turned dark red and become tattered and worn. Once in their native water, the salmon pair up to spawn. The females prepare nests and lay eggs — about 500 to 700 at a time — and the males fight off other fish and fertilize the eggs. The spawning process lasts for a few days, until both the female and male fish are exhausted. When the fish die, their bodies decompose in the water or get washed to the shore, where they provide food for bald eagles, bears, and other birds and animals. The eggs hatch, develop into "fry," and eventually head out to sea.

If you want to watch the salmon, there's a viewing platform at Rearguard Falls, on the south side of Highway 16, just west of the park. Visitors are asked to watch quietly, to avoid running along the riverbanks, and to stay out of the water so as not to disturb the fish.

Rafting

Mount Robson Whitewater Rafting (☎ **888-566-7238,** 250-566-4879), based at the Mount Robson Lodge (see "Where to Stay" below), offers 14-km (9-mile), three-hour whitewater rafting trips (class I or mild rapids, to class III, or wilder rapids) on the Fraser River between late May and mid-September. Trips depart at 9:30 a.m. and 1:00 p.m. daily and cost C$65 (US$46) or C$75 (US$53) with a lunch barbecue. As well as enjoying stellar views of Mount Robson, you pass Rearguard Falls, where you may see spawning salmon at the end of the journey home from the Pacific. The company also offers a gentle, 2.5-hour sight-seeing float trip (no rapids) for C$49 (US$34).

Where to stay in Mount Robson Provincial Park

Aside from campsites in Mount Robson Provincial Park, the closest beds are along Highway 16, just west of the park, where you can book a room in a log cabin or B&B. For a wider selection of hotels, drive farther west and south (about half an hour) to the village of Valemount.

Mountain River Lodge

$$ West of Mount Robson Provincial Park

This semi-isolated spot just west of the park is peaceful and wild, with a forested, riverside setting and marvelous views of Mount Robson. Bed-and-breakfast accommodation is offered in a bright, roomy main lodge. The rooms all have private baths, and two open onto balconies with mountain panoramas. Log cabins with kitchens are also available. Guests in the cabins can have breakfast for an additional C$10 (US$7).

On Hwy. 16 and Swift Current Creek, 4km (2.5 miles) west of Mount Robson Park Information Centre. ☎ *888-566-9899, 250-566-9899. Fax: 250-566-9899. Internet:* www.mtrobson.com. *Rack rates: B&B: C$105 (US$74) double, including breakfast. Cabin: C$125 (US$88). MC, V.*

Mount Robson Lodge

$$ West of Mount Robson Provincial Park

Wander through fields of lupins while you contemplate your visit to Mount Robson. Log cabins, some with kitchens, are situated on spacious grounds overlooking the Fraser River. The cozy cabins have large windows from which you can savor the mountain views. You can also camp here, at the **Robson Shadows Campground.** Campsites are beside the river, and washrooms and showers are available.

Hwy. 16, 5km (3 miles) west of Mount Robson Park. ☎ *888-566-4821, 250-566-4821. Fax: 250-566-9190. Internet:* www.mountrobsonlodge.com. *Rack rates: C$125 (US$88) double. Camping: C$15 (US$11) per vehicle. MC, V. May–Oct.*

In Mount Robson Provincial Park, the main campground is **Robson Meadows,** a treed site along the Fraser River with 125 camping spots. The site has hot showers, flush toilets, and you can walk to the visitor center and convenience store. You're also near hiking trails and interpretive walks. Rates are C$17 (US$12) per night. To reserve a spot, call ☎ **800-689-9025** or visit Internet: www.discovercamping.ca. You can book up to three months before your trip, and you pay by credit card (MasterCard or Visa) at time of booking. You also pay a reservation fee of C$6.42 (US$4.49) per night, to a maximum of C$19.26 (US$13).

Two other campgrounds are located in the park. Both are first-come, first-served. You can pitch your tent in a small campground (19 sites) along the **Robson River,** where you find flush toilets and hot showers, or at the more basic **Lucerne** campsite (34 sites) in the eastern end of the park on Yellowhead Lake. Camping fees are C$17 (US$12) at Robson River and C$14 (US$10) at Lucerne. Credit cards are not accepted.

Where to eat in Mount Robson Provincial Park

Aside from the cafeteria beside the visitor center, no restaurants are located in the park. You find groceries and some casual restaurants in Valemount, about 40km (25 miles) southwest of the park.

Fast Facts: British Columbia Provincial Parks

Area Code

☎ 250.

ATMs

If you're traveling to Hamber Provincial Park, stop in Jasper, Alberta, or Golden, B.C. If you're heading to Mount Assiniboine Provincial Park, the handiest ATMs are in Canmore or Kananaskis Country, Alberta. For visitors to Mount Robson Provincial Park, ATMs are in Jasper, Alberta or Valemount, B.C.

Emergencies

Hamber and mount Robson Provincial Parks: Valemount RCMP ☎ 250-566-4466. Mount Assiniboine Provincial Park: Mount Assiniboine Lodge ☎ 403-678-2883

Fees

No park admission fee. Backcountry campsites cost C$5 (US$3.50) per night.

Fishing Licenses

B.C. residents pay C$10 (US$7), non-residents C$20 (US$14), for one-day. Annual licenses: B.C. residents: C$36 (US$25), other Canadians: C$55 (US$39), visitors: C$80 (US$56).

Hospitals

Seaton General Hospital (☎ 708-852-3344), McBride and District Hospital (☎ 250-569-2251) in the village of McBride, 90km (56 miles) west of Mount Robson on Highway 16.

Information

Hamber Provincial Park: Jasper National Park Information Centre ☎ 780-852-6176; Fortress Lake Wilderness Retreat ☎ 250-344-2639. Mount Assiniboine Provincial Park: Mount Assiniboine Lodge ☎ 403-678-2883. Mount Robson Park Headquarters ☎ 250-566-4325.

Road Conditions and Weather

Jasper/Banff highway conditions: ☎ 403-762-1450. Weather in Jasper ☎ 780-852-3185. Weather in Banff/Kootenay region: ☎ 403-762-2088.

Taxes

British Columbia's provincial sales tax is 7.5%. The 7% national Goods & Services tax (GST) applies to most goods and services, although visitors to Canada can apply for a rebate on some purchases. Most hotels charge an 8% hotel room tax.

Time Zone

Mount Robson Provincial Park: Pacific Standard Time; Mount Assiniboine and Hamber provincial parks: Mountain Standard Time.

Web Site

www.bcparks.ca

Part VI
The Part of Tens

The 5th Wave   By Rich Tennant

"Okay—here they come. Remember, it's alot
like catching salmon only spit out the poles."

In this part...

*I*f I hadn't included this section, you'd still be able to find your way to the Canadian Rockies, check in to some terrific hotels, and enjoy meals in the best restaurants. Essential trip-planning advice and information is all spelled out before you even get to this bonus part of the book. The Rocky Mountain Highs and Stellar Vistas listed in the following pages are also described in other chapters. I highlight them here because I think they're standout places and experiences. The Treats to Take on a Day Hike are just that — a few extra goodies.

Chapter 22

Ten Stellar Vistas

*W*hen you travel through a region of rugged mountains, jewel-colored lakes, wild rivers, pine forests, and flower-filled meadows, it's impossible *not* to be awed by the remarkable scenery. Every turn in the road unveils another stellar view.

All the same, certain scenes do stand out. In this chapter, I tell you about some quintessential Canadian Rocky Mountain landscapes that qualify as postcard images. Those places have delighted explorers, captivated artists and writers, and inspired entrepreneurs. It's no surprise that the list also includes regional superlatives: the highest peak, the largest lake.

As well as being impressive, these places are accessible. No need to climb hills, ford rivers, cross glaciers, or hire a helicopter to take in the views. You can drive right in (or up, or past, or through).

Add to this the very real possibility of a deer, elk, mountain goat, or bighorn sheep wandering into your field of view, and you begin to understand why the Canadian Rockies are world famous for scenery.

Banff Townsite

Towns aren't usually regarded as scenic highlights. Especially towns descended on by 4 million tourists a year. Then again, few towns can boast a setting to rival that of Banff. It's situated along the Bow River in the southeastern corner of Banff National Park, with **Cascade Mountain** to the north, in line with Banff Avenue; **Tunnel Mountain** to the east; and **Mount Rundle** (the one you often see on postcards, towering above the town) to the south. On the western edge of Banff, on the lower slopes of **Sulphur Mountain,** you find the hot springs that led to the creation of a national park here in the first place. Sure, it's commercialized and touristy. But the town of Banff is also surrounded by beauty. So before you head for Starbucks or McDonald's, be sure to stand back and take in the view. See Chapter 13.

Kananaskis Valley

Highway 40 through Alberta's Kananaskis Country escorts you along the eastern slopes of the Canadian Rockies through a landscape so wild and beautiful that it's tricky to keep your eyes on the road. Heading south from Highway 1 (the Trans-Canada), Highway 40 skirts past Barrier Lake and parallels the Kananaskis River on its journey to the Kananaskis Lakes, passing numerous picturesque peaks (**Mount Kidd,** for instance, west of the highway in the Kananaskis Village area, and **Mount McDougal** to the east). This region of mountains and foothills was set aside for outdoor recreation to "rejuvenate people's spirits." Kananaskis Country is inspiring any time of year, whether you venture into the wilderness or just motor along the highway and contemplate the possibilities. See Chapter 16.

Lake Louise

When you stand on the shore of Lake Louise in Banff National Park, the elements of a classic Rocky Mountain postcard setting are assembled before your eyes: the famous lake, whose waters are a rich blue-green, and beyond it, on the opposite shore, the glacier-clad Mount Victoria and the neighboring peaks of Fairview and Lefroy. The grand Chateau Lake Louise overlooks it all. If you visit in winter, when the lake is a sheet of ice and the hotel grounds are draped in snow, the scene is all the more enchanting, especially in January, when you can catch a professional ice carvers' competition (Ice Magic) and watch the lakeshore transformed into a gallery of cool, clear art. Granted, all this beauty does attract a lot of people. But to be frank, against a backdrop of glaciers and 11,000-foot (3,353-meter) peaks, they look rather insignificant. See Chapter 12.

Maligne Canyon and Maligne Lake

This 55-meter (165-foot) limestone canyon, carved by the waters of the Maligne River, is the deepest canyon in Jasper National Park and one of the most fascinating gorges in the Canadian Rockies. Follow the interpretive trail to get a good look. Various footbridges cross the canyon. The scenery is dramatically different in winter, and it's possible to walk on the frozen canyon floor if you do so with a guide. While you're in the Maligne Valley region, make a stop at Maligne Lake, the longest lake in Jasper (22 km/13.6 miles long) and the second-largest glacial lake in the world. It's also one of the most picturesque places in the park, and a popular spot for boat tours. Many of the mountains around Maligne Lake, including **Leah Peak** and **Samson Peak,** were named by Mary Schaffer, a Quaker from Philadelphia who explored the Rockies in the early 1900s and was the first non-Native woman to visit much of Banff and Jasper national parks. See Chapter 14.

Moraine Lake

Who's the fairest of them all? In Banff National Park, it's hard to imagine a dreamier lake than Louise . . . until you take a tour to nearby Moraine Lake. Hmm. This smaller lake, encircled by the glaciated mountains of the **Valley of the Ten Peaks** (the Wenkchemna Valley), definitely stops you in your tracks. "No scene has ever given me an equal impression of inspiring solitude and rugged grandeur," wrote Walter Wilcox, an American mountaineering enthusiast who spent considerable time in the Canadian Rockies in the late 1800s and was among the first to visit the Valley of the Ten Peaks. It was Wilcox who named the lake "Moraine," after a rock pile, or moraine, deposited by the **Wenkchemna Glacier.** Today, a lakeshore trail to the rock pile allows you to appreciate the scene Wilcox raved about from various vantage points. To the north (behind Moraine Lake Lodge), you can see the towering summit of **Mount Temple,** the tallest mountain in the area (11,650 feet/3,551 meters) and the third highest peak in the park. See Chapter 12.

Mount Edith Cavell

You can spot the snow-capped Mount Edith Cavell from Jasper Townsite. In fact, you can't miss it. The tallest peak in the area (3,363 meters/11,030 feet), Edith Cavell defines Jasper's southern skyline. For a closer look, drive up a winding 14.5-km (9-mile) road to the north side of the massive mountain, where you can gape at **Angel Glacier** hanging between two peaks. See Chapter 14.

Mount Robson

It isn't difficult to imagine that this mountain is the highest in the Canadian Rockies — at 3,954 meters (12,972 feet) it towers over neighboring peaks. It isn't the tallest in Canada, however. That's Mount Logan, in the Yukon, which rises another 2,000 meters (6,561 feet) higher. All the same, Mount Robson is so massive that it creates its own climate. Its summit is frequently covered in cloud. For those who aspire to climb the mountain, unpredictable weather is a major challenge. If you simply want to stand in Mount Robson's presence, follow the Yellowhead Highway into Mount Robson Provincial Park and head for the visitor center near the park's western entrance. There's an excellent viewing area here. See Chapter 21.

Sinclair Canyon

You drive through the sheer rock cliffs of Sinclair Canyon at the southern entrance to Kootenay National Park in B.C. The narrow gorge makes for a stately welcome to the park, even if you stay in your car, but to really soak up this vista, slip into your swimsuit and sink into the Radium Hot Springs pool, where you can eyeball the canyon walls through a curtain of steam. After all, you *are* on vacation. Sinclair Canyon is popular not only with mineral-water loving tourists, but with bighorn sheep. See Chapter 20.

Takakkaw Falls

You appreciate the awesome power of a mountainous environment even more when, along with *observing* nature, you can *hear* it. If you get close enough to Takakkaw Falls in Yoho National Park, where melt water from the **Daly Glacier** thunders through a U-shaped hanging valley, dropping 254 meters (833 feet) into the Yoho River Valley, you can't hear much else. So don't try to talk. Just stay in the moment. See Chapter 19.

Waterton Townsite

The grounds of the rustic Prince of Wales Hotel, perched high on a bluff, make an ideal vantage point from which to survey the town of Waterton, and Upper Waterton Lake, the deepest lake in the Canadian Rockies. The tiny wind-battered townsite shrinks against the vastness of the surrounding wilderness. Did I mention the *wind?* Hold onto your hat and cling to your traveling companion. The wail of the wind contributes to the wildness of this out-of-the way park, home to bears, coyotes, deer, and wolves. It's all very romantic, or just downright tempestuous, depending on your perspective. The Prince of Wales Hotel itself strikes a stunning pose when viewed from the entrance road into town. See Chapter 17.

Chapter 23

Ten Rocky Mountain Highs

As you've probably already gleaned from flipping through this book, the Rockies are brimming with opportunities for exhilarating adventure. Nevertheless, you certainly don't have to scale a glacier-covered peak or hang glide off a cliff to be moved by the mountains — all of the following experiences leave you breathless.

Capture the Local Wildlife

As long as you can operate a camera, you have a good shot at bringing home impressive wildlife photos as souvenirs from the Canadian Rockies. You're almost certain to spot elk, deer, and bighorn sheep on your travels. Maybe even mountain sheep or bears. If you venture far on foot, you're apt to encounter numerous photogenic smaller critters, such as chipmunks, marmots, and squirrels. Early and late in the day are the best times to spot and photograph wildlife. That's when the animals are most active. The light's nicer, too. A telephoto lens is a great asset; these animals are called *wild* for a reason, and you need to keep your distance. Park officials suggest that you stay 30 meters (98 feet), or about three bus lengths, away from elk, deer, sheep, goats, and moose. I probably don't need to tell you that you should allow a lot *more* space if you happen to see a bear, cougar, or wolf. The good news is that it's okay to get a little chummier with the squirrels. Remember, though, you're not allowed to feed park animals, large or small.

Cycle the Golden Triangle

If you like to tour on two wheels and can budget three to five days for an excursion, consider the popular "golden triangle" route, which loops through three Canadian Rockies national parks (Banff, Kootenay, and Yoho). It's a long haul (320km/198 miles), but the scenery is so stunning that you'll ignore your aching quads. At any rate, you can take a dip in the mineral pools and get a massage when you get to Radium Hot Springs.

Dine at the Top

Canada's highest mountaintop restaurant, the Eagle's Eye at the Kicking Horse Mountain Resort in Golden, British Columbia, serves up a breathtaking 360-degree panorama of the Rocky, Selkirk, and Purcell mountain ranges. And the food, when you manage to tear yourself away from the view, is excellent.

Hike to Crypt Lake

To really appreciate the Canadian Rockies (and life in general), you have to get out of your car. Scramble up a mountain. Dip your toes in a stream. Picnic on the shores of an alpine lake. The deservedly popular day trip to Crypt Lake in Waterton National Park is one hike you won't forget. Other lakes in the mountains are equally lovely, but the exhilarating trek to Crypt Lake makes you feel particularly adventurous since you have to reach the trailhead by boat and ascend a trail that features a tunnel and a very narrow ledge. You should, of course, have some hiking experience before you head for this trail.

Lodge in a Log Cabin

While you can find many fine hotels in the Rockies, few offer the romance and atmosphere of a stay in a log cabin. For one thing, when you step outside your door, you're not in a hallway to the front lobby, you're right in a forest. Or on the banks of a river. A cabin or chalet usually contains the same conveniences you enjoy in a hotel, along with a wood-burning fireplace and in some cases a spiffy kitchen, but in a beautiful secluded setting. Some terrific cabins are hidden along the Icefields Parkway, just south of Jasper Townsite, along the Bow Valley Parkway in Banff National Park, and west of Mount Robson Provincial Park on Highway 16.

Meet Elk on the Course

If you already golf, you probably know that the Canadian Rockies are among the top spots anywhere to hit the links. If you don't golf, perhaps this would be a good time to start. If you aren't successful, you can always blame the distractions, which include snow-topped summits, postcard-pretty streams, bunkers that match the contours of surrounding mountain ranges, and companions such as deer and elk.

Run the River on the Kicking Horse

The fittingly named Kicking Horse River, which courses through Yoho National Park and hurtles west to Golden where it meets with the Columbia River, is renowned for whitewater rafting action. To really get acquainted with the Kicking Horse, book a trip on the lower canyon section, noted for class IV rapids. If you're new to the sport, rivers are rated on a scale of I (little or no current) to VI (significantly steep vertical drops and boulders). For a gentler introduction to the river, sign up for a sight-seeing float trip on smooth water.

Savor Fall Colors

Brilliant yellow and blazing gold aren't shades that spring to mind when you envision hiking in the Rockies . . . unless you're talking about trekking through a valley of alpine larches in the autumn. Larch trees turn a beautiful golden-orange color before they drop their needles. It's a seasonal spectacle that brings hikers back again and again. Trails in the Moraine Lake region in Banff National Park are top choices for larch lovers.

Hit the Summit of Sulphur Mountain

For a remarkable view of Banff Townsite and nearby mountain ranges, ride the gondola to the top of Sulphur Mountain, one of the tallest peaks in Banff (2,270 meters/7,445 feet). The trip up takes about eight minutes and costs C$25 (US$18). If you're energetic (or frugal), walk up. Then you can take the gondola back down for free.

Travel the Icefields Parkway

That's ice field . . . as in a field of ice? Yes, actually about 325 sq. km (125 sq. miles) of ice and snow, straddling the Continental Divide. The Columbia Icefield is a highlight of the spectacular, 230-km (143-mile) highway between Banff and Jasper. Several glaciers are visible from the highway. You also pass some awesome waterfalls on the route. Whether you're traveling by car or on a bike, the Icefields Parkway is rated one of the top journeys in the country.

Chapter 24

Ten Treats to Take on a Day Hike

· ·

In This Chapter

▶ Locating local goodies

▶ Trying new takes on trail favorites

▶ Pleasing gourmet tastes

· ·

*U*nlike on a backcountry trip, where weight and space considerations influence what you bring along for sustenance, on a day hike you have the luxury of munching on just about anything you like. Pack some high-energy snacks — such as the foods in this chapter — and be sure to drink lots of water. You may want to snack throughout the day instead of taking a formal lunch break. Whatever you bring, be sure to pack out (take away with you) any leftovers — including the pistachio shells and orange peels.

Beef Jerky

Beef jerky from the ranching community of Longview in the Rocky Mountain foothills of southern Alberta has reportedly sustained mountaineers on expeditions to Mount Everest. It certainly should provide sufficient fuel for your day hike. **Longview beef jerky,** made from thin strips of Alberta beef that's marinated and cooked, is widely available in gas stations and convenience stores throughout Alberta and elsewhere in western Canada. In addition to the original version, you can buy pepper, honey garlic, sweet and spicy, and buffalo flavors.

Chocolate from Banff

Ever tasted a bear paw? It's a chewy caramel-cashew concoction covered in smooth Belgian chocolate, and one of numerous decadent treasures created by the chocolate and candy shops along Banff Avenue. Strolling past **Mountain Chocolates, The Fudgery,** and **Bernard**

Callebaut, you see chunks of dense, luscious fudge, stacked in mouth-watering displays; almonds and cashews, drowned in creamy milk chocolate; crisp apples dipped in candy coatings. Go ahead. Buy one. By the time you've logged six hours on the trail, you'll have earned it.

Energy Bars

For emergency supplies, toss in one or two energy bars. Unlike chocolate bars, these high-carbohydrate snack bars, formulated for endurance athletes such as marathon runners, will never, ever, break or melt. Taste-wise, energy bars have come a long way since the original *PowerBar* (which you wouldn't mistake for a trail treat) came on the market more than a decade ago. Try Clif, Balance, Boulder . . .

Fruit Leather

Yet another option in the tough-and-durable category, dried strips of pureed fruit (apple, strawberry, banana, and others) deliver quick energy along with a vitamin boost. Fruit leather requires considerable effort to chew — so you become oblivious to the fact that you've slogged a few more kilometers in the process of eating a piece.

Gourmet GORP

I'm not suggesting that there's anything wrong with Good Old Raisins and Peanuts, but the makings of innovative trail blends (dried cranberries, pumpkin seeds, macadamia nuts, roasted soybeans, dried pears, pretzels) are easy to come by. Investigate the bulk food sections of major grocery stores or stock up in natural food shops such as **Community Natural Foods** at 1304–10th Avenue SW in Calgary or **Nutter's Bulk and Natural Foods** in Canmore (900 Railway Avenue) and Jasper (622 Patricia Street).

Hummus

Why stick with plain old PB when you can slather this tasty and easy-to-spread Mediterranean blend of chickpeas (garbanzos) and tahini (sesame butter) on your crackers, grainy breads, or bagels? Unlike peanut butter, where your options are basically crunchy or smooth, hummus is whipped up in endless variations, such as roasted garlic, roasted red pepper, and black olive.

Maple Bears

A little sugar is often just what you need to boost you up that final switchback to the summit. Maple sugar is the logical choice when you're hiking in Canada, which produces more than 85% of the world's supply. **Welch's Chocolate Shop** in Waterton Lakes (Wind Flower Avenue at Cameron Falls Drive: just follow your nose) carries an excellent selection of maple sugar candies (bear-shaped and others). While you're there you can also buy gummy bears, candy bones, and many other candy classics. Welch's also has a shop in Banff (123 Banff Avenue).

Pea Butter

This Canadian-made alternative to peanut butter is produced from a special variety of peas that turn brown when they're ripe. Look for the **NoNuts** brand in major grocery stores. Developed for people with nut allergies, pea butter makes an interesting sandwich spread — and a good conversation starter!

Sesame Seed Bagels

Bagels offer the considerable advantage of looking and tasting pretty much the same after six hours of hiking as they do when you first hit the trail. In addition to being nearly indestructible, even if they get smooshed, bagels are easy to come by, and convenient to pack and carry. You can even pop into a bagel shop and buy a fully loaded one to go. (Choose from many varieties; I just happen to prefer sesame.)

Smoked Salmon with Lime Wasabi Mustard on Rye Crisps

Why not?

Quick Concierge

Fast Facts

American Express

An American Express Travel Service office is located at 421 7th Ave. SW in Calgary (☎ 403-261-5982). To report a lost or stolen card: ☎ 800-268-9824.

Area Codes

The area code for Calgary and southern Alberta (including Kananaskis Country and Banff National Park) is 403. For Edmonton and northern Alberta (including Jasper National Park), dial area code 780. In British Columbia, the area code for destinations in the Canadian Rockies is 250. You don't need the area code to dial local numbers. To call long distance within Canada or the U.S., dial 1, plus the area code, plus the 7-digit local number.

ATMs

Automated banking machines are widely available in Calgary and throughout the Canadian Rockies.

Avalanche Hazards

Call ☎ 403-762-1460 for information about hazards in the Banff/Kootenay/Yoho area and ☎ 780-852-6176 for Jasper. You can also get avalanche situation updates by visiting the Canadian Avalanche Association's Web site at www. avalanche.ca/weather/bulletins.

Credit Cards

American Express, MasterCard, and Visa are widely accepted. If your credit card is lost or stolen, call the issuing company immediately. American Express ☎ 800-268-9824, MasterCard ☎ 800-307-7309, Visa ☎ 800-847-2911.

Backcountry Fees

A Wilderness Pass to stay in the backcountry overnight in a national park costs C$8 (US$5.60).

Business Hours

The national parks are open year round, although certain attractions and establishments in some parks are closed in winter. Most hotels and restaurants in Waterton Lakes National Park close for the winter. In Calgary, shopping centers are generally open Monday to Friday from 10 a.m. to 9 p.m., Saturday from 10 a.m. to 6 p.m., and Sunday and holidays from 11 a.m. to 5 p.m. Most banks are open weekdays, 10 a.m. to 4 p.m., with extended hours, including weekends, at some locations.

Directory Assistance

Dial ☎ 411 to obtain local and long distance (Canada and the U.S.) telephone numbers and addresses. There's a charge for this directory assistance if you're calling from a residential or private phone but not if you call from a pay phone or a hospital.

Doctors

Your hotel may be able to recommend a physician. Or, for minor medical problems, visit a pharmacy. In Calgary, many are open weekends and evenings. Shoppers Drug Mart has 24-hour locations in Chinook Centre (☎ 403-253-2424) and in North Hill Shopping Centre (☎ 403-289-6761). In the national parks, you find pharmacies in Banff, Jasper, and Waterton Lakes townsites. For hospital locations, refer to the chapters on individual parks.

Emergencies

For medical, fire, or crime emergencies, dial ☎ 911.

Fishing Licenses

A fishing license in the national park costs C$7 (US$4.20) per day or C$20 for an annual pass. Licenses are sold at visitor information centres and fishing supply stores.

Internet Access

To check your e-mail during your travels, visit one of the numerous cyber cafes throughout the parks and neighboring communities. In Calgary, try **Cinescape** (☎ 403-265-4511). In Banff Townsite, computer terminals are located in **Cascade Plaza**, lower level.

Liquor Laws

The legal age to purchase liquor in Alberta is 18. It's 19 in British Columbia. Most beer and wine shops in Calgary and Banff are open daily.

Mail

The cost to mail a postcard or standard-size letter is 48 cents within Canada, 65 cents to the U.S., and $1.25 for airmail service to other countries.

Maps

Maps are widely available in convenience stores, service stations, and outdoor shops, and from tourist information offices.

Newspapers

Calgary's daily papers are the ***Calgary Herald*** and the ***Calgary Sun***. Many other national and international papers are sold in magazine shops and book stores. In smaller communities, weekly newspapers carry information on local happenings and events. National newspapers (the *Globe and Mail* and the *National Post*) are also widely available in the main commercial centers in the parks.

Park Passes

You can buy either a daily or an annual pass to visit the national parks in the Canadian Rockies. A daily pass costs C$7 (US$4.90) per person or C$14 (C$9) for groups of between 2 and 7 people in the same vehicle. An annual pass (good for 27 national parks in Canada) is valid for one year from the date on which you purchase it, and sells for C$45 (US$36) per person or C$89 (US$63) for groups. Passes are sold at park gates and visitor information centres.

Road Conditions

For conditions in Banff, Jasper, Kootenay, and Yoho national parks, call ☎ 403-762-1450. To check on highways outside the national parks call ☎ 800-550-4997 in British Columbia, and ☎ 403-246-5853 (Calgary area) or ☎ 780-471-6056 (Edmonton area) in Alberta.

Taxes

The 7% Goods and Services Tax (GST) applies to most products and services you buy in Canada. Visitors to Canada can claim a rebate on the GST they pay on many purchases—mainly things purchased to take out of the country. You find rebate application forms at most visitor centers and in duty-free shops. For further information, go to www.ccra.gc.ca/visitors.

In Alberta, there's no provincial sales tax, but hotels charge a 5% accommodation tax. In British Columbia, you pay a retail sales tax of 7.5%. The hotel tax in B.C. is 8%. The provincial taxes are not refundable.

Time Zones

Alberta (Banff, Jasper, and Wateron Lakes national parks and Kananaskis Country) is in the Mountain standard time zone, as are Yoho and Kootenay national parks in British Columbia. Most of British Columbia, however, including Mount Robson Provincial Park, is on Pacific standard time, which is one hour behind Mountain time.

Temperature

Canada uses the Celsius system, where the freezing point is 0 degrees. To convert Celsius to Fahrenheit, multiply by 9/5 and then add 32. For example, 22 degrees C is a pleasant summer morning (72 degrees F) while −5 degrees C in February is great skiing weather (23 degrees F).

Tipping

Tips or service charges are not usually included in your restaurant tab (unless you're dining with a large group). The usual practice for good service in a restaurant is to tip your server 15 to 20%.

Weather

Call ☎ 403-762-2088 to hear a weather forecast for the Banff/Kootenay/Jasper region. Dial ☎ 780-852-3185 for weather conditions in Jasper. To check the weather outlook online, go to Environment Canada's Web site at www.weatheroffice.com.

Toll-Free Numbers and Web Sites

Major airlines

Air Canada
☎ 888-247-2262
www.aircanada.ca

Alaska Airlines
☎ 800-252-7522
www.alaska-air.com

American Airlines
☎ 800-433-7300
www.aa.com

America West Airlines
☎ 800-363-2597
www.americawest.com

Continental Airlines
☎ 800-231-0856
www.continental.com

Delta Air Lines
☎ 800-221-1212
www.delta.com

Horizon Airlines
☎ 800-547-9308
www.horizonair.com

Northwest Airlines
☎ 888-225-2525
www.nwa.com

United Airlines
☎ 800-864-8331
www.united.com

WestJet
☎ 888-937-8538
www.westjet.ca

Major car rental agencies

Avis
☎ 800-230-4898 in the U.S.
☎ 800-272-5871 in Canada
www.avis.com

Alamo
☎ 800 GO ALAMO (☎ 800-462-5266)
www.goalamo.com

Budget
☎ 800-268-8900
www.budgetrentacar.com

Enterprise
☎ 800-RENT-A-CAR (☎ 800-736-8222)
www.enterprise.com

Hertz
☎ 800-236-0600
www.hertz.com

National
☎ 800 CAR RENT (☎ 800-227-7368)
www.nationalcar.com

Thrifty
☎ 800 THRIFTY (☎ 800-847-4389)
www.thrifty.com

Major hotel and motel chains

Best Western International
☎ 800-780-7234
www.bestwestern.com

Coast Hotels and Resorts
☎ 800-663-1144
www.coasthotels.com

Comfort Inns
☎ 877-424-6423
www.choicehotels.com

Courtyard by Marriott
☎ 888-231-2211
www.courtyard.com

Days Inn
☎ 800-329-7466
www.daysinn.com

Delta Hotels
☎ 877-814-7706
www.deltahotels.com

Econo Lodges
☎ 877-424-6423
www.choicehotels.com

Fairmont Hotels and Resorts
☎ 800-257-7544
www.fairmont.com

Hampton Inn
☎ 800-445-8667
www.hampton-inn.com

Hilton Hotels
☎ 800-445-8667
www.hilton.com

Holiday Inn
☎ 800-465-4329
www.holiday-inn.com

Howard Johnson
☎ 800-446-4656
www.hojo.com

Hyatt Hotels and Resorts
☎ 800-663-7313
www.hyatt.com

Marriott Hotels
☎ 888-236-2427
www.marriott.com

Prestige Inns
☎ 877-737-8443
www.prestigeinn.com

Residence Inn by Marriott
☎ 888-236-2427
www.residenceinn.com

Quality Inn
☎ 800-228-5151
www.choicehotels.com

Sheraton Hotels and Resorts
☎ 888-625-5144
www.starwood.com/sheraton

Radisson Hotels International
☎ 888-201-1718
www.radisson.com

Travelodge
☎ 800-578-7878
www.travelodge.com

Red Carpet Inns
☎ 800-251-1962
www.reservahost.com

Westin Hotels and Resorts
☎ 888-625-5144
www.starwood.com/westin

Where to Get More Information

The **Parks Canada** Web site, which has information for visitors to Canada's national parks along with links to individual national park sites, is www.parkscanada.gc.ca.

You also find lots of useful links at the **Canadian Tourism Commission** Web site, www.travelcanada.ca.

To obtain brochures and information on the province of Alberta, call ☎ 800-252-3782 or visit www.travelalberta.com. **Travel Alberta** produces three handy publications: the *Vacation Guide*, *Accommodation Guide*, and the *Campground Guide*. To order copies, call the toll-free number or go to the Web site and click on Free Vacation Guides.

To contact **Tourism British Columbia,** call ☎ 800-435-5622 or visit www.hellobc.com. Call the toll-free number or visit the site to order an accommodation guide and other free publications.

Helpful visitor information, including tips from locals, can be found at www.canadianrockies.com.

You may also want to contact some of the following visitor centers and tourism bureaus when you're planning your trip:

✔ **Tourism Calgary,** ☎ 800-661-1678; Internet: www.tourismcalgary.com

✔ **Banff and Lake Louise Tourism,** ☎ 403-762-1550 (Banff), ☎ 403-522-3833 (Lake Louise); Internet: www.banfflakelouise.com

- ✔ **Jasper Tourism,** ☎ 780-852-3858; Internet: www.jaspercanadianrockies.com

- ✔ **Tourism Canmore,** ☎ 866-226-6673; Internet: tourismcanmore.com

- ✔ **Golden Tourism,** ☎ 800-622-4653; Internet: www.goldenchamber.bc.ca or www.go2rockies.com.

Index

• K •

• *M* •

• N •

• O •